Jürgen Habermas

Key Concepts

Jürgen Habermas

Key Concepts

Edited by

Barbara Fultner

RAWAT PUBLICATIONS

Jaipur · New Delhi · Bangalore · Hyderabad · Guwahati

ISBN 978-81-316-0477-9

First Indian Reprint, 2012

First published in 2011 by Acumen

Acumen Publishing Limited
4 Saddler Street, Durham, DH1 3NP
www.acumenpublishing.co.uk

Published by
Prem Rawat for **Rawat Publications**
Satyam Apts., Sector 3, Jawahar Nagar, Jaipur - 302 004 (India)
Phone: 0141 265 1748 / 7006 Fax: 0141 265 1748
E-mail : info@rawatbooks.com
Website: rawatbooks.com

New Delhi Office
4858/24, Ansari Road, Daryaganj, New Delhi 110 002
Phone: 011-23263290

Also at *Bangalore*, *Hyderabad* and *Guwahati*

Printed at Chaman Enterprises, New Delhi

Contents

Contributors

Joel Anderson was educated at Princeton, Northwestern and Frankfurt Universities and taught at Washington University in St Louis before joining the Philosophy Department of Utrecht University. His research focuses on questions of autonomy, agency, normativity and recognition in philosophical anthropology, ethics and social theory. He edited *Free Will as Part of Nature: Habermas and His Critics* (special issue of *Philosophical Explorations*, March 2007) and *Autonomy and the Challenges to Liberalism* (with John Christman; 2005). His current book project is entitled *Scaffolded Autonomy: The Construction, Impairment, and Enhancement of Human Agency*.

Ciaran Cronin is a freelance translator and author and is a research associate at the Centre Marc Bloch in Berlin. He previously taught philosophy at the University of Illinois in Chicago and at Grinnell College in Iowa. He has published a number of papers on Habermas and political philosophy and is co-editor (with Pablo De Greiff) of *Global Justice and Transnational Politics* (2002).

Barbara Fultner is Associate Professor of Philosophy at Denison University. She is the translator of, among other volumes, Jürgen Habermas's *Truth and Justification* (2003). She works on topics in philosophy of language and social theory, with a special interest in intersubjectivity. Her articles have appeared in journals including *Philosophical Studies*, *The International Journal of Philosophical Studies* and *Continental Philosophy Review*. In 2008–9, she was a Fellow at the University of Connecticut Humanities Institute.

Keith Haysom is a recent graduate of the New School for Social Research. He is currently teaching at the School for Political Studies, University of Ottawa and the Department of Political Science, Carleton University, in Ottawa, Canada. His research interests include critical theory, theories of intersubjectivity and language, social movements and global justice.

Joseph Heath is Professor of Philosophy at the University of Toronto. He is the author of *Communicative Action and Rational Choice* (2001), *Following the Rules* (2008) and various scholarly articles on the subject of critical theory, Habermas and practical rationality.

Eduardo Mendieta is Professor of Philosophy at the State University of New York, Stony Brook. He is the author of *The Adventures of Transcendental Philosophy* (2002) and *Global Fragments: Globalizations, Latinamericanisms, and Critical Theory* (2007). He recently co-edited (with Chad Kautzer) *Pragmatism, Nation, and Race: Community in the Age of Empire* (2009). He is presently at work on another book entitled *Philosophy's War: Logos, Polemos, Topos*.

Kevin Olson is Associate Professor of Political Science at the University of California, Irvine. He is the author of *Reflexive Democracy: Political Equality and the Welfare State* (2006) and editor of *Adding Insult to Injury: Nancy Fraser Debates Her Critics* (2008). His work has also been published in the *American Journal of Political Science*, the *Journal of Politics*, *Constellations* and the *Journal of Political Philosophy*. In 2006–7 he was an Erasmus Mundus Scholar at Utrecht University, The Netherlands.

Max Pensky is Professor of Philosophy at Binghamton University, State University of New York. His recent works include *The Ends of Solidarity: Discourse Theory in Ethics and Politics* (2008). Current research projects include a study of the role of memory and forgetting in critical theory, and the status of amnesties for international crimes.

William Rehg is Professor of Philosophy at Saint Louis University. He is the author of *Cogent Science in Context: The Science Wars, Argumentation Theory, and Habermas* (2009) and *Insight and Solidarity: The Discourse Ethics of Jürgen Habermas* (1994); the translator of Habermas's *Between Facts and Norms* (1996); and co-editor (with James Bohman) of *Deliberative Democracy* (1997) and *Pluralism and the Pragmatic Turn* (2001).

Melissa Yates is Assistant Professor of Philosophy at Rutgers University in Camden, New Jersey. She specializes in social and political philosophy, with particular interests in the works of Habermas and Rawls.

Christopher Zurn is Associate Professor of Philosophy at the University of Massachusetts Boston. He works on topics in constitutional democracy and in contemporary critical theory. He has authored *Deliberative Democracy and the Institutions of Judicial Review* (2007); co-edited (with Boudewijn de Bruin) *New Waves in Political Philosophy* (2009); and co-edited (with Hans-Christoph Schmidt am Busch) *The Philosophy of Recognition: Historical and Contemporary Perspectives* (2010).

Acknowledgements

This project has been nothing if not collaborative. From start to finish, it has been a great pleasure and an honour to work with this set of authors. Thanks to their collective effort, this book presents the kind of comprehensive conceptual map of Jürgen Habermas's philosophy that I envisaged at the outset. Several authors advised me on shaping the volume early on and on various other matters along the way. Special thanks to Bill Rehg for stepping into the breach late in the game and expanding the scope of his chapter. Thanks also to the anonymous reviewers for their thoughtful comments and suggestions. I would like to thank Melissa Rubins for her assistance with compiling the bibliographic database and with formatting; Bridget Tyznik for help with the indexing of names; Judy Napper for her fine copy-editing; and Kate Williams at Acumen for seeing the manuscript through its final stages. I am grateful to my editor, Tristan Palmer, for inviting me to undertake this project as well as for his patience and support in bringing it to completion. Throughout, my life-partner Jonathan Maskit has been my sounding board, on matters philosophical and otherwise, and my mooring. I cannot imagine not having him at my side. Finally, I would not be who and where I am today without the love and care of my mother, Hanna Fultner. I dedicate my portion of the labour that went into this volume to her.

Abbreviations

The following abbreviations are used for frequently cited works by Jürgen Habermas. Full bibliographical details can be found in the Bibliography. Dates in square brackets are the dates of publication in English.

BFN	*Between Facts and Norms* (1992 [1998])
BNR	*Between Naturalism and Religion* (2005 [2008])
CES	*Communication and the Evolution of Society* (1976 [1979])
DW	*The Divided West* (2004 [2007]
IO	*The Inclusion of the Other* (1996 [1998]
JA	*Justification and Application* [1993]
LC	*Legitimation Crisis* (1973 [1975])
KHI	*Knowledge and Human Interests* (1968 [1971])
MCCA	*Moral Consciousness and Communicative Action* (1983 [1990])
OPC	*On the Pragmatics of Communication* [1998)]
PDM	*The Philosophical Discourse of Modernity* (1985 [1990])
PMT	*Postmetaphysical Thinking* (1988 [1992])
PNC	*The Postnational Constellation* (1998 [2001])
STPS	*The Structural Transformation of the Public Sphere* (1962 [1989])
TCA	*The Theory of Communicative Action* (1981 [1984/1987])
TRS	*Toward a Rational Society* [1970]
TJ	*Truth and Justification* (1999 [2003])

Introduction

Barbara Fultner

Jürgen Habermas is without a doubt the most important German philosopher living today and one of the most important social theorists in the world. Heir to the founders of the Frankfurt School, Max Horkheimer and Theodor Adorno, his is one of the first names that come to mind at the mention of critical theory. His influence, like theirs, extends across the social sciences and humanities. Moreover, he has lived the life of a public intellectual *par excellence*, contributing on a regular basis to the editorial pages of major newspapers and engaging in public dialogue with other major figures ranging from Jacques Derrida, Michel Foucault and Richard Rorty to then Cardinal Ratzinger, now Pope Benedict XVI. He is a deeply systematic thinker and a consummate synthesizer, bringing together concepts from sociology, Marxist theory and continental as well as analytic philosophy: a fact that makes his work often challenging to read.

Habermas was born in 1929 in Düsseldorf and grew up in the small town of Gummersbach, where his father, Ernst Habermas, was director of the Bureau of Trade and Industry. After the Second World War, he studied in Göttingen, Zürich and Bonn. Horrified at the atrocities of the Nazis and at having been deceived about them, Habermas was appalled to realize that many academics, most notoriously Martin Heidegger, were silently complicit with if not actively supportive of the regime. He became a prominent critical voice of his generation, active in the anti-nuclear movement in the 1950s and in the student protests of the 1960s. After completing his *Habilitationsschrift* (a postdoctoral dissertation required for appointment to a professorship in Germany) in Marburg, he held a brief appointment in Heidelberg and, in 1964, was appointed professor of sociology and philosophy at the Institute for Social Research in Frankfurt as Horkheimer's successor. He became director of the Max Planck Institute for Research on Conditions of Life in the Scientific-Technological World in Starnberg from 1971 until 1982, when he returned to Frankfurt. He retired from that position in 1994 and has been writing and guest lecturing at various universities since then, notably Northwestern University in Evanston, Illinois, New York's New School for Social Research and Stony Brook University.

The essays in this volume aim to present a conceptual map of his capacious, and still growing, intellectual output. Over the past fifty years, he has produced numerous landmark books that have left an indelible impression on their respective domains of enquiry, often setting the agenda of what people think about and how they think about it. His influence is most palpable in critical theory and social-political philosophy. However, as the contributions in this volume show, the theory of communicative action, with its theory of linguistically embodied rationality, has much to bring to the table for ethics, epistemology, philosophy of mind and philosophy of language as well. The most important of his works probably remains *The Theory of Communicative Action*, where Habermas presents a comprehensive formulation of his theory of society, modernization and rationality which is the foundation for his subsequent elaboration of his moral theory, his political theory and his theory of law.

Evolution of a theory

While the organization of this volume is conceptual, it is worth examining Habermas's intellectual development from a historical perspective. What is striking about Habermas's corpus is its systematicity and continuity, on the one hand, and its dynamic nature on the other. His views and interests have evolved not only according to their own internal logic but also, crucially, in response to criticisms by and dialogue with others. He is not only a dialectical, but a dialogical thinker. His work can be segmented into roughly four distinct periods.[1] They represent shifts in focus and emphasis more than changes in his basic views and, as with most such periodizations, are somewhat arbitrary, as the strands of Habermas's thinking cut across them.

1. Philosophical anthropology: critique of philosophy of consciousness and of positivism (1954–70)

The first period spans roughly the time from his dissertation to the publication of *Knowledge and Human Interests*. It includes *The Structural Transformation of the Public Sphere* (1962 [1989]),[2] *Theory and Practice* (1963 [1973]), *On the Logic of the Social Sciences* (1967 [1988]) and the essays published in *Philosophical-Political Profiles* (1971 [1983]). During this time, Habermas develops a critique of the transcendental subject as found in both German idealism (Kant, Fichte, Hegel) and Husserlian phenomenology. Informed by hermeneutics and historical materialism, he rejects philosophy of consciousness as a viable starting point for social theory in favour of an emphasis on social evolution and human history. The detailed analysis of eighteenth-century coffee house culture in *The Structural Transformation of the Public Sphere*, a canonical text in critical theory and literary studies, demonstrates how the bourgeois public sphere emerges from historically specific material conditions and is tied to particular economic changes that were taking place at the time (capitalism, global trade, etc.). This means that the very structures of the public sphere are historically conditioned. *The Structural Transformation of the Public Sphere* also, of course, establishes the public sphere as a lifelong interest for Habermas and prefigures much of what is to come. His critique of the commodification of culture, for example, can be seen to prefigure the later thesis of the colonization of the lifeworld; and he is already concerned with the relationship between the public and the private as well as with social constructions of subjectivity that will occupy him in greater detail in the 1980s.

At the same time, Habermas mounts a critique of positivism in the sciences. He rejects the notion of a false objectivity in science on similar grounds as the philosophy of consciousness, namely, its ahistoricity, as well as its failure to appreciate fully the ineliminable role that culture plays in determining our nature. The transcendental – disembodied – subject and the objective, unbiased – and equally disembodied – scientist are replaced by a human, embodied and historically situated knowing subject that is the product of evolution, mediated by sociocultural processes. Hence the cognitive competencies of such a subject are not inscribed in some sort of immutable nature, but are *learned*. The project of accounting for these competencies and how they are acquired is what Habermas's long-time colleague and friend Karl-Otto Apel called *Erkenntnisanthropologie*, or anthropological epistemology.

Knowledge and Human Interests, too, lays the groundwork for future theory. Habermas here regards human interests as constitutive of spheres of human knowledge and identifies three such fundamental knowledge-constituting interests: technical, practical and emancipatory. The "orientation[s] toward technical control, toward mutual understanding in the conduct of life, and toward emancipation from seemingly 'natural' constraint" (KHI: 311) augur, even if they may not precisely map onto, the subsequent tripartite distinctions between theoretical, practical and aesthetic discourse and between the three corresponding validity claims to truth, normative rightness and sincerity. Perhaps most importantly, *Knowledge and Human Interests* introduces language as "the only thing whose nature we can know" (314), thus signalling the linguistic turn that will be the foundation for the theory of communicative action. Nonetheless, *Knowledge and Human Interests* raised some methodological issues and does not provide Habermas with the right theoretical framework for formulating an empirically grounded theory of society that can also incorporate a normative critical analysis of modernity.

2. From the reconstruction of historical materialism towards a theory of communicative action (1971–82)

After *Knowledge and Human Interests*, Habermas turns to transforming and updating Marxism by drawing on systems theory (Luhmann), developmental psychology (Piaget, Kohlberg) and social theory (Weber, Durkheim, Parsons, Mead, etc.). *Legitimation Crisis* (1971 [1973]), his 1971 Princeton Gauss Lectures, published in *On the Pragmatics of Social Interaction* (1984 [2001]), and the essays published in *Communication and the Evolution of Society* (1976 [1979]) belong to this period. The Gauss lectures mark a significant shift in Habermas's thinking and his search for an appropriate conceptual framework. For it is here that he proposes that social theory take a "linguistic turn", arguing that human action and understanding can be fruitfully analysed as having a linguistic structure. This preliminary attempt to rework the foundations of social theory resulted in the pivotal 1976 essay, "What is Universal Pragmatics?" (CES: 1–94; OPC: 21–103), in which he lays the foundations for his theory of communicative competence.

Towering at the end of this period as its culmination is, of course, *The Theory of Communicative Action*. Habermas identifies three goals of the two-volume book, namely, to develop:

> first, a concept of communicative rationality that is sufficiently skeptical in its development but is nevertheless resistant to cognitive-instrumental abridgments of reason; second, a two-level concept of society that connects the "lifeworld" and "system"

> paradigms in more than a rhetorical fashion; and finally, a theory of modernity that explains the type of social pathologies that are today becoming increasingly visible, by way of the assumption that communicatively structured domains of life are being subordinated to the imperatives of autonomous, formally organized systems of action. Thus the theory of communicative action is intended to make possible a conceptualization of the social-life context that is tailored to the paradoxes of modernity.
> (TCA 1: xlii)

At the core of the theoretical model introduced in *The Theory of Communicative Action* lies Habermas's conception of communicative rationality and the dichotomy of lifeworld and system. Habermas understands social evolution as a form of societal learning, and this learning is sedimented in social systems. Such systems, as they become increasingly complex and differentiated, take on a logic of their own and may no longer be subject to the control of individual or even collective social agents. Socialization and individuation processes, by contrast, take place in the lifeworld, a notion that Habermas adopts from Husserl, but reconceives in formal-pragmatic terms.

3. Postmetaphysical thinking: rationality, morality and democracy (1982–2000)

Following the publication of *The Theory of Communicative Action*, Habermas continues to elaborate the theory of rationality and modernity and to shore up its conceptual foundations. He develops critiques of postmodernism, scepticism, historicizing relativism and positivist dogmatism. In *Truth and Justification* (1999 [2003]), he reformulates his account of truth and articulates his "weak naturalism" (see below). At the same time, *The Theory of Communicative Action*'s conceptual framework – given its broad scope and ambitions – is designed to be applied to all kinds of domains of human activity. Turning to ethics and social-political philosophy, Habermas uses it to develop his distinctive moral theory in the form of discourse ethics, a theory of deliberative democracy, and a discourse theory of law. In all three arenas, he is concerned not only with an analysis of the norms of any of these forms of discourse and rationalities, but also with the kinds of social structures that are necessary to produce subjects with the competencies required to engage in them.

This period includes *Moral Consciousness and Communicative Action* (1983 [1990]), *The Philosophical Discourse of Modernity* (1985

[1987]), *Postmetaphysical Thinking* (1988 [1992]), *Justification and Application* (1991 [1993]), *Inclusion of the Other* (1996 [1998]) and his monumental work on political and legal theory, *Between Facts and Norms* (1992 [1996]).

4. Postsecular and postnational thinking (2001–)

Entering the twenty-first century brings somewhat of a return to philosophical anthropology for Habermas, as he takes up the relationship between reason and faith. Discussions of discourse ethics in particular often raise the problem of motivation: why ought one to act rationally and do what is morally right? Habermas has been criticized for having an overly rationalist and universalist Kantian conception of the knowing and acting subject. Yet in his work of the last ten years or so, his appreciation of the corporeality of human beings, and the vulnerability that comes with it, emerges with greater clarity. This latest development arguably begins with his acceptance speech for the 2001 Peace Prize of the German Book Trade Association, titled "Faith and Knowledge". It has appeared, along with a lengthy essay on "The Debate on the Ethical Self-Understanding of the Species" in *The Future of Human Nature* (2001 [2003b]). He argues against cloning and pre-implantation genetic testing on the basis that we have an ethical self-understanding of our species that is shared by all moral persons and in which morality is embedded. He worries, roughly, that interference with the given biological constitution of a future subject (who cannot give her consent) may threaten our – and that subject's – conception of autonomous agency and our experience of ourselves as free agents. In addition to contributing to the bioethics debate, Habermas writes on the problem of free will and the role of religion in what he terms a "postsecular" society, taking up what he describes as "a peculiar dialectic between the philosophically enlightened self-understanding of modernity and the theological self-understanding of the major world religions that protrude into this modernity as the most unwieldy (*sperrigste*) element from its past" (Habermas 2010: 16, trans. mod.). His postmetaphysical philosophical commitments as well as the proceduralism of his discourse theories of morality, democracy and law clearly converge with what he regards as the postsecular self-understanding of modern societies in *Between Naturalism and Religion* (2005 [2008]).

The attempt to articulate a model of a postsecular society and to engage questions of religion is driven not only by issues internal to discourse ethics (such as the motivation problem mentioned above), but also by the consideration of concrete political circumstances. Germany and the rest of Europe are marked by increasing religious pluralism. The expansion of the European Union in the wake of the collapse of the Soviet Union and Eastern bloc placed new strains on the concept of European unity. On a global scale, religion was clearly a factor in the Yugoslav wars, the 9/11 terrorist attacks and the ongoing conflict in Iraq. Habermas's own support for the NATO intervention and bombing in Kosovo in 1999, on the one hand, and his opposition to the US invasion of Iraq in 2003, on the other, required justification and prompted him to examine international law, its normative force, and how it is to be upheld and applied. In short, Habermas has sought to determine whether social democracy can be extended beyond the boundaries of nation-states and what a cosmopolitan democracy in a global political order would look like. Thus in his most recent writings, he has apparently returned not only to a form of philosophical anthropology but also to a more explicitly normative critical theory.

Unifying themes and thematic overview

Despite the above shifts in interests and emphasis, the remarkable systematicity of Habermas's work and its consistency over time is striking. Certain themes reverberate throughout Habermas's *oeuvre* and hence throughout this volume. Many of the themes he develops in painstaking detail subsequently are already contained *in nuce* in his first major work, *The Structural Transformation of the Public Sphere*. Foremost of these is the interest in the public sphere. This concern drives his emphasis on intersubjective communication that is the hallmark of his thought. Social actors are who they are because they interact with one another, and the norms whereby they abide are normatively binding if they are or can be backed by reasons. A healthy public sphere where such argumentation can take place, however, depends on other socio-structural conditions. Another important aspect, also already present in *Structural Transformation of the Public Sphere*, is the recognition of the historically conditioned nature of human activity and of the importance of social structures in shaping that activity and thus the agents engaged in it. This is a feature of Habermas's thought that critics of some of his later work have often neglected or forgotten. The notion of structural transformation is crucial to Habermas's understanding of modernity and rationalization in *The Theory of Communicative Action*; it lies at the forefront of his recent writings on globalization, which he regards as a process of modernization.

Philosophically, a key theme is Habermas's Kantian pragmatism. His project can be described as a reconciliation of Kant, Darwin and Marx (cf. TJ: 9). His discourse ethics, his cosmopolitanism and his concept of communicative reason are most certainly deeply Kantian. He is unwilling to yield either to relativism with regard to truth or morality, on the one hand, or to any kind of naturalistic reductionism, on the other. Philosophy, for him, is a normative enterprise; the ideal of critical theory, after all, is to provide a *critical* diagnosis of the times, which is to say, a diagnosis from a normative standpoint from which how things could be better becomes visible. Thus, Habermas has argued against a reductionist "strong" naturalism as well as against a "postmodern 'overcoming' of a normative self-understanding of modernity" (PNC: 130), endorsing instead a "soft" or "weak" naturalism articulated most clearly in *Truth and Justification* and *Beyond Naturalism and Religion*. He remains committed to the idea that the universalist and normative claims of reason are context-transcendent and unconditionally valid and that it is possible to reach consensus about such claims. By the same token, his Kantianism is "detranscendentalized" by the influence of classical pragmatism. Kant's "cosmological idea" of the unity of the world, for example, is replaced by the pragmatic presupposition of an objective world; the "idea of freedom" as a postulate of practical reason by the pragmatic presupposition of the rationality of accountable agents; and reason as a "faculty of ideas" by a discursive, linguistically embodied and historically situated reason (TJ: 87). In the wake of Darwin, Marx and Peirce, Habermas takes seriously the idea that our practices evolve and are historically situated and that there are facts of the matter about our evolutionary history, both in terms of biological and cultural evolution, that make us who we are.

As the foundations of Habermas's mature conceptual framework are laid in *The Theory of Communicative Action*, most of the essays in this volume focus on it and subsequent work. In Chapter 1, Max Pensky provides a more detailed intellectual biography of Habermas and situates his work in its socio-historical context, particularly with reference to the Frankfurt School of critical theory. Chapters 2–5 deal with issues relating to Habermas's concept of communicative rationality and outline the basic concepts of the theory of communicative action. In Chapter 2, Melissa Yates explains Habermas's critique of metaphysics and his account of social science and elaborates Habermas's "soft" naturalism and weak or "quasi"-transcendentalism. She also takes up methodological issues regarding his approach such as the concept of rational reconstruction and what he means by postmetaphysical thinking. Formal pragmatics, which is crucial to the detranscendentalized conception of reason Yates explicates, is the topic of my Chapter 3. It articulates the necessary conditions under which it is possible for agents in interaction to reach mutual understanding. Habermas's hallmark concept of communicative action refers to the linguistically mediated interaction of social agents oriented towards reaching mutual understanding. The notions of validity and intersubjectivity play a central role in this account. Habermas argues that in order to understand one another's utterances, we must know what makes them acceptable. That is, we must understand the reasons that could be garnered to make good on the claims we raise, explicitly or implicitly, in what we say. In this way, rationality is embodied in linguistic communication. Chapter 3 also illustrates how Habermas's thinking transcends the divide between "continental" and "analytic" or Anglo-American theorizing by drawing on both hermeneutics and analytic philosophy of language. The distinction between communicative and strategic action, fundamental to Habermas's social theory, is introduced in Chapter 3 and taken up again in Chapter 4 by Joe Heath. Communicative action, of course, is but one form of action coordination. Societies are also organized by systemic structures. To develop this aspect of his theory of society, Habermas modifies the classical social theories of Weber and Durkheim by drawing on Talcott Parsons's functionalist theory. Heath explains Habermas's distinction between system and lifeworld, outlining both the strengths and limitations of Habermas's functionalism. A widely endorsed objection against functionalist theories of society is that they leave no room for the agency and autonomy of individuals. One of the goals of Habermas's two-tiered model of society is, in fact, to explain how it is possible to retain the notion of autonomous agency against the background of functionally organized societal structures. In Chapter 5, Joel Anderson spells out Habermas's intersubjective conception of autonomy, identity and the self. He distinguishes between political, moral and personal autonomy, as well as accountable agency and authentic identity. On Habermas's intersubjectivist account, we, as subjects, are socioculturally and historically situated. Autonomy is therefore not something we are simply born with, but something that must be fostered and nurtured as we mature. Its development also relies on our social environment being appropriately structured. The mature subjects that emerge from these processes of socialization are capable of engaging in discourse.

The conditions of possibility of communicative action outlined in Chapter 3 are the most basic, but different types of discourse will have their own particular conditions of possibility. The next section of the book thus turns to Habermas's discourse theories of morality, democracy and law. All three of these can be understood as applications or, as Habermas puts it, "operationalizations" (BFN: 103) of his "discourse principle" which stipulates that "just those norms are valid to which all those possibly affected could agree as participants in rational discourses" (BFN: 107; see Chapter 6 in this volume, p. 120). As I have already indicated, Habermas rejects the idea that there is some kind of transcendent truth or morality in favour of the view that what is morally right or politically correct or legally legitimate is determined discursively, which is to say, through rational argumentation. William Rehg explicates Habermas's moral theory, "discourse ethics", in Chapter 6. Habermas endorses a Kantian proceduralist model of moral justification according to which moral claims carry universal intersubjective validity. A norm or moral rule is justified if it is "acceptable to all those concerned". Hence discourse about the validity of moral norms is to be carried out from an impartial perspective, taking into account the interests and values of all concerned. Rehg shows how morality differs from ethics which, as Habermas defines it, has to do with conceptions of the good life and happiness. Especially in modern, pluralistic societies, we tolerate and, indeed, expect multiple conceptions of and reasonable disagreements about the latter, whereas in the moral domain, discourse aims at universal consensus. In Chapter 7, using some of the same proceduralist notions, Kevin Olson outlines Habermas's theory of deliberative democracy. In contrast to morality, which is governed by the principle of universalization, politics is (or ought to be) governed by the principle of democracy, which serves to establish principles of legitimate lawmaking. Moral discourse is oriented towards norms and values and aims at the rational consensus of all *persons*; political discourse is oriented towards the legitimacy of laws and aims at the consensus of all citizens of a "legally constituted" political community. Hence, the principle of democracy captures "the performative meaning of the practice of [political] self-determination" (BFN: 110). Olson shows how rational and political will formation can be institutionalized according to Habermas by means of a system of rights that ensures the access to equal political participation for all citizens. He elaborates on the notion of political autonomy introduced in Chapter 5 and on how rights institutionalize the ideals of equality, reciprocity and inclusion. Political legitimacy, on this account, ultimately derives from communicative power, which in turn is generated through public discourse. Olson thus closes his chapter with a discussion of the public sphere.

We might say that the subjects of communicative action are rationally accountable subjects in interaction, those of moral discourse persons, and those of political discourse citizens. Since Habermas conceives political discourse as legally constituted inasmuch as legitimate democratic procedures require institutionalization, he needs to have a theory of law. In Chapter 8, Chris Zurn's presentation of Habermas's discourse theory of law is organized along the perspectives of sociology, philosophy and legal adjudication. Sociologically, Habermas thinks of the law as a "transmission belt" that interacts with both system and lifeworld, connecting communicative and functional forms of social integration (solidarity, money, power). Law is a potential emancipatory mechanism because it embodies moral norms and societal values, but can also be used to the benefit of powerful lobbies because it is couched in the specialized economic and administrative vocabularies. Philosophically, Habermas aims to overcome the divide between legal positivism and natural law theory. He argues that law and morality are independent, equiprimordial spheres of discourse. Finally, adjudication discourse theory spells out the logic of applying laws and of how judges and legal scholars in the legal public sphere assess the legitimacy not only of particular legal decisions but of the laws being applied themselves.

The final three essays, perhaps more than the others, illustrate how Habermas's theoretical work emerges from his engagement with the socio-political and cultural questions of the day. Keith Haysom, in Chapter 9, takes up the topic of the public sphere and traces Habermas's evolving conception of civil society, his analysis of the crisis of the welfare state and his diagnosis of social pathologies by examining his treatment of social movements over the course of his career, starting with his involvement in the 1960s' student protests. Haysom makes the case that, in his later work, Habermas "rediscovers" the public sphere and civil society, no longer in its *bourgeois* form, as it figured in *Structural Transformation*, but in the form of voluntary and grassroots organizations. In some respects picking up where Haysom leaves off, Ciaran Cronin presents Habermas's highly complex model of what a "postnational" political order might look like in Chapter 10. The model of cosmopolitan democracy Habermas defends is the result of his reflection on economic globalization, the collapse of the Soviet system, the Balkan wars as well as the US-led invasion of and ensuing war in Iraq. In Chapter 11, Eduardo Mendieta identifies Habermas's other recent concern, namely, the role of religion in society. Not unlike the way in which Haysom uses social movements, Mendieta uses secularization as a lens through which to examine Habermas's concept of social evolution and the way in which he has rethought his thesis that modernization is a form of rationalization over the years. Mendieta traces the role of religion in Habermas's thinking from being a catalyst for rationalization in the early years, to a source of social order (a function subsequently shifted increasingly onto law in modernity), to an independent sphere of discourse and social practice that philosophy cannot displace but has to learn to live with, to, finally, a source of action motivation and value and thus perhaps something on which philosophy in fact might depend. In this final phase, religion could again be regarded as a kind of catalyst. This closing chapter therefore shows not only the ultimately unified nature of Habermas's *oeuvre*, but also, since his work on religion is still in progress at the time of this writing, points in the direction of what we can expect Habermas's next major and no doubt influential tome to be.

Notes

1. This periodization is adapted from one proposed by Eduardo Mendieta.
2. Dates in square brackets are the English publication dates.

ONE

Historical and intellectual contexts

Max Pensky

It is not unusual, when reading about the lives and works of influential philosophers, to encounter the view that their work transcends the times that the authors live in; that the most influential philosophers think and write about highly abstract metaphysical or universal ideas and problems that are not specific to any particular historical or social context, and that for this reason they and their texts are "in conversation", not with their own contemporaries but with their philosophical predecessors, however historically remote they may be. One implication of this view is that there are other philosophers, perhaps those who have less of an interest in abstract, metaphysical, or "timeless" questions, who therefore have a correspondingly thicker and more influential relationship with their own historical context; they're "in conversation" with those among whom they live, rather than with the great figures of the history of philosophy.

If this view is correct, then the first set of context-transcending philosophers may sacrifice their relevance for their own contemporaries, but they are rewarded by the timeless and universal significance of what they think and write about. Conversely, the context-immanent philosophers may not age especially well, since they think and write about problems that may be specific to their own times, but they are rewarded by the relevance and influence they can assert within their own society. It is easy to see how this view implies a conclusion about the difference between these two types of thinkers: timeless philosophy is serious or important philosophy, the real work of the perennial search for transcendent truth. And if one cannot or will not manage this kind of achievement, there is always the time-bound, useful but forgettable kind of philosophy as a kind of consolation prize.

But this view and its implications have a lot of serious problems. For one thing, it is simply analytically true that philosophers *always* write fully enmeshed in their own times and their own societies, and unless they remain entirely obscure, they are therefore always formed by, and in turn influence, their own social contexts. The very notion of transcendence presupposes this embeddedness. Moreover, philosophy is very much a public, social activity itself. Even the most apparently context-transcending, metaphysical philosophical problems of truth, reason or being are not the sole property of aloof philosophers, but are published, sent out to mingle in a shared intellectual environment where they are, and are meant to be, accepted or rejected, debated and argued over, transformed and refashioned.

When it comes to philosophical concepts, then, there is no "either/or" between context-transcending universals and context-immanent particulars, but rather a "both/and", a give-and-take or a dialectic.

Claims of universality are claims made to others with whom one lives in particular circumstances, with an eye towards transforming those circumstances. Even Plato and Descartes, the very models of the metaphysical thinker, wrote what they wrote in some significant degree in order to criticize and transform crucial elements of their own societies, which for them had fallen into forms of moral and epistemic relativism crying out for philosophy to intervene. Conversely, even the most socially and politically committed philosophers are precisely philosophers, rather than, say, social activists or politicians, just because they understand their work not just as offering opinions, suggestions or insights about their own times, but indeed because their relationship with those times is one that can produce a claim to truth, or justifiability, which in turn contains a moment of context-transcendence as well.

Therefore the key distinction is not, ultimately, between context-transcendent and context-immanent philosophers, and certainly not between the seriousness and rigour of context-transcendence and the more casual or unambitious nature of context-immanence. Rather, philosophers differ greatly on *the attitude they assume* towards the relationship between philosophical truth and social influence; some take this relationship as an evident but ultimately surmountable aspect of their work, while others see it as an essential, indeed the primary focus of their energies as thinkers.

Habermas's historical and intellectual influences

Any discussion of the influences upon and impact of the philosophical writings of Jürgen Habermas must proceed on the basis of this corrected view of the philosopher's work, since Habermas's half-century of philosophizing so strongly exemplifies the second, engaged paradigm I discussed above. For Habermas, the dialectical relationship between the philosopher's preoccupation with the context-transcending truth or universal justifiability of our claims and norms, and the context-immanence of the social world in which such claims and norms are offered and received, indeed lies at the very core of his conception of the philosopher's task. And this means that when we begin to catalogue the many and varied intellectual influences and sources that Habermas quite consciously gathered and refashioned in his own work, we must bear in mind his conviction that a new, up-to-date vision of the proper tasks and scope of philosophizing arises only from an overarching, one might say metaphilosophical, view of the philosopher's own times, intellectual landscape, historical situation and social demands.

Habermas is, arguably, the most diversely influenced of all contemporary philosophers, in the sense that the sources he brought together in his work, both philosophical and non-philosophical, are remarkably broad; indeed some might complain that they are too broad, too various and diverse. But this breadth of influences makes sense once we bear in mind the deliberate task of making the philosopher's influential relationship with his or her own times the centre, rather than the by-product, of the activity of philosophy itself.

All biographical discussion of Habermas must begin at what in German is sometimes still referred to as "*Stunde null*": "zero hour", the moment of war's end in 1945, with German culture and society in ruins both physically and spiritually. Born in 1929, Habermas grew up in the small provincial town of Gummersbach, in the "everyday life" of National Socialism. He was enrolled in the Hitler Youth and briefly served in an anti-aircraft artillery unit in the closing months of the Second World War. As a sixteen-year-old at war's end, Habermas was deeply affected by the revelations of the nature and extent of the Holocaust and the moral depravity of the leadership of the Nazi regime as he followed the Nuremberg Trials on radio.[1]

Moreover, his birth year of 1929 marked Habermas as a member of a very specific generational cohort that has played a distinctive and crucial role in post-war German culture and politics. On one side, Habermas and his generational peers were too young to have any memories of the Weimar Republic or to have taken any active part in the National

Socialist regime that would incur adult responsibility. But on the other hand they were old enough to have direct, personal experiences of the horrible and fatal collapse of German society, to have participated in the final stages of the war effort, and to see firsthand the enormous task of rebuilding a physically and morally shattered society.[2]

For this generation in particular, the question of Germany's political and indeed spiritual future was paramount. How could Germany build a stable, peaceful democratic society from the ruins of fascism? How could the elements of German culture worth saving – the elements of political and moral modernity, and above all the tradition of Enlightenment, of Kant and Goethe, Schiller and Bach – be picked from this rubble and included in the foundation of a new social order? There are very few modern examples of a generation that so self-consciously recognized itself challenged with such an enormous task of social rebuilding and reinvention. For a culture that had so valued the activity of philosophy, and had embraced its own philosophical tradition as a primary source of collective identity and self-understanding, it is not surprising that this generation also regarded the task of social rebirth as implying a collective reorientation to its philosophical heritage.

As a young university and graduate student in philosophy, in the early 1950s, and especially one deeply influenced by Martin Heidegger, Habermas was shocked to discover that this generational task, re-envisioning Germany's relationship with its own philosophical heritage, was not in fact taking place. Instead, as he bitterly noted at the time, the ingrained conservatism of the German academy in the post-war years helped sponsor a head-in-the-sand culture of denial and evasion, one that mirrored the broader post-war trend towards suppressing and silencing, rather than openly debating, Germany's immediate past. Prominent philosophers, including some of Habermas's own professors, had affiliations with National Socialism that were pointedly not discussed or even divulged.

Perhaps more tellingly, the very idea that philosophy must transform itself in response to the German disaster met with deep resistance. As a university student Habermas was far from alone in his dismay and frustration with the idea that philosophy in post-war Germany could carry on business as usual, as though the period between 1933 and 1945 could simply be bracketed out of consideration. German philosophy had produced not just Kant and Hegel, but (indirectly, surely) Marx as well. It was a tradition not only of deep insularity, of conservative academic self-sufficiency, but of its own internal radical critique as well. Moreover, the heritage of Enlightenment itself contained at its core the very dialectic between philosophical insight and calls for progressive social reform that I discussed earlier: Kant was not just the author of the *Critique of Pure Reason* but of essays such as "An Answer to the Question: What is Enlightenment?" (1996: 11–22), which demand the *general* social encounter with a conception of public reasoning, enquiry and tolerance that Kant's philosophy had discovered in the universal features of human cognitive faculties.

The question facing Habermas and his like-minded philosophical colleagues in the early years of the Federal Republic was how the pertinent dimensions of this eighteenth-century tradition of intellectual and political Enlightenment could be rendered serviceable for a society with such unprecedented damages and needs. How could the Enlightenment's commitment to core human values such as secularism, rationality, tolerance, representative republican governance, universal and equal moral and legal rights, and broad social inclusion be reappropriated in a way that would resonate with the needs of the times?

The answer to this question is highly complex, but in one sense it can be summarized reasonably well with three linked claims. First, recovering and promoting the values of Enlightenment modernity for the post-war world required that philosophy be gently but firmly knocked off its pedestal as a discipline with a special claim to transcendent, foundational truth, and assigned a more humble but more socially significant role, one that was tailored specifically to the values and challenges of a secular, "postmetaphysical", democratic society. Second, in order to fulfil this role, philosophy, above all the notoriously insular philosophy as it developed in the German universities, must engage in substantive and productive reciprocal dialogue with the newer, adjacent disciplines that it had traditionally held at arm's length. In his earliest work Habermas had already pointed to the primary candidate for this kind of partnership: social science, above all those branches of political sociology that he later termed "reconstructive", that is, sciences that aim at explaining those dimensions of human interaction that have a putative claim to universality. Third, Habermas understood that specifically German (or perhaps better, European) philosophy in the post-war era had to open itself up to the influence of parallel philosophical traditions, above all the tradition of American pragmatism, which had taken the productive relationship between philosophy and democracy as one of its most basic problems. In doing so, Habermas saw himself as bringing in the kind of fresh material and problems that would compel European philosophy to move decisively away from theoretical models that had become exhausted: the model of the solitary, autonomous ego as the "basic unit" of philosophical analysis, and the model of consciousness as the mode in which this ego relates both to itself and to its external world.

In the following, I will first offer some brief comments on Habermas's commitment to a new, humble and interactive mode of philosophy. A longer discussion of Habermas's project of opening dialogue between philosophy and the reconstructive and critical social sciences recalls Habermas's early and fraught collaboration with the post-war Frankfurt School of critical theory and its prominent figures, Max Horkheimer and Theodor Adorno. Finally, I will turn to Habermas's development of a theory of linguistic competence and communicative rationality in the 1970s and 1980s that meets the requirements of a philosophy that has definitively broken both with the philosophy of the subject and the philosophy of consciousness.

The reconception of philosophy and its role

In an essay entitled "Philosophy as Stand-In and Interpreter" from the early 1980s, Habermas declared that philosophy, above all the magisterial style of academic philosophy so familiar in the German tradition culminating in Kant and Hegel, could no longer plausibly claim a role as a judge, determining once and for all what the natural sciences may and may not legitimately know, and how the sciences may and may not legitimately take their place within a broader canopy of cultural learning (MCCA: 1–21).

Given the conditions of modernity, Habermas insisted, philosophy must take on humbler but still crucial ambitions: to "stand in" for the reconstructive social sciences. By this he meant that philosophy ought to explain and analyse, and thereby hold open a space for, the contributions of empirically grounded theories of human action that have strong universalistic claims. It is precisely here, Habermas believed, that a humble but still viable version of the older Enlightenment account of rationality still had a sharp relevance. Such theories – for instance, theories of linguistic competence – do not simply conjecture *ex cathedra* about the sovereign power of reason in the world, *à la* Kant and Hegel, but begin with basic human competencies that already present strong empirical grounds for universality, that is, competencies lacking any identifiable alternative if we are to consider ourselves and one another as responsible subjects.

Language and communication, of course, are the chief candidates for such competencies, and Habermas suggests that the reconstructive sciences that explore them ought to turn to philosophy as a helper and adjunct in expressing and disseminating the full significance of their universalistic claims. And a philosophy that seeks to fulfil this helper role will have to drop its self-understanding as offering those sciences their "permit" and their space for legitimacy, and learn them in order to make their own claims of rationality (for that in the end is precisely what such universal competencies are) intelligible.

The legacy and transformation of critical theory

This brings Habermas to the second revision in philosophy's self-understanding. Rather than appoint itself as the sovereign judge that will decree how scientific knowledge will find its proper relationship to the sum of human cultural understanding, Habermas instead suggests that philosophy serves as an *interpreter*, communicating and transmitting insights from the specialized and technical language of the reconstructive sciences to the "normal" discourse of the everyday lived world of adult citizens, that is, the democratic public sphere where the normative and political implications of scientific progress find their proper forum for debate.

The implications of Habermas's argument in "Philosophy as Stand-In and Interpreter" are that philosophy's disciplinary core consists in a specific ongoing relationship with parallel disciplines in the natural and above all in the social sciences. Philosophy's purpose is therefore impossible without an ongoing conversation with social theory. It is a position that has guided Habermas's own intellectual trajectory as early as the 1950s.[3]

This argument for a supple, curious and self-limiting philosophy certainly does not originate with Habermas. But it does help to explain why the young Habermas, following his PhD in philosophy and some years as a journalist, found a home (although as we will see an uneasy one) at the Institute for Social Research in Frankfurt. For as we will see, the famous "Frankfurt School" of critical social theory seems an excellent fit for Habermas's reformed vision of a socially committed, interdisciplinary philosophy.

Founded in the 1920s, the Institute for Social Research at the University of Frankfurt began as an interdisciplinary research centre where philosophers, sociologists, economists, legal scholars and even students of psychiatry and literature would collaborate on large-scale studies of the sources and structure of contemporary social pathologies. Under the directorship of Max Horkheimer in the 1930s, the Institute was innovative in synthesizing philosophical analysis with empirical social research, with the goal of critically identifying and indicting sources of injustice, domination and oppression.

Although deeply influenced by Marxist theory, few of the Institute's members were overt Marxists. But in his influential inaugural lecture, Horkheimer pledged to work toward the development of a "critical theory" that would expose the illusions and deceptions that made capitalist society able to survive, and that, in the view of the critical theorists, made a transition from liberal democracy to totalitarianism inevitable (Horkheimer 1972: 188–243).

Synthesizing impulses in both Marx and Freud, Frankfurt School members such as Horkheimer, Theodor W. Adorno, Herbert Marcuse, Erich Fromm and Friedrich Pollack designed often ingenious methods for observing how social pathologies arose and spread at both the "micro" and the "macro" levels; that is, both in terms of the suite of neuroses and affective and cognitive disorders of individual subjects that arose among a manipulated and oppressed mass of citizenry, leading them to renounce their own independence and political rights and capitulate in the face of domination, and on the institutional level, as constitutional democracy was undermined by a potent mix of state-run markets and mass loyalty to one-party rule. They analysed and observed the "authoritarian personality" in Germany and the United States, sought to uncover the psychological and social enabling conditions for anti-Semitism as a political force, and worked to uncover the otherwise hidden mechanisms whereby capitalism and democracy, ostensibly devoted to a society of material plenty and political freedom, seemed to collude in order to deny persons both of these.

But this interdisciplinary research programme, while always alert to the sources of normativity within Enlightenment modernity, grew increasingly sceptical regarding the project of Enlightenment modernity as a whole. Already in the 1930s and especially thereafter, in the face of the evident success of Nazism and the lead-up to global war, the writings of the Institute members grew increasingly dark. In their classic wartime study, *Dialectic of Enlightenment* (2002), Horkheimer and his colleague Theodor W. Adorno were no longer willing to see the tradition of European Enlightenment as a resource for political demands for justice and equality based on a universal form of human reason. Instead, they observed that since the beginning of modern history and indeed since before the beginning of recorded human history, "reason" has been in a process of mutual intertwinement with "myth": the urge to emancipate subjectivity from its subjection to the forces of nature drives humans to develop a mode of rationality as anti-natural, as a force to separate from nature by dominating it. But time and again, this very drive to domesticate and control nature – both external environments and the "inner nature" of humans' natural drives, desires and longings – leads to newer, harsher and more subtle forms of domination and control (Horkheimer & Adorno 2002). By the time Horkheimer and Adorno returned to Frankfurt and re-established the Institute for Social Research in the

1950s, the radical, Marxist influence on their and the Institute's work was largely absent. Although the Institute and its members continued its empirical work on the social-psychological dimensions of social domination, and although its members continued to play a largely progressive role in the volatile political culture of the new Federal Republic of Germany, philosophy itself largely abandoned any radical political ambitions of its own. In the post-war work of Horkheimer himself, and even more so in the case of Adorno in fact, philosophy often appeared to return to its older conservative function, safeguarding the values of truth and beauty from a modern social reality inimical to them.

Habermas is often thought of as representing a "second generation" of the critical theory of the Frankfurt School and it is certainly true that the works of key members of the Institute for Social Research were already a deep influence on Habermas's philosophical development even prior to his two-year stint as Adorno's assistant in Frankfurt. However, while critical theory is undoubtedly a key influence, it is also frequently overestimated and its influence was in many ways as negative on the development of Habermas's mature theory as it was positive. The more nuanced role that the Frankfurt School's thought had for Habermas requires a more elaborate explanation.

After undergraduate study in philosophy at universities in Göttingen, Zürich and Bonn, Habermas received his PhD in philosophy from the University of Bonn in 1954. His thesis was a study of the philosophy of history of the German idealist philosopher Schelling. He developed a deep interest in the work of Martin Heidegger. But even before his doctoral work was complete, Habermas's disillusionment with German philosophy's inability even to acknowledge, let alone examine its own relation to its (Nazi) times had led him away from Heidegger, and toward an engagement with the tradition of radical philosophical critique that his own student and university years had not offered him. He discovered the core writings of Western Marxism in the course of the middle of the 1950s, not only Horkheimer and Adorno but also their important precursors and contemporaries: Georg Lukács, Ernst Bloch, Herbert Marcuse, Walter Benjamin, and Marxist existentialists in France such as Jean-Paul Sartre and Maurice Merleau-Ponty.

In 1956, Habermas moved to Frankfurt, to serve as Adorno's academic assistant and to begin work on his "habilitation", the book-length post-doctoral thesis required in Germany to enter the ranks of university professors. From the beginning of his Frankfurt stay, however, Habermas's relations with Max Horkheimer were tense. Indeed, Horkheimer had strongly opposed Adorno's invitation to Habermas to work at the Institute and in a strongly worded letter to his friend, argued that the young Habermas was too radical, strongly influenced by Marx, to be a suitable Institute member.

Nevertheless, Horkheimer became Habermas's academic supervisor, with predictable consequences. The two clashed and after two years Habermas left Frankfurt and the Institute for Social Research, moving to the University of Marburg, where he completed his habilitation thesis under the direction of Wolfgang Abendroth, one of the very few openly Marxist philosophy professors in the generally conservative and strongly anti-communist West Germany of the mid-1950s.

Quite apart from any personal difficulties, however, Habermas's relationship to the Frankfurt School was bound to be difficult. Following the publication of *Dialectic of Enlightenment*, after all, Horkheimer and Adorno had largely abandoned the original project of a critical theory of society in which philosophy and empirical sociology would mutually reinforce and challenge one another, and had steadily moved back towards a more traditional disciplinary focus in philosophy. Both had been sharply critical of the goals and tactics of the radical student movement that swept through the cities and university campuses of Germany in 1968.[4] Habermas, for his part, was unwilling to accept the global rejection of the emancipatory dimension of socially embodied human rationality, and with it the core normative claim of the Kantian version of intellectual and political Enlightenment; the pessimistic work of Horkheimer and Adorno was thus bound to be a challenge and an ongoing obstacle as much as an intellectual inheritance. Thus the thesis that he produced under Abendroth's direction expresses a genuinely dialectical relationship with the influence of critical theory.

That thesis, entitled *Structural Transformation of the Public Sphere* (1962 [1989]), was a resounding success and quickly established Habermas as among the most promising philosophers and intellectuals in West Germany. In its argument and method, the book also made good on Habermas's ambitions to begin to produce social and political theory that would preserve the Enlightenment's core assertion of the internal connection between reason, freedom and dignity while jettisoning the philosophical trappings of that assertion that had become untenable.

Analysing the development of informal sites for political debate in eighteenth-century Europe such as salons, coffee houses, clubs and newspapers, Habermas observed that such informal venues offered spaces outside of the institutionalized political system for citizens to inform themselves of the issues of the day, debate these issues among themselves, and to form political opinions that could then be transmitted through various democratic access points to the political system. Such a "grassroots" source of political opinion formation operated on the very same procedural principles of open discourse that Habermas would later analyse as key elements of communicative rationality itself. Speakers and listeners in the public sphere were oriented by a shared, reciprocal willingness and desire to participate, by the recognition of the rough equivalence of their discursive status, and via a broadly shared insight into the consensual goals and fair practices of coming-to-understanding that took precedence over any particular political position or interest. In other words, they operated both reasonably and democratically, in a sense that revealed the strong conceptual interdependence of reason and democracy. Procedurally correct participation in a political public sphere required a specific range of skills, insights and behaviours. Democratic participation rests on discursive exchange, based on the giving and taking of reasons and oriented towards consensus.

In this way, the European political public sphere is the early stage of a phenomenon that Habermas's later work would explore theoretically, rather than historically. The public sphere is the space that participatory modern politics opens up between the everyday lived world of shared particular experiences and attitudes, on the one side, and the hierarchical, bureaucratic institutions of modern governance, on the other. This narrow and fragile space constitutes the arena where subjects, as citizens, exercise their rational agency by participating in informal discourses on matters of shared interest.

But as its title implied, *Structural Transformation of the Public Sphere* did not just analyse the normative foundations of early democratic communication, but also the decline of the public sphere, which was imperilled by the rise of the complex bureaucracies and highly organized state apparatuses that arose over the course of the nineteenth and twentieth centuries. These new "steering media" of state power and large market economies arose as linked responses to social complexity, and offered increasingly sophisticated and effective responses to the coordination problems of advanced national-state societies. But state bureaucracies and market economies also had the parallel undesirable effect of squeezing shut the narrow public space between state and market economy, transforming active citizens into passive clients and economic consumers.[5]

While Habermas's early work tends in some important sense to mirror the bleak diagnoses of social pathology so prevalent in the wartime writings of the "first generation" of critical theory, his understanding of the crisis tendencies and the structural deficiencies of modern democratic societies never assumed that rationality itself was the core problem. Instead, he was convinced that the form of calculative control that made effective bureaucratic power possible was distinct in important ways from the capacity for reason-giving and reason-taking that characterized the successful communicative steering of equally situated citizens. Hence the philosophical task of identifying just what this rationality consisted of, and how it could continue as a resource for democratic forms of life, put Habermas fundamentally at odds with the diagnosis of modernity offered by Horkheimer and Adorno. It also set the course for the collaborative effort between philosophy and the reconstructive, empirical social sciences that was discussed above.

In the works of the following decade, Habermas would turn to social theory and other reconstructive sciences as the primary tools for exploring both the pathologies of modern societies and their indwelling potentials for rationality and reform. In *Knowledge and Human Interests* (1968 [1971]), his most important philosophical work of the 1960s, Habermas turns to a number of other reconstructive sciences, including philosophical anthropology, historiography and even psychoanalytic theory, to justify the claim that "anthropologically deep-seated" interests acted as universal enabling conditions for the possibility of knowledge, and that these interests could be identified and distinguished from one another on the basis of the validity conditions of the kinds of knowledge that they enabled. These interests were neither reducible to physical features of the natural history of the human species, nor were identical to the various institutions that embodied them. Instead, knowledge-constitutive interests were, pragmatically speaking, the transcendental foundations of human knowing.

Habermas argues that three such interests are identifiable: a *technical* interest in the manipulation and control of external nature; a *practical* interest in intersubjective understanding, and an *emancipatory* interest in liberation from various forms of domination, coercion and control. Technical interest blossoms in modernity into the complex of science and technology, with its internal, interest-specific criteria of what counts as expertise, truth, success and progress. The practical interest in turn yields the range of hermeneutic-interpretive sciences that the nineteenth century had grouped together as the *Geisteswissenschaften* or the humanities: disciplines such as historiography, literary criticism or cultural studies whose goal is not to predict and control their objects of study but to generate understanding of them among qualified participants.

The institutions that the emancipatory interest gives rise to presented Habermas with a serious problem, however, since in some sense the identification of this third, openly normative and political interest was as aspirational as it was descriptive. Clearly Habermas could and did identify Marxist-inspired social criticism as a form of organized knowledge dedicated to revealing and overcoming modes of unnecessary domination, rather than control or understanding. But he also argued that Freudian psychoanalysis could be seen in this light, despite the obvious problems of how the outcome of (potentially interminable) psychotherapy could count as knowledge, and how the radically asymmetrical relationship between analyst and analysand could be seen as a paradigmatic example of (presumably egalitarian and general) emancipation.

Theory of communicative reason

Knowledge and Human Interests was generally regarded as unsuccessful in its attempt to identify the bases of modern forms of knowledge. But it served a crucial function in moving Habermas definitively from the kind of historical and contextual analysis of social knowledge that he had presented in *Structural Transformation of the Public Sphere* to the project that would occupy him throughout the 1970s and 1980s: a theory of communicative reason that encompassed both the "micrological" level of the actual epistemic foundations for differentiated modes of human knowing and acting, and the "macrological" level of the rise of social modernity, with its suite of new institutions and practices that embody, in various forms, these foundations.

Recognizing that the anthropological orientation of *Knowledge and Human Interests* was insufficiently conceptually clear for a critical social science, Habermas next turned to the neighbour discipline of linguistics, and especially the pragmatic branch of speech act theory, to find resources for a theory of rationality as a socially embedded suite of universal competencies. Regarding language as a system of intersubjective, coordinated actions, rather than a lexicon of meanings, Habermas investigated how speech is actually used to coordinate action: what core competencies speakers and hearers must have to communicate successfully with one another (see CES).

The account that emerged was one heavily influenced by both contemporary linguistics and by the tradition of American pragmatism. Underlying all natural languages, Habermas argued, is a set of universal, that is, pragmatically unavoidable, skills and competencies, in whose absence no coordination of actions by the medium of the exchange of speech acts is possible. The ability to assume alternate positions within a system of personal pronouns – to alternate between the "I" of speaker and the "you" of hearer – to understand what it means to justify the validity of an utterance through the giving of the right kind of reasons, to grasp the symmetrical and reciprocal demands of intersubjective speech acts, count as universal competence in a way that highlights the ultimately practical and social dimension of true or justified utterances.[6]

In his landmark two-volume *Theory of Communicative Action* (1981 [1984/1987]), therefore, Habermas is able to demonstrate the close collaborative relationship between philosophy and the reconstructive sciences that had motivated him since his earliest work, and that we have summarized in the discussion of the essay "Philosophy as Stand-In and Interpreter".

As in his earlier work, Habermas develops a theory of socially embedded rationality by analysing the universal linguistic competencies that adult speakers and hearers must ascribe to themselves and one another, in order to coordinate their collective behaviour. The reconstruction of universal linguistic competence requires Habermas to delve still more deeply into linguistics and theories of action and argumentation; into social-psychological theories of developmental psychology and related theoretical approaches to cognitive and moral learning processes; into speech act theory (which analyses human communication as intersubjective acts, rather than only as the mastery of a natural language); and into empirically based theories of natural argumentation.

The Theory of Communicative Action also constitutes a profound and sustained interrogation of the history, structure and goals of the discipline of sociology, including a deep reading of the theory of modernity as rationalization in the work of Max Weber, the symbolic interactionism of George Herbert Mead, the theories of secularization and transformation of a collective consciousness in Émile Durkheim, and the functionalist theory of Talcott Parsons. This extraordinary set of varied influences threatens to overwhelm the project as a whole, leaving it without centre or guiding thread. But understanding Habermas's larger conception of the transformed role of philosophy in the modern world allows us to perceive that *The Theory of Communicative Action* is ultimately a profoundly philosophical endeavour.

At every step, whether working through the fine details of the universal pragmatics of linguistic competence or entering longstanding methodological debates in interpretive sociology, the theory remains consistent in its objective of locating, identifying and elaborating the potential for rational conduct within the very structures of the modern subject and modern forms of social life; identifying the principal threats to this potential, and indicating how these threats can be responded to.

Habermas's intellectual impact

The question of Habermas's most significant and lasting impact on philosophy and on larger social areas is of course difficult to estimate. But a few generalities can serve as a good introduction.

From *Structural Transformation of the Public Sphere* through *The Theory of Communicative Action* and *Between Facts and Norms*, Habermas's published works in philosophy and political theory have played a crucial role in the transformation of Western philosophy in the post-war half-century and through the beginning of the twenty-first century. Three aspects of this influence stand out.

Cross-disciplinary engagement

First, as discussed above, Habermas's deliberately syncretistic, cross-disciplinary and encyclopaedic, wide-ranging approach to philosophy introduced a deliberate alternative to the image of the solitary, self-reflective philosopher conjuring profound truths from the depths of his internal consciousness, a model (and at times a caricature) of philosophical activity that remained largely intact as late as Wittgenstein and Heidegger in the post-war era. The popularity of Habermas's philosophical writings have definitively contradicted this image of methodological isolation, offering in its place a model of philosophy as a part of a multi-voiced conversation among and between related areas of human enquiry, with perhaps a special responsibility to serve as an interpreter or even perhaps as a referee between them when necessary and, if possible, to offer assistance in translating the findings of the natural and social sciences from the special technical vocabularies appropriate to them into the everyday language of public debate. Philosophy on this model is perhaps distinguished from, say, sociology or history by its awareness of its great age, its long institutional history and the enduring quality of the questions that it addresses, and a heightened degree of self-reflexivity and self-awareness about the nature and limitations of academic or scientific enquiry. But it has renounced both the principle and the method that presupposes some exclusive access to truth that other related disciplines lack. This is perhaps a deflationary view of the nature and purpose of philosophy. But it is also one that offers the discipline a far better chance for continued relevance in a scientific age.

Rehabilitation of reason

Second, Habermas's philosophical works as a whole represent what I will call the rehabilitation of reason. As Habermas had put it in his essay on "Philosophy as Stand-In and Interpreter", the need to abandon philosophy's pretensions to serve in the dual role as final judge of what the other sciences may legitimately know, and of how the sciences are to be related to all other spheres of human culture, does not imply that philosophy should also abandon its status as the "guardian of rationality". On the contrary.

In contrast to the trajectories of both Anglo-American analytic epistemology and philosophy of language and logic, and continental "post-modern" theories of the indeterminacy of the subject and its supposedly rational core, Habermas's discourse theory takes up without apology the ancient philosophical claim of reason's centrality in the human adventure. What is more, the reason that Habermas defends is a foundational power or aptitude of the human species. Reason is *universal*, in the sense that we have grounds to regard it as the origin of the exception-less and compulsory norms and claims associated with the conscious regulation of human affairs. It is *foundational* in the sense that it cannot be naturalized; that is, human reason and its status as a source for universal claims cannot be adequately accounted for by regarding it naturalistically as an outcome of contingent processes of either natural or social evolution. Finally, reason is *normative* in so far as it is the identifiable source of demands for the justification of our social and personal norms and not just of the capacity for rational calculation of strategic success or prudence.

This second claim regarding the rehabilitation of reason in Habermas's work may at first glance seem to conflict with the first, his demythologization of the practice of philosophy and his demand that philosophy become a good interaction partner with other adjacent disciplines in the humanities and social sciences. In fact, much of the distinctiveness of Habermas's philosophical project can be seen as the harmonization of these two. A deflationary account of the role and methods of philosophy that moves beyond claims for its distinctiveness and autonomy harmonizes with a rehabilitation of the centrality of reason in so far as Habermas's work breaks with both the "philosophy of the subject" in which reason is seen in the first instance as the property of the autonomous subject, and only derivatively as a feature of intersubjective interaction, and the "philosophy of consciousness", in which the internal life of the self-reflecting mind is taken as the primary forum for philosophical exploration, while the linguistically mediated interaction between subjects in society is taken as derivative of, and patterned after, subjects' self-relations.

Reason, for Habermas, is primarily a feature of human interaction, guided by the giving and taking of reasons in interpersonal communication. For this kind of interaction to succeed, the communication that coordinates it must be oriented towards consensus among those included in the relevant discursive procedures. Those procedures, if they are to appear reasonable, must tacitly or explicitly adopt rules of equality, reciprocity, openness or non-deceit, and fair inclusion of all concerned. And these rules, finally, can be taken as universal, unavoidable conditions for the possibility of justifiable outcomes, and hence as the foundations for "downstream" normative claims such as moral rightness, political justice and legal fairness.[7]

Habermas's famous "discourse principle", that norms by which we see courses of action as right or wrong are to be considered as justified only if all those affected by them could agree to them in a discourse that incorporates just these conditions, is the kernel of a claim that reasonableness is internally linked to rightness. It also renders in philosophically precise terms our everyday intuition that reasonableness is, in the end, simply the ability and willingness of a group of people to conduct themselves in a certain demanding but hardly impossible way; something that everyone is capable of, that everyone knows how to do without any special qualifications, and that people in just societies are well advised to institutionalize in their political systems as much as they realistically can. Domination, whether in the overt form of political systems that deny people the basic freedoms to act in uncoerced concert with one another, or in more insidious forms where the communicative resources of the lifeworld have dried up, leaving people no access to rational discourse, is thus in the final analysis a frustration of society's rational potential. The internal connection between reason and democracy – Habermas's great theme from *Structural Transformation of the Public Sphere* to *Between Facts and Norms* – is philosophy's contribution to the project of Enlightenment: democracy is not merely one of many plausible contenders in modes of political authority, nor the historically accidental and transitory "current favourite". It is reasonable as compared to all identifiable alternatives. As much as Habermas has devoted himself to a philosophical reconstruction of the reasonableness of democratic life, he has defended this vision against all opponents, most influentially perhaps against "postmodern" theorists such as Michel Foucault and Jacques Derrida, whom Habermas castigates for their abandonment of the promise of a robust and overtly rational defence of democratic life (see PDM).

This rehabilitated communicative, procedural and formal conception of reason does not aspire to the kind of foundational proof that would have been the ambition of an earlier form of philosophy. But as we will see, a core element of Habermas's influence on contemporary philosophy in particular, and indeed on contemporary thought in general, is the re-envisioning of the nature of socially embodied, intersubjective reason, a vision that navigates between the overly substantive, exclusionary and ultimately insidious effort to reanimate a holism that our times will not support, on the one side, and on the other an easy cynicism that finds in the pluralism of modern forms of life a justification for a wholesale abandonment of the discourse of rationality altogether.

Postmetaphysical thinking

This introduces the third and final aspect of Habermas's philosophical influence. For decades Habermas himself has consistently defined his philosophical project as "postmetaphysical" (PMT). Although a central term for all of Habermas's thinking, "post-metaphysical thinking" lacks a precise definition and may be better seen as a reigning spirit or broad postulate for how to think and write philosophically, rather than a specific philosophical claim.

To begin, postmetaphysical thinking certainly entails the Kantian claim that the traditional matters of philosophical metaphysics, that is, the immortal soul, or the existence of an omnipotent and omniscient Creator, or the fact of the freedom of the moral will, do not admit of definitive answers and ought to be taken instead as various expressions of the perennial human interest in the limits of what can be definitively known, or more specifically of the peculiar situation where one's interest in knowing something fundamental to the human conditions is evidently at complete odds with one's capacity to know it. But more pointedly, Habermas's vision of the postmetaphysical refers to the transformed role of philosophy in a transformed modern world. Paralleling the work of John Rawls in his "non-ideal" political theory, Habermas observes that philosophy confronts a modern social reality that has itself undergone dramatic and irreversible developments toward complexity, pluralism and diversity. These developments place strong limits on what philosophy can legitimately aspire to explain. Just as Rawls argued that the irreducible fact of value pluralism rules out the very possibility of a holistic value consensus within modern, democratic societies, so Habermas, too, frequently describes a "de-centred" self-understanding of modernity, where there is no real possibility of a broad and uncoerced consensus on basic orientations toward life, values, or ideals of the good.

Under conditions of irreducible pluralism and conflicting conceptions of the good life, the rationality of modern forms of life can consist only in reasonable procedures for regulating conflict and generating social solidarity, and these reasonable procedures are nothing other than the forms of communicative rationality that succeed in installing themselves durably into the practices of democratic self-governance and the attitudes of tolerance and humility of modern democratic citizens. Philosophy, like modern society itself, must abandon its ambitions toward a transcendent truth and all-embracing meaning, in order to re-appropriate its far humbler but still-crucial mission: identifying, articulating and, if possible, promoting the rationality of modern social existence.

Public intellectual and mentor

Beyond the broad influence Habermas has exercised on post-war philosophy in these intertwined ways, no discussion of his overall influence would be complete unless it mentioned two other areas. First, Habermas has had a very considerable impact as an engaged public intellectual in the very same "political public sphere" that he theorized as a philosopher. Indeed there has been virtually no debate of broad international concern over the past half-century that Habermas has not participated in, via opinion pieces in newspapers and journals, conferences and discussions, both in his native Germany and increasingly to a global audience.

It would be impossible to detail the number and range of the debates that Habermas has participated in, but even the briefest of highlights demonstrates this crucial dimension of his influence: as early as the 1950s Habermas was a key voice in debates over the transition of the political culture of the new Federal Republic to embrace, rather than merely tolerate, the demands of democratic governance. From curricular reform in secondary schools, through West Germany's international alliances, the sweep of its domestic politics, to its policies of reparation and commemoration, Habermas has consistently demanded an open society. As the Cold War ended Habermas was a vocal advocate for a self-reflective and deliberation-based model for German unification, and since then has been a tireless commentator on Germany's role in the European Union and the importance of the Union's political consolidation and expansion (DW). More recently, Habermas has been a high-profile participant in debates concerning the moral and political dimensions of new genetic technologies (FHN) and of the role of religion and religious values in public life in the "postsecular" societies of Western Europe.[8] In all these interventions, Habermas's work as a public philosopher and as a public intellectual merge: he insists that, in a postmetaphysical democratic world, only good reasons can provide the ultimate warrant.

Second, Habermas's half-century as an active philosopher has also been extremely influential in moulding and promoting the intellectual careers of a wide and international spectrum of younger scholars. Indeed an entire "third generation" of critical theorists can be said to exist, comprising former students of Habermas such as Axel Honneth, Hauke Brunkhorst and Rainer Forst in Germany, and Thomas McCarthy, Seyla Benhabib and Nancy Fraser in the United States.

Notes

1. There are relatively few good biographical studies of Habermas in English. For an account of Habermas's early years and his reactions to his experiences of National Socialism, see his interview with Peter Dews (Habermas 1986: esp. 149–90).
2. A thorough discussion of Habermas's role in the early years of the Federal Republic of Germany can be found in Moses (2007: esp. 105–30).
3. For further discussion of Habermas's conception of detranscendentalized reason and postmetaphysical thinking, see Chapter 2 in this volume.
4. Chapter 7 in this volume further addresses Habermas's involvement in the student protests.
5. The later Habermas theorizes this phenomenon in terms of the colonization of the lifeworld by the system. See Chapter 4 in this volume.
6. For a discussion of Habermas's linguistic turn and its development, see Chapter 3.
7. See Chapters 6, 7 and 9, respectively.
8. Habermas, "Pre-political Foundations of the Democratic Constitutional State?" (Habermas & Ratzinger 2006: 19–52).

PART I

Communicative rationality

TWO

Postmetaphysical thinking

Melissa Yates

The development of empirical research methods in both the social and the natural sciences has had a deep impact on the self-conception of philosophy. Jürgen Habermas aims to strike a balance between two ways of understanding the relationship between philosophy and the sciences: between a conception of philosophy as an Archimedean point from which to view the human condition and a conception of philosophy as a mere artefact of Western culturally embedded assumptions. Against the first, Habermas aims to integrate the resources and methods of the social sciences into philosophy and to deny that philosophy can proceed outside of historical and social contexts. On his view, philosophical knowledge is produced communicatively, through socially embedded dialogue. Against the second, Habermas claims fundamental questions about the human condition cannot be answered by purely social or natural scientific approaches. His "postmetaphysical" methodology aims to integrate empirical resources into philosophy without losing sight of what is unique to philosophy: namely, its ability to step back from the empirical data in order to reconstruct in a systematic way underlying universal truths about us, our societies and our place in the world.

Criticism of metaphysical philosophy

In "Themes in Postmetaphysical Thinking" Habermas claims that since Hegel there has been "no alternative to postmetaphysical thinking" (PMT: 29). He means two things by this statement. First, postmetaphysical thinking is something that has developed from specific social and historical processes. Postmetaphysical philosophy is not merely a philosophical method but a philosophical movement that evolved in response to critiques of what came before. But second, it is not a normatively empty historical development. Postmetaphysical thinking reflects an acceptance of principled critiques of earlier, more metaphysical approaches to philosophical questions.

For Habermas, postmetaphysical philosophy is as much descriptive of our social and historical time as it is descriptive of a valid philosophical methodology. Metaphysical philosophy is, in a sense, stuck in the past. Historical figures that count as metaphysical thinkers include Plato, Plotinus, Neo-Platonists, Augustine, Aquinas, Cusanus, Pico de Mirandola, Descartes, Spinoza, Leibniz, Kant, Fichte and Hegel. Against these, ancient materialism, scepticism, late-medieval nominalism and modern empiricism count as antimetaphysical countermovements (PMT: 29). Since postmetaphysical philosophy is the rejection of metaphysical thinking it is important to begin with a brief discussion of the critiques of metaphysics that Habermas takes for granted.[1]

The term "postmetaphysical" might already strike one as misleading, particularly since there are many contemporary philosophers who consider themselves to be metaphysicians. Metaphysics is defined by its ambition to provide a totalizing account of the whole from a transcendent point of view in which ideas are the model or blueprint for matter. The material world is measured against the perfection of an all-encompassing conception of the universe as a whole, supported from an objective, universal perspective above or outside the world. This approach typically elevates the contemplative life of the philosopher as the exemplary or privileged way of life. According to Habermas, what is dangerous about this understanding of philosophy is that it embeds theory itself in a way of life "that promises contact with the extra-ordinary" (PMT: 32). There is an escapism and contempt for the material world in this way of thinking, evidenced by the accounts of salvation that often accompany metaphysical thinking:

> Each of the great world religions stakes out a privileged and particularly demanding path to the attainment of individual salvation – e.g., the way to salvation of the wandering Buddhist monk or that of the Christian eremite. Philosophy recommends as its path to salvation the life dedicated to contemplation – the *bios theoretikos*. (PMT: 32)[2]

It is not simply that postmetaphysical philosophy rejects these accounts of salvation. Habermas emphasizes further that philosophy is itself distorted by the drive to purify itself of reliance on the material world. Purity in a metaphysical system is only attainable if philosophy defines the terms of its own debate in a self-justifying way without reliance on sensory experience.[3] To attain objective knowledge about the world, on this view, the philosopher should strive to be disembodied, to occupy a neutral or transcendent position outside her cultural and historical context.[4]

Postmetaphysical philosophy presupposes that there is no such observer-position available for the philosopher because we are all deeply conditioned by our historical contexts. In Habermas's terms, we are all participants, embedded in a world that serves as the presupposed background for all of our judgements, philosophical or otherwise.[5] Our linguistic context is one of the most important features of this background, since it makes possible our philosophical projects; for Habermas, there is no way for us to get behind that, so to speak. So, according to postmetaphysical philosophy, we must begin philosophy with a sober acceptance of the fact that philosophical reasoning is deeply embedded in particular linguistic contexts.[6] This "linguistic turn" in philosophy effectively shifted metaphysical thinking away from the solipsistic philosopher, instead conceiving of philosophy as a communicative process.

Postmetaphysical philosophy still occupies a unique position and has a distinctive purpose, however, independent of empirical science. As Habermas puts it:

> What remains for philosophy, and what is within its capabilities, is to mediate interpretively between expert knowledge and an everyday practice in need of orientation. What remains for philosophy is an illuminating furtherance of lifeworld processes of achieving self-understanding, processes that are related to totality. For the lifeworld must be defended against extreme alienation at the hands of the objectivating, the moralizing, *and* the aestheticizing interventions of expert cultures. (PMT: 17–18)

The image of a philosopher–mediator requires of postmetaphysical thinking an engagement and responsiveness to social and natural sciences unprecedented in philosophical thinking. The goal for postmetaphysical philosophers remains to analyse lifeworld structures from a critical distance, to systematize fundamental human conditions: but this time without the pretence of occupying an extraordinary vantage point.

Habermas uses the term postmetaphysical thinking to describe the kind of philosophy that can still be done even in light of the deep social embeddedness of the practice of philosophy. This chapter explicates five key ideas that constitute Habermas's postmetaphysical approach to philosophy: (i) the detranscendentalized use of reason, (ii) rational reconstruction, (iii) weak transcendentalism, (iv) context-transcending validity, and (v) soft naturalism.

The detranscendentalized use of reason

Habermas rejects the metaphysical pretence of purification from bodily elements to occupy a position above or beyond the world. Rationality is itself embedded in historically conditioned practices, which contain assumptions about the right kinds of questions, the appropriate kinds of evidence, and the legitimate philosophical agendas. By speaking of the "use of reason" Habermas emphasizes a *practice* of reasoning that is not capable of being purified or rendered neutral of its historical conditions. In this way the subject of knowledge is "detranscendentalized": finite and only capable of philosophical reflection because she has a wealth of everyday and common-sense knowledge already.[7]

For Habermas, one of the most significant components of our inescapable historical embeddedness is that our communicative practices enable knowledge. In "Communicative Action and the 'Use of Reason'" Habermas explains, "Detranscendentalization leads, on the one hand, to the embedding of socialized subjects into the context of a lifeworld and, on the other hand, to the entwinement of cognition with speech and action" (BNR: 30). Everyone reaches adulthood with fundamental communicative assumptions and over the course of everyday life competent language users adopt a wide range of complicated communicative norms. In many ways, human embeddedness in specific linguistic background cultures is the starting point for Habermas's philosophical project. When we advance knowledge claims, such as when we say that "germs do not spontaneously generate", we can do so only from within highly regulated communicative structures on the assumption that these claims are evaluable by others within our linguistic communities. It is in this sense that philosophers can advance knowledge claims only as participants within the context of communicative practices.

According to Habermas, two important assumptions make possible the communicative practice of advancing knowledge claims. First, detranscendentalized subjects presuppose a common world shared by others. For instance, we pragmatically presuppose that the world is "objective" in the sense that it is "the same for everyone", whenever we refer to something in the world.[8] When someone refers to a chair as being made of wood the presupposition is that there are objects in our world that we can all identify as chairs. In addition, Habermas argues that we presuppose a shared social world in our practices of justifying moral claims. Postmetaphysical thinking takes for granted this presupposition of a shared world that is knowable by all of us in common (BNR: 43).

Second, a detranscendentalized use of reason proceeds on the assumption that philosophical knowledge claims must be justified in the form of reasons advanced *to* others. Habermas explains:

> As speakers and addressees ... communicatively acting subjects encounter one another literally at eye level by taking on first- and *second*-person roles. By reaching an understanding about something in the objective world and adopting the same relation to the world, they enter into an interpersonal relationship. In this performative attitude *toward* one another, they share communicative experiences *with* one another against the background of an intersubjectively shared – that is, sufficiently overlapping – lifeworld. (BNR: 40)

Instead of aiming to remove philosophical thought from the impurity of everyday contexts, postmetaphysical thinking proceeds on the assumption that all knowledge claims are advanced in the context of our relationships with other communicating subjects. Our claims can only be understood, or rationally redeemed, against the backdrop of a wide range of pretheoretical assumptions about our shared world. Meeting each other "at eye level" contradicts the conception of the theorist as metaphorically outside or above the material world.

Rational reconstruction

While Habermas accepts that philosophy cannot proceed from a vantage point that transcends historical context, he also aims to preserve philosophy's ability to critically examine background cultures. We are all embedded in contexts that we cannot analyse from the outside, but we should not conclude that we cannot rationally understand these contexts, or that we are unable to criticize them. Instead, philosophy can take a critical distance on these background assumptions from within by rationally reconstructing their basic features.

Rational reconstruction begins with empirical investigation. For instance, a rational reconstruction of communicative practices begins with an analysis of the uses of language by everyday speakers.[9] Competently communicating subjects abide by wide-ranging rules that structure their communication. Everyday speakers have an implicit knowledge of these deeper structures and rules, and the task of rational reconstruction is to make explicit this tacit knowledge. Habermas describes this point in "Historical Materialism and the Development of Normative Structures": "*reconstruction* signifies taking a theory apart and putting it back together again in a new form in order to attain more fully the goal it has set for itself" (CES: 95). When someone advances a claim about the temperature outside they do so as a participant in a communicative practice regulated by assumptions about what counts as reasons for knowledge claims about temperatures.[10] At the surface level communicative subjects do not know these rules and structures, but in practice their action presupposes an implicit understanding of them. As Thomas McCarthy puts it, the goal of rational reconstruction "is not a paraphrase or a translation of an originally unclear meaning but an explicit knowledge of rules and structures, the mastery of which underlies the competence of a subject to generate meaningful expressions" (1993: 131).[11] Rational reconstruction does not attempt to improve language or speech; it is a theoretical method for analysing the *conditions of possibility* for language and speech with the aim of discovering universal presuppositions adopted by communicative subjects.

Habermas describes the task of rational reconstruction as a twofold process of making explicit the implicit rational structure of language and speech. The first depends on formal pragmatic analyses, where the theoretical aim is to develop an account of the universal rules that must be presupposed to make sense of different kinds of communicative acts. Rather than merely giving an account of how subjects use language and speech in everyday contexts, formal pragmatics attempts to systematically organize and articulate fundamental conditions of everyday speech and language. For instance, communicative action oriented towards understanding is only possible on the background assumption that speakers should offer reasons for the knowledge claims that they advance. The success of reconstructions of formal pragmatic conditions of language and speech depends crucially on how well the reconstructive theory provides the rational grounds for the empirically observable uses of language and speech in everyday contexts.

But rational reconstruction does not merely aim to provide a deeper understanding of these empirically observable communicative acts. A second component of Habermas's reconstructive project concerns the historic evolution of species-wide competences of communicating subjects (McCarthy 1993: 138). Habermas refers to this second component of rational reconstruction as an attempt to understand the *generation* of the formal pragmatic presuppositions of competent communicatively acting subjects in the essay "What is Universal Pragmatics?" (CES: 13).

The process of rational reconstruction addresses a transcendental question. The reconstructive task is to determine the conditions of possibility of, in this case, communicative action. These conditions are meant to have the force of universally presupposed rules and structures, but they are not knowable *a priori*, independently of experience. This is a crucial contrast with transcendentalist approaches adopted by earlier metaphysical thinkers. McCarthy explains that, in contrast with the Kantian transcendental project, Habermas's rational reconstructions "are advanced in a hypothetical attitude and must be checked and revised in the light of the data, which are gathered a posteriori from the actual performances and considered appraisals of competent subjects" (1993: 131). Reconstructive theories can be assessed only by real-world communicative actions. This resonates with several important commitments of postmetaphysical thinking. Reconstructive projects can only be taken up from within the conditions of communicative action under the reconstructive lens, not from a transcendent position outside these structures. Moreover, instead of treating empirical experience as something that distorts the purity of rational projects, reconstructive approaches in philosophy explicitly depend on these experiences and observations as necessary data to check the success of the theories.

Weak transcendentalism

The transcendental nature of rational reconstruction might make it appear that Habermas is himself using the metaphysical methods that he has criticized. Kant called his project transcendental because it sought the *a priori* conditions that make experience of the world possible. While Habermas's understanding of rational reconstruction also aims to discover "conditions of possibility", his approach does not attempt to discover the conditions of experience in general. Instead, he poses a different transcendental question: "How is mutual understanding (among speaking and acting subjects) possible in general?" (*ibid.*: 130). This question cannot be addressed aprioristically because it depends on an analysis of the use of language and speech by communicatively acting subjects (which is only knowable *a posteriori*). This *weak* version of a transcendental question relies on empirical experience at two different points. First, reconstructing the conditions of mutual understanding requires analysing communication among everyday speakers. Second, conclusions advanced about these conditions through reconstructive arguments must continuously be tested against everyday experience. The results of reconstructive projects cannot be demonstrated *a priori*. Instead, as Habermas explains in "What is Universal Pragmatics?", "we term *transcendental* the conceptual structure recurring in all coherent experiences" (CES: 21–2).

For Kant, there was a stark distinction between empirical investigation and transcendental philosophy.[12] For this reason, Habermas is sometimes reluctant to use the term transcendental at all because he worries that it might lead to a misunderstanding of his project (CES: 25). But Habermas is committed to the idea that postmetaphysical philosophy can make use of weakly transcendental approaches. For instance, he defends our presupposition of a shared objective world as transcendentally necessary in this weaker sense because "it cannot be corrected by experiences that would not be possible without it" (BNR: 41). Any attempt to deny the idea of a shared objective world could only be advanced communicatively. And, if Habermas is right, any communicative action can only be made sense of against the backdrop of an assumption of a shared objective world. This means that we cannot but assume that there *is* such a world whenever we attempt communicative action. He explains, "The formal-pragmatic supposition of the world creates placeholders for objects to which speaking and acting subjects can refer. However, grammar cannot 'impose' any laws on nature. A 'transcendental projection' in the weak sense depends on nature 'meeting us halfway'" (BNR: 42). The objects in our shared world are not constituted by the fact that we refer to them; our *knowledge* of them is so constituted.

Another weakly transcendental supposition that Habermas supports is the claim that we must all presuppose we are engaged with rational beings when we communicate:

> In their cooperative interactions each must ascribe rationality to the other, at least provisionally. In certain circumstances, it may turn out that such a presupposition was unwarranted. Contrary to expectation, it might happen that the other person cannot account for her actions and utterances and that we cannot see how she could justify her behavior. ... This supposition states that a subject who is acting intentionally is capable, in the right circumstances, of providing a more or less plausible reason for why she did or did not behave or express herself this way rather than some other way. Unintelligible, odd, bizarre, or enigmatic expressions prompt follow-up questions because they implicitly

> contradict an unavoidable presupposition of communication and therefore trigger puzzled or irritated reactions. (BNR: 36)

The presupposition of rationality in others (until proven otherwise) is here defended by reference to examples of irrationality. This kind of rationality is primarily practical: we presuppose that people generally can justify their actions to others. If we encounter a person who is sleep-walking and cannot explain what he is doing, we look for an unusual explanation for his action because we presuppose that unless something unusual is going on the person could give reasons for what he is doing.

Habermas uses his weakly transcendental approach to derive significant moral and political conclusions. In addition to the presupposition of a shared objective world Habermas also thinks we necessarily presuppose a shared "social world", regulated by an understanding of legitimate interpersonal relationships (BNR: 46; cf. also TCA 2: 127). If we take for granted that all persons are capable of rationally justifying their actions then we need an understanding of how we adjudicate this exchange of reasons in a social context. Habermas argues that:

> If the process of argumentation is to live up to its meaning, communication in the form of rational discourse must allow, if possible, all relevant information and explanations to be brought up and weighed so that the stance participants take can be inherently motivated solely by the revisionary power of free-floating reasons. (BNR: 49)

Speakers necessarily presuppose that others are rationally capable of justifying action; they also presuppose that rational discourse involves an exchange of reasons that is improved by the incorporation of as much relevant information as possible. In the context of democratic deliberations Habermas advances four further transcendental presuppositions. The first is that democratic deliberations are public and inclusive, such that everyone who could make a contribution that pertains to a controversial matter is included. The second is that everyone has equal rights to engage in communication and an equal opportunity to speak. The third is that participants exclude deception and illusion from their arguments. And the fourth is that communication is not coerced, but is instead "free from restrictions that prevent the better argument from being raised and determining the outcome of the discussion" (BNR: 52). Seyla Benhabib defends these weakly transcendental presuppositions in *The Claims of Culture* as the norms that are "in a minimal sense necessary for us to distinguish a consensus, rationally and freely attained among participants, from other forms of agreements that may be based on power and violence, tradition and custom, ruses of egoistic self-interest as well as moral indifference" (2002: 67). According to Benhabib, we cannot deny the difference between rationally motivated consensus, as opposed to agreement that results from force and manipulation.[13] This supports a weakly transcendental account of the norms necessary for rationally motivated agreements. As she puts it:

> This would not be a strong transcendental argument proving the necessity and singularity of certain conditions without which some aspect of our world, conduct, and consciousness *could* not be what it is. A weak transcendental argument would demonstrate more modestly that certain conditions need to be fulfilled for us to judge those practices to be of a certain sort rather than of a different kind. For example, without showing equal respect for one's conversation partners, without an equal distribution of these rights to speak, interrogate, and propose alternatives, we would find it hard to call the agreement reached at the end of a conversation fair, rational, or free. This does not mean that these conditions do not themselves permit interpretation, disagreement, or contention, or that they are rooted in the deep structure of human consciousness. (2002: 38)

Speakers will no doubt find themselves disappointed by actual democratic deliberation for failing to live up to these regulative ideals. For Habermas, these suppositions are examples of the conditions of possibility for legitimate democratic deliberation. The fact that we experience disappointment with our actual experiences in their failure to live up to our expectations serves as further evidence that we presupposed them in the first place.[14]

Context-transcending validity

Habermas's philosophical methodology is transcendental because it questions the conditions of possibility of mutual understanding; it is *weakly* transcendental because it abandons the goal of aprioristically determined conditions of experience and instead takes as its point of departure analyses of the use of language and speech by everyday communicative actors. This is a broadly postmetaphysical approach because it takes for granted that the subjects of transcendental knowledge are themselves embedded in historical contexts and that rational reconstruction cannot be pursued from a God's-eye point of view. At the same time, Habermas denies that postmetaphysical thinking undermines our ability to reconstruct the transcendental presuppositions, in particular the conditions of mutual understanding, as *universally valid*. Transcendental conditions are not knowable independent of experience but they admit of context-transcending validity, according to Habermas. This is crucial if rational reconstruction is to serve as a resource for moral and political criticism of dominant cultural practices, which he thinks it should. Habermas's approach thus requires a delicate balance between his rejection of metaphysical attempts to theorize from a transcendent perspective and his defence of the postmetaphysical attempt to defend transcendental knowledge claims as valid in a context-transcendent way.

Habermas describes context-transcendent validity as a process of "immanent transcendence" (BNR: 35). Rational reconstruction of fundamental communicative structures is a project undertaken by a philosopher-participant who is a competent language user in a specific social and historical context. She cannot occupy a context-independent perspective on the world, nor can her references to objects in the world be experienced independently of habits and anticipations about the world. All knowledge of the world, according to postmetaphysical thinking, is constituted communicatively (BNR: 35–6). That means that the process of knowledge-acquisition is itself a communicative process: it develops in the course of an exchange of reasons and evidence among communicatively competent speakers and addressees who advance *knowledge claims*.[15] When we advance knowledge claims *as valid* we pragmatically presuppose that validity claims are universally valid within a relevant domain. As William Mark Hohengarten puts it, "Validity means validity for every subject capable of speech and action" (PMT: ix). The presuppositions of these validity claims depend on the context of the claim: whether it refers to the objective world, the social world, or the subjective world. In each system of reference we presuppose different conditions of validity. When a geologist claims that continents continuously move by a process of plate tectonics he advances a knowledge claim that presupposes a shared objective world with continents such that the referent is the same for all of us. He also advances the claim as universally valid: if it is a true claim then it reflects something true about the earth and the continents. The geologist advances this claim from within the context of a social and historical context of scientific theories and assumptions, but the claim advanced is meant as a context-transcending claim about the objective world. By reconstructing the communicative practice of justifying a claim about the objective world *as valid* we discover presuppositions of this practice.[16]

According to Habermas, we can also rationally reconstruct the transcendental conditions of validity claims advanced about the social world, the world constituted by *normatively* sanctioned actions. This reconstructive task also begins with empirical experience of communicative processes employed by speakers when advancing moral validity claims. Such claims also refer to a shared world and aim for universal validity, but the referents of moral terms are more ambiguous because they do not admit of the kind of scientific analysis that validity claims about the objective world do. So, for instance, when someone advances the moral claim that all persons should be afforded freedom of conscience they do so not as a claim that is only valid *for us* but instead as a context-transcendent validity claim about all persons. The question for Habermas is, then, under what conditions can moral claims be valid in this way?[17] In the context of moral discourse his answer to this transcendental question depends on his reconstruction of what he calls the "moral point of view", or the ideal speech conditions under which communicatively acting subjects could arrive at morally valid conclusions. These ideal speech conditions systematically account for the rules of moral discourse in a context-transcending way.[18] The process of *justifying* a moral claim *as valid* is one that must be structured to satisfy these ideal speech conditions, to the extent possible.[19]

Habermas's defence of the possibility of postmetaphysical context-transcendent validity claims rejects the idea of cultural incommensurability. While he takes for granted the criticism of metaphysical thinking for its pretence of purity and cultural neutrality, he warns against the conclusion that we lack access to universally valid knowledge claims about the objective world.[20] There are inevitable challenges in attempts to translate knowledge claims from one linguistic community to another, but Habermas argues that people can achieve mutual understanding because "in presupposing a shared objective world, they orient themselves toward the claim to truth, that is, to the unconditional validity they claim when they make a statement" (BNR: 36). Claims to context-transcendent validity, because they refer to our shared world, remain open to criticism from all perspectives. This is why exposure to different cultural contexts provides an important resource for subverting dogmatic and conservative assumptions.[21]

Soft naturalism

Postmetaphysical thinking proceeds from the criticism of metaphysical philosophy in terms of its commitments to totalizing worldviews, solipsistic accounts of self-consciousness, denunciations of the material lives of everyday practices in favour of purified rationality, and the pretence to occupy an extra-worldly objective vantage point. Philosophy today can only proceed postmetaphysically, according to Habermas. In the place of metaphysical approaches to philosophy, Habermas endorses a weakly transcendental project of rationally reconstructing fundamental presuppositions of implicit commonsense knowledge claims. This approach rejects the Kantian aim of apriorism in favour of an empirical starting point: the analysis of everyday intuitions about communicative practices from the participant perspective. Not surprisingly this admission of an empirical starting point has required that his philosophical project be interdisciplinary, drawing from resources in social and natural sciences. It is, however, important to stress that philosophy retains a unique role and a research project distinct from the empirical sciences. Philosophy will continue to thrive in a postmetaphysical age.

Habermas demarcates this unique role for philosophy from empirical science in his rejection of a brand of naturalism that seeks to reduce all knowledge to scientifically demonstrable knowledge. In response to this reductionism Habermas defends what he calls a "soft naturalist" position against "hard naturalism".[22] Naturalism holds that everything that exists is a part of the natural world. Habermas accepts this, but denies it makes transcendental claims unjustified or unintelligible. Instead he posits the presupposition of a shared objective world as a condition of communicative rationality and conceives of this world as something we inevitably refer to in the course of advancing knowledge claims.[23] This sort of transcendentalism grants an epistemic priority to well-justified claims about the natural world. In response to religious fundamentalist critics of his political philosophy, for example, he unapologetically sides with the best theories supported by natural science as deserving of unqualified political support: we should take for granted that dinosaurs existed even if that conflicts with some fundamentalist religious views.[24]

Hard naturalists support the stronger view that all knowledge claims must be reduced to scientific knowledge claims, often leading to a deep scepticism about the force of *normative* knowledge claims. In various places Habermas refers to hard naturalism also as "scientistic naturalism". "'Scientism' means science's belief in itself: that is, the conviction that we can no longer understand science as one form of possible knowledge, but rather must identify knowledge with science" (KHI: 4). In *Knowledge and Human Interests* Habermas argues that philosophy of science and positivism fail to question the legitimacy and presuppositions of scientific methodology, instead taking for granted an objective and universal methodological stance. For this reason, he argues, early positivism "succumbs to the same sentence of extravagance and meaninglessness that it once passed on metaphysics" (KHI: 67).[25] Habermas rejects the assumption that the merits of naturalism vindicate a broad-based reduction of all knowledge claims to scientific knowledge claims. In particular, he thinks that humans have developed so that we take for granted a shared social world too. According to soft naturalism, scientific approaches remain appropriate for claims about our shared objective world but do not exhaust what we can know about our shared social world. In his terms, "reality is not exhausted by the totality of scientific statements that count as true according to current empirical scientific standards" (BNR: 153).

A classic example of the tension between hard and soft naturalist approaches is evidenced in the philosophical debate about the compatibility of freedom and determinism. According to hard naturalism, humans must be conceived as part of the natural world in a way that focuses on the material aspects of humans: we have bodies that are moved to act by other material causes, whether those causes are internal (brain functions) or external (other bodies) to us. Hard naturalists might, for example, explain what we take to be intentional movements in neurobiological terms: we lift our hand because our brain sends a signal to our hand and causes it to move. According to a narrowly determinist explanation our actions are causally explained by previous material events. We are not "free" to choose one among many courses of action because whatever we do will always have been caused by material causes. Hard naturalism, according to Habermas, takes for granted that accounts of free will or "reasons for action" are pseudo-scientific explanations that should be reduced to their scientific, material explanations (BNR: 207). Soft naturalism does not compete with attempts to scientifically understand material causality or neurobiology, but also does not reduce our everyday understanding of "acting on reasons" to these causes.[26]

A soft naturalist accepts that humans exist in the natural world, and that empirical studies can serve as an important corrective to socially accepted and commonsense beliefs. But according to the soft naturalist we must also be able to account for our non-scientific experiential assumption that we view ourselves as free. When we give explanations for running five miles we do not typically give the material causal story, even if it is a true one. We give *reasons* for our *choice* to run five miles.[27] A soft naturalist assumes that these kinds of explanations are also crucial to understanding why we do things and that the scientistic reduction of such explanations to neurobiological functions of the body misses the target. According to Habermas:

> A will is formed, however imperceptively, *in the course of* deliberations. And because a decision *comes about* as the result of deliberations, however fleeting and unclear they may be, we experience ourselves as free only in the actions that we perform to some degree consciously. … Only a reflective will is free.
> (BNR 155–6)

This is not a claim about biology, but rather a claim about our practical knowledge of ourselves.[28]

For Habermas, hard naturalists mistakenly overextend the lessons of science. Scientific knowledge is itself communicatively structured by participants taking part in processes of argumentation and justification. Scientific research cannot proceed wholly outside this participant perspective, as if from a pure observer's point of view.[29] The problem evidenced by the hard naturalist parallels Habermas's analysis of a problem with some religious fundamentalists. A religious fundamentalist who denies that dinosaurs existed millions of years ago for the reason that it conflicts with religious texts fails to accept the burden of justifying claims about the objective world according to the methods of empirical science, a cognitive requirement given the evolution of knowledge claims in modern times. The hard scientist who denies that there are any claims of justice because claims about justice cannot be vindicated by reference to objects in the natural world has also failed to accept the division of labour between kinds of knowledge claims. Normative knowledge claims require normative reasons and cannot be settled by mere reference to empirical evidence.

This account of the demarcation of science and philosophy plays an important role in Habermas's conception of the transcendental requirements of citizenship in pluralistic democracies. For example, his defence of the separation of church and state presupposes that all citizens have "self-modernized". A crucial component of self-modernization is the acceptance of secular knowledge in scientific domains. In particular, religious citizens must distinguish between the kinds of evidence and reasons that can be used in favour of claims about the objective world and the kinds of justifications for dogmatic claims of faith. This is relevant in public debates over educational policies concerning evolution, for instance. While he does not characterize adoption of this epistemic stance as a civic duty, Habermas does see it as a necessary precondition for legitimate civic engagement ("Religion in the Public Sphere", BNR: 137).

Despite this, Habermas also insists that religious language has an important and perhaps irreplaceable role to play in public deliberation.[30]

He takes for granted that religious language sometimes conceals deep, universal moral truths that have not yet been adequately understood in secular terms. In "Religion in the Public Sphere" he explains:

> Religious traditions have a special power to articulate moral intuitions, especially with regard to vulnerable forms of communal life. In corresponding political debates, this potential makes religious speech into a serious vehicle for possible truths contents, which can then be translated from the vocabulary of a particular religious community into a generally accessible language. (BNR: 131)

Religious citizens should, on his account, provide religious reasons for their positions on laws and policies to make possible processes of public learning. Secular citizens, moreover, are tasked with helping translate religious reasons that arise in informal public debate into secular alternatives for the purposes of formal processes of legislation. This approach demonstrates Habermas's commitment to the idea that science does not have priority in moral deliberation, and that philosophy cannot presuppose clean demarcations between secular and religious moral deliberation.

Philosophic discourse is itself embedded in contingent historical contexts. According to postmetaphysical thinking, philosophy should take for granted the priority of scientific claims about the objective world. But this does not entail a priority of scientific claims about the social world, nor does it rule out the possibility that religious claims contain important universal moral truths. By rationally reconstructing communicative assumptions within scientific, moral and religious discourse, philosophers can provide universal insights about the kinds of deliberative contexts that are oriented towards understanding without the pretence of occupying a transcendent vantage point. Weakly transcendental claims about communicative rationality shed light on processes of scientific justification no less than on processes of moral justification. Our presupposition of a shared objective and social world makes possible communicative acts of justification and points the way to a uniquely philosophic task, namely, reconstruction of the universal conditions of scientific and moral understanding.[31]

Notes

1. Habermas does not take himself to be advancing these criticisms in a unique way. Instead, in "Themes in Postmetaphysical Thinking" Habermas takes himself

to be surveying successful objections advanced by a wide range of historians, sociologists, psychologists and philosophers.

2. See also KHI: 301, on the religious origins of the word "theory".
3. In "Metaphysics after Kant" Habermas writes: "Philosophy no longer directs its own pieces. This holds true even for the one role in which philosophy does step out of the system of sciences, in order to answer *unavoidable* questions by enlightening the lifeworld about itself as a whole. For, in the midst of certainties, the lifeworld is opaque" (PMT: 16).
4. Habermas's criticism of the objectivism of metaphysics can be traced back to *Knowledge and Human Interests*: "[A]s long as philosophy remains caught in ontology, it is itself subject to an objectivism that disguises the connection of its knowledge with the human interest in autonomy and responsibility (*Mündigkeit*). There is only one way in which it can acquire the power that it vainly claims for itself in virtue of its seeming freedom from presuppositions: by acknowledging its dependence on this interest and turning against its own illusion of pure theory the critique it directs at the objectivism of the sciences" (KHI: 311).
5. Jeffrey Flynn's (2009) book review of Jürgen Habermas's *Between Naturalism and Religion* makes clear the significance of the participant and observer perspectives in Habermas's communicative theory of rationality.
6. In "Themes in Postmetaphysical Thinking", Habermas writes, "The embedding of theoretical accomplishments in the practical contexts of their genesis and employment gave rise to an awareness of the relevance of everyday contexts of action and communication. These contexts attain a philosophical status in, for example, the concept of a *lifeworld background*" (PMT: 34). For a discussion of the lifeworld, see Chapter 4 by Heath in this volume. For a discussion of the pragmatics of communication, see Chapter 3 by Fultner.
7. See KHI: ch. 6, "The Self-Reflection of the Natural Sciences: The Pragmatist Critique of Meaning".
8. In "Communicative Action and the 'Use of Reason'" Habermas argues: "To say that the world is 'objective' means that it is 'given' to us as 'the same for everyone.' It is linguistic practice – especially the use of singular terms – that compels us to make the pragmatic presupposition that such a world is shared by all. The referential system built into natural languages ensures that any given speaker can formally anticipate possible objects of reference. Through this formal presupposition of the world, communication about something in the world is intertwined with practical interventions in the world. Speakers and actors reach an understanding about and intervene in one and the same objective world" (BNR: 31). Cf. also discussion of worlds in TCA 2. For a discussion of the presuppositions of communications, see Chapter 3 in this volume.
9. Habermas takes the idea of rational reconstruction from Chomsky, who developed the idea in the context of grammatical theory (CES: 14–20). Thomas McCarthy explains this point in *The Critical Theory of Jürgen Habermas*: "Habermas's conception of a universal pragmatics rests on the contention that not only phonetic, syntactic, and semantic features of *sentences* but also certain pragmatic features of *utterance* – that is, not only language but speech, not only linguistic competence but 'communicative competence' – admit of rational reconstruction in universal terms" ([1978] 1996: 274).
10. Habermas attributes this idea to Dieter Heinrich in "Metaphysics after Kant": "*All* species competences of subjects capable of speech and action are accessible to a rational reconstruction if, namely, we recur to the practical knowledge to

which we intuitively lay claim in tried-and-true productive accomplishments" (PMT: 14).

11. See also McCarthy ([1981] 1996: 277).
12. See CES: ch. 1 for further discussion of weak transcendentalism in contrast with Kantian transcendentalism: "From now on, transcendental investigation must rely on the competence of knowing subjects who judge which experiences may be called coherent experiences in order to analyze this material for general and necessary categorical presuppositions. Every reconstruction of a basic conceptual system of possible experience has to be regarded as a hypothetical proposal that can be tested against new experiences. As long as the assertion of its necessity and universality has not been refuted, we term *transcendental* the conceptual structure recurring in all coherent experiences. In this weaker version, the claim that structure can be demonstrated a priori is dropped" (CES: 21).
13. See Benhabib's defence of "weak justification" (2002: 30–31).
14. Cf. Chapter 7 by Olson in this volume.
15. Habermas terms this "immanent transcendence" in an ironic way, inasmuch as transcendence is traditionally opposed to immanence.
16. As described above, one of these presuppositions is that all persons share this objective world; it would not make sense to advance the claim that the continents are moving in a non-context-transcending sense ("the continents are moving *to me* but not *to you*").
17. He accepts that many claims about our social world do not have these universal goals, such as when we advance claims about norms that apply to culturally specific groups, which he calls ethical (as opposed to moral) claims. For Habermas, the validity of ethical claims cannot be determined in a context-transcendent way.
18. The concept of ideal speech conditions varies in different discourse contexts. The above example applies specifically to moral discourse, but Habermas also extends this idea to other forms of discourse, including legal discourse, religious discourse and discourse concerning international relations. See this volume, Chapters 8, 11 and 10, respectively.
19. See the section on weak transcendence above for examples about these context-transcendent conditions of moral discourse.
20. William Mark Hohengarten further explains this point in the introduction to *Postmetaphysical Thinking*: "Validity claims can of course only be raised within particular language games and forms of life; yet, while *immanent* in particular contexts of communication, they can always claim a validity that *transcends* any and all of them" (PMT: xi).
21. Thomas McCarthy explains this point in *Ideals and Illusions*: "It is important to see that the context transcendence of the ideas of reason harbours not only a dogmatic but also a subversive potential: claims to validity are permanently exposed to criticism from all sides. ... it invites an ongoing critique of dogmatism, prejudice, self-deception, and error in all their forms" (1993: 5).
22. See also *Truth and Justification*.
23. Against idealism, he thinks that we constitute our knowledge of the objects in the natural world through communication, but not the objects themselves. When we advance claims about the natural world, nature has to meet us halfway.
24. See Habermas's essay, "Religion in the Public Sphere" (BNR: 114–47).
25. For a discussion of the connections between the rejection of epistemology by positivism and philosophy of science see ch. 4 of KHI, "Comte and Mach: The Intention of Early Positivism".

26. Cf. Habermas (2003b). Habermas develops his account of soft naturalism in response to issues raised by Searle in contemporary philosophy of mind.
27. Cf. Habermas's discussion of Putnam, "Norms and Values: On Hilary Putnam's Kantian Pragmatism" (TJ: 213–36).
28. Habermas responds to reductions of reasons to neurobiological processes: "In tracing all mental process back to the causal interaction between the brain and its environment in a deterministic manner and in denying the capacity of the 'space of reasons' – or, if you will, the level of culture and society – to intervene, reductionism seems no less dogmatic than idealism, which sees the originary power of the mind also at work in all natural processes. But bottom-up monism is only more scientific than top-down monism in its procedure, not in its conclusions" (BNR: 165).
29. Failing to accept this feature of scientific knowledge leads to the same problems suffered by metaphysical thought in the attempt to present knowledge claims with the force of a God's-eye point of view.
30. For further discussion, see Chapter 11 in this volume.
31. I would like to thank Jon Garthoff and Barbara Fultner for useful and provocative comments on this chapter.

THREE

Communicative action and formal pragmatics

Barbara Fultner

In the early 1970s, Jürgen Habermas undertook a *linguistic turn* in critical theory. Motivated by the fact that humans engage in activities that are meaningful to them, he argued that social actions and interactions can be fruitfully analysed as having a linguistic structure. He developed an account of communicative competence, called formal pragmatics, and elaborated the concept of communicative action, which he had used less systematically until that time. These lie at the core not only of what eventually became *The Theory of Communicative Action*, but also of his discourse ethics, elaborated in the 1980s, his theory of democracy, and his theory of law, developed in the 1990s. It is fair to say that Habermas's entire theoretical edifice stands on the foundation of his account of human communication, more specifically, of how we use language in order to reach mutual understanding with one another. This, to him, is the most fundamental form of action coordination. Although formal pragmatics did not begin as a theory of meaning *per se*, it has implications for such a theory, and the linguistic turn in social theory corresponds to a *pragmatic* turn in the theory of meaning. An adequate theory of meaning, for Habermas, must account for the socially binding force and action-coordinating function of language, and it must do so by subsuming its semantic dimension in the narrow sense of how words hook up to the world under formal pragmatics, which takes into account how words are used. Furthermore, such a theory must do justice to the objective, intersubjective and subjective aspects of language and communication. The corresponding triad of world, other and self runs throughout Habermas's understanding of communicative action and of the lifeworld. It is captured by the slogan that in communicative action, a speaker reaches a mutual understanding with another about something in the world. In other words, she represents a state of affairs, establishes an intersubjective relation with a hearer, and expresses her intention. Correspondingly, Habermas identifies truth, normative rightness and sincerity as the three types of validity claim that are raised in speech acts, provides a tripartite typology of speech acts (constatives, regulatives and expressives) and identifies three types of discourse (theoretical, practical and aesthetic).

Habermas draws on a wide range of theories to develop his account, including speech act theory (J. L. Austin, John Searle), transformational grammar (Noam Chomsky), formal semantics (Gottlob Frege, Michael Dummett), intentionalist semantics (H. P. Grice), use theories of meaning (Wittgenstein), hermeneutics (Wilhelm Dilthey, Hans-Georg Gadamer), transcendental pragmatics (Karl-Otto Apel) and, most recently, inferential semantics (Robert Brandom). Since Habermas's linguistic turn is motivated by concerns in social theory and philosophy of action, I shall begin with the fundamental distinction he draws between strategic and communicative action. I then turn to an elucidation of his formal pragmatics, his adoption of speech act theory, the validity basis of speech, the three types of validity claim and the notion of the ideal speech situation. Finally, I conclude with a look at his critique of extant theories of meaning and his recent differentiation between truth and rightness. For Habermas not only appropriates the conceptual resources of analytic philosophy of language, but is also critical of much of this tradition, particularly its tendency to ignore or misunderstand the intersubjective, that is communicative, nature of language.

Communicative and strategic action

Habermas, as social theorist, is interested in how social order is possible. How are modern societies structured? What are the mechanisms of action coordination and what makes them binding? In the early 1970s, Habermas described two basic approaches to the analysis of society in the social sciences: one *objectivist*, the other *subjectivist*.[1] The bifurcation depended on the answer to the question of whether meaning – the meaningfulness of actions to agents – should be treated as primitive or as reducible to something else, such as causal relations. Subjectivist approaches are paradigmatically represented by the kinds of phenomenological social theories pioneered by Alfred Schutz, Peter Berger and Thomas Luckmann (Schutz & Luckmann 1973; Berger & Luckmann 1966). They analyse societies in terms of the ways in which social practices are meaningful to the agents involved in them. In contrast, objectivist social theories take an objectivating attitude towards agents and seek to explain their actions in terms of nomological regularities. Albeit in different ways, both these approaches have a monadological or individualistic starting point and therefore fail to do justice to a key element of social action coordination, namely, intersubjectivity.

All action, according to Habermas, is teleological in the sense that it is goal-oriented. However, depending on whether the action is social or not, and depending on what the goal is and how an actor believes it to be attainable, different action types emerge. A first distinction can be drawn between non-social and social actions, depending on whether they involve other individuals at all. We can further distinguish between action oriented towards success and action oriented towards mutual understanding. In the case of success-oriented action, an agent has a goal or purpose in mind, identifies the means to attain it, and then (causally) intervenes in the world accordingly. Going for a walk by oneself in order to get exercise or hammering in a nail to hang a picture are non-social actions oriented toward success.[2] Their fulfilment is a matter of how the world is: one's heart rate is sufficiently raised, the picture stays on the wall. Non-social purposive activity oriented towards success is instrumental action, in Habermas's terminology (OPC: 118).[3] Social action, on the other hand, involves some sort of action coordination. Habermas recognizes, however, that the actions of multiple individuals can be coordinated in different ways. In particular, the individuals can take different attitudes toward one another, which result in two different types of action. They can regard one another with an "objectivating" attitude from a third-person observer perspective and aim to affect one another causally; in the most extreme cases physically pushing the other around or holding a gun to the other's head. This kind of action is performed with an orientation towards success; it is strategic social action. Or they can regard one another from an "intersubjective" or second-person participant point of view, not trying to realize their own individual purposive goals, but with an orientation towards reaching mutual understanding (*Verständigung*).[4] This type of social action is communicative. An agent acting strategically is merely seeking to exert causal influence on another; in the context of language use, this reduces language to a mere mechanism of information transmission as opposed to a means of reaching understanding. Unlike strategic action, communicative action functions as a means of social integration. In other words, it forges social bonds. This is because Habermas takes there to be a rational basis for reaching mutual understanding; whatever agreement is attained is to be rationally motivated and cannot be established through force. It is in order to ground this claim that he develops formal pragmatics. He argues that the paradigmatic model, and indeed the source, of social coordination is communicative action, that is, linguistically mediated interaction.

Formal pragmatics

In *Truth and Justification*, Habermas describes his view as a form of "linguistic Kantianism" and writes that formal pragmatics was "meant to elucidate the socially integrating and binding force of speech acts with which speakers raise validity claims that are subject to critique and with which they make their hearers take a rationally motivated stance" (TJ: 7). Reaching mutual understanding is "the inherent telos of human language" (OPC: 120). Thus, in a detranscendentalizing move, Habermas grounds the concept of communicative action in the very structure of speech.

In the landmark 1976 essay "What Is Universal Pragmatics?"[5] Habermas distinguishes between language (*Sprache*) and speech (*Rede*). Language can be regarded as the system of syntactic and semantic rules constituting a language; speech refers to how that system is applied in order to communicate. The goal of formal pragmatics is to spell out the general conditions of possibility, or presuppositions, of communicative action (OPC: 21). In other words, formal pragmatics is supposed to yield a rational reconstruction[6] of communicative competence, of what it means to understand and to be able to employ an utterance. This rational reconstruction is based on an understanding of communicative practice and hence fallible. Whereas linguistic competence refers to the ability to produce syntactically well-formed sentences, communicative competence refers to our ability to produce context-appropriate utterances. The basic unit of analysis, for pragmatics, then, is the speech act or utterance rather than the sentence. Already in *The Theory of Communicative Action*, however, Habermas recognized that the distinction between semantics (what sentences mean) and pragmatics (how they are used):

> cannot be developed into a methodological separation between the formal analysis of sentence meanings and the empirical analysis of speakers' meanings in utterances; for the literal meaning of a sentence cannot be explained at all independently of the standard conditions of its communicative employment. (TCA 1: 297)

Very much influenced by the later Wittgenstein, Habermas thus recognizes the inherent connection between meaning and use. Even though he introduces the programme as constituting a theory of communication, as the theoretical framework develops it becomes clear that it has implications for a theory of meaning.

Communication is not merely a matter of transmitting information for Habermas, but of establishing (or maintaining) a relationship with another person.[7] When a speaker is trying to reach an understanding with an interlocutor about something in the world, he argues, there is a "double structure of speech": the two people communicate simultaneously at the level of what they are talking about (the propositional content) and at the intersubjective level of their relationship (OPC: 64). Initially, Habermas identifies two uses of language based on this double structure: interactive and cognitive (OPC: 75). These two functions mutually presuppose one another and are therefore best understood as analytically rather than empirically distinct. They also figure in speech act theory as introduced by J. L. Austin (1962) and subsequently elaborated by John Searle (1969). Subsequently, Habermas refers to them as the communicative and representational functions of speech and adds a third, the expressive function.[8] Thus through language, we represent the world, establish relationships with one another, and express our feelings, emotions and other internal states.

Speech act theory

Habermas takes speech act theory to be an important step in the right direction from semantics to pragmatics. Austin rightly recognized that we use language not merely to describe the world or to state truths, but also to *do* things: speech is a type of action.[9] Hence speech act theory is an ideal vehicle for linking philosophy of action and language. According to the theory, an utterance or speech act Mp has two primary components: propositional content p (the traditional purview of semantics) and illocutionary force (M), which indicates what action the speaker is performing in making the utterance. For example, the propositional content *that* the roads are icy can be used in different types of speech act with different types of illocutionary force. It can be used to make a descriptive assertion ("The roads are icy"), or to ask a question ("Are the roads icy?"), or to issue a warning ("The roads are icy!"), and so on. These two components correspond to the representational and communicative functions of speech introduced above. The propositional content of an utterance provides a representation of the world, whereas "the illocutionary force of a speech act", Habermas writes, "consists in fixing the communicative function of the content uttered" (OPC: 56).

Of course, people do not always speak truthfully or use language to reach understanding. We can also use language to manipulate, to flatter, to lie, and so on: in other words, to further our own individual interests. In the terminology introduced above, we can use language *strategically* as well as *communicatively*. Habermas adapts Austin's distinction between illocution and perlocution to account for this fact.

Illocutionary acts, according to Austin, are those that we perform *in* making utterances. The paradigmatic example is promising: to utter "I promise" simply *is* to make a promise. Its illocutionary effect is that I am now bound to do as I promised. *By* making this promise, I may also make you happy. This is a *perlocutionary* effect. What distinguishes perlocutionary from illocutionary effects is that the latter but not the former are internally connected to the meaning of what is said. It is evident from what the speaker says whether she is making a promise, asking a question, and so on, and the illocutionary effect of making a promise is that one is now under an obligation to do what one said. The obligation follows from the utterance of the promise. This is the sense in which Habermas claims that illocutionary acts are "self-identifying". Unlike nonlinguistic actions, speech acts require no interpretation to figure out what act was performed or what the utterance means. Perlocutionary effects, in contrast, depend on circumstances external to the utterance's meaning and hence are identified through inference. Habermas departs from Austin in two regards. First, he holds that illocution and perlocution are mutually exclusive attitudes from the perspective of the agent (OPC: 128). Second, he maintains that perlocutionary language use oriented towards attaining success is parasitic on illocutionary use oriented towards reaching understanding (OPC: 122). It is only possible, Habermas argues, to use language perlocutionarily because its primary use is illocutionary. If someone is lying, she can only do so successfully if her true intentions remain hidden from her interlocutor and if the words she uses carry their illocutionary meaning.[10]

In *The Theory of Communicative Action*, Habermas defines communicative action as the unreserved pursuit of illocutionary aims (OPC: 128). The illocutionary force of speech acts has an action-coordinating role and they have what he calls a binding/bonding effect (OPC: 223). In order to explain this action-coordinating function and the binding nature of speech acts – which serves the purpose of social integration – Habermas appeals to what he calls the validity basis of speech.

Validity claims

The questions of what makes speech acts binding on interlocutors and what Habermas means by validity are closely connected to the debate in philosophy of language about semantic normativity. At issue in that debate is whether meanings, understood as semantic rules, should be conceived as being the sorts of rules we *ought* to obey, that are *binding*, and, if so, in what sense. Habermas clearly sides with normativists such as Dummett and Brandom and against anti-normativists such as Davidson.[11]

Habermas makes validity a core notion of formal pragmatics by arguing that in performing a speech act, a speaker raises three mutually irreducible types of *validity claims*: a claim to truth, a claim to normative rightness, and a claim to sincerity. Not all of these are foregrounded in the speech act. Habermas categorizes speech acts into three types, depending on which kind of validity claim is explicit. Consider these examples:

(a) It is raining.
(b) Please fetch the mail!
(c) I am sorry.

The assertion in (a) is what Habermas calls a constative speech act, the request in (b) is a regulative, and the apology in (c) is an expressive speech act. (a) thematizes a truth claim: it asserts that a particular state of affairs in the world obtains, namely, that it is raining. And it is true if and only if that state in fact obtains. In raising a claim to truth, a speaker undertakes a commitment that what she says is true, in other words, that it correctly represents the world. By contrast, neither (b) nor (c) are subject to truth conditions in that sense. As Austin already pointed out, (b) cannot be true or false, although it can be an appropriate or inappropriate request, right or wrong. That is, it raises what Habermas terms a claim to normative rightness: the speaker is requesting someone else to do something and thus establishes, seeks to establish, or draws upon a particular relationship with that person. In raising a claim to normative rightness, she claims that what she says is context-appropriate, that she is authorized to be performing this kind of speech act, and so on. (c) expresses a claim to sincerity or truthfulness; after all, a genuine apology or expression of sympathy requires the speaker in fact to really mean it. In raising a claim to sincerity, she claims that she is not lying but sincerely expressing her mental states. Utterances expressing intentions fall into this category for Habermas: claims to intend to do this or that are neither true nor false but sincere or insincere. The three types of validity claim make reference to the objective world of states of affairs, the social world of the totality of intersubjective relations, and the subjective world of internal mental states, emotions, and so on, respectively (TCA 2: 127; OPC: 295). It is important to realize that Habermas does not mean to reify what he is calling worlds here or to postulate them as Platonic realms of some kind. This can perhaps be most clearly illustrated by the way in which sincerity claims refer to the subjective world. The mental states and emotions that constitute that world are not to be understood as a class of entities. If they were, then, presumably, expressive speech acts *would* have truth conditions: they would be true if the speech act correctly *represented* the speaker's internal states. But this is precisely the kind of philosophy of mind Habermas eschews. Normative rightness and sincerity are merely *analogous* to truth, they are not equivalent to it, a point to which I shall return.

All three types of claims are at least implicit in all speech acts. The expressive "I am sorry" presupposes a claim to truth (e.g. that the speaker has done something for which she apologizes) as well as a claim to normative rightness (e.g. that the addressee is the appropriate individual to whom to apologize). This feature of speech acts is also demonstrated by the fact that a speech act can be challenged in different ways. If *A* asks *B*, for instance, "Please open the window!", *B* can refuse to do so by rejecting any of the three validity claims:

> "But it's already open." [truth]
> "I don't have to do what you tell me." [rightness]
> "You just want me to get up so you can take my seat." [sincerity]

Interlocutors accept or reject each other's validity claims in the course of their interactions. They take, as Habermas puts it, a *yes- or no-attitude* towards them or accept or reject the offer contained in the speech act.

Whether or not a claim is challenged, in making a claim a speaker always takes on the warrant to vindicate it, if necessary, with reasons. In other words, she can be called upon to justify her claims. This in turn requires that to understand an utterance is to know its conditions of acceptability. To explain what this means, Habermas draws on Michael Dummett's assertibilist semantics. Dummett argues that the notion of assertibility is an epistemic one, whereas the notion of truth is not.[12] We may not (even in principle) be in a position to ascertain whether a sentence that is counterfactual, contains universal existentials, or is time-indexed, say, is true or not; a sentence's truth conditions may be epistemically inaccessible to us. Meaning, however, cannot be epistemically inaccessible in this way, lest we risk not knowing what our words really mean. Dummett therefore proposes a theory of meaning according to which the meaning of a sentence is given not by its truth-conditions, but by the conditions under which it would be legitimately *assertible* (Dummett 1993: 45ff.). Generalizing Dummett's account, Habermas holds that to understand an utterance is to know the conditions under which it is acceptable. This means knowing "the kinds of reasons that a speaker could provide in order to convince a hearer that she is entitled in the given circumstances to claim validity for her utterance" (OPC: 297). This understanding is intrinsically pragmatic and intersubjective:

> To understand an expression is to know how one can make use of it in order to reach understanding with somebody about something ... One simply would not know what it is to understand the meaning of an utterance if one did not know that the utterance can and should serve to bring about an agreement; moreover, it is part of the concept of agreement that it "holds" (*gilt*) [i.e. is valid] for the participants. The dimension of validity is thus inherent in language. The orientation toward validity claims is part of the pragmatic conditions of possible mutual understanding – and of linguistic understanding itself. (OPC: 298)

Thus Habermas links the theory of communication with the theory of meaning. Acceptability implicitly refers to a second person inasmuch as understanding an utterance involves knowing the conditions under which a *hearer* may accept it. Acceptability conditions comprise not only "grammatical conditions of well-formedness and general contextual conditions" but also "those *essential conditions* under which he could be motivated by the speaker to take an affirmative position" (TCA 1: 298). Conversely, Habermas writes, "To understand an assertion is to know when a speaker has good grounds to undertake a warrant that the conditions for the truth of the asserted sentences are satisfied" (TCA 1: 318). The same is said to hold analogously for expressive and normative sentences. Acceptability conditions are therefore fundamentally tied to issues of rational motivation, to reason giving and argumentation. The warrant undertaken in an utterance amounts to a promise to make good on the claims raised if asked.

In smoothly running communication, the validity claims interlocutors raise are generally intersubjectively recognized. When glitches or breakdowns are minor enough, interlocutors routinely engage in repair work. If *B*, in response to *A*'s request, points out to *A* that the door is already open, *A* may simply acknowledge that fact ("Oh, I hadn't noticed") and carry on. If simple repair work is not successful, in more serious cases of communication breakdown or disagreement, interlocutors must resort to *discourse*. For Habermas this is a quasi-technical term, referring to argumentation and rational justification. Depending on which type of claim is being challenged, a different type of discourse is called for. Challenges of claims to truth call for theoretical discourse about factual evidence and states of affairs in the world. Normative rightness claims are justified in practical discourse about the validity of the (moral) norms in question. Even sincerity claims are subject to aesthetic-existential discourse, although they are vindicated, according to Habermas, in the first instance not by providing reasons but by one's subsequent actions. The fact that all three validity claims are criticizable means that they are *cognitive* claims in the sense that they are subject to rational scrutiny and assessment.[13]

Ideal speech situation

There are other formal-pragmatic presuppositions of communicative action that constitute communicative competence. They include the assumption that speakers' respective interpretations of the speech situation and of their diffuse environments largely coincide, that their lifeworld perspectives converge, that their validity claims can, at least in principle, be vindicated, and that interlocutors mean the same thing by their words. The insistence that interlocutors must presuppose that they attach the same meanings to the utterances they make sets Habermas apart from philosophers of language as diverse as Jacques Derrida and Donald Davidson. The latter take the fact that what speakers mean by their utterances is unstable from one speaker or situation to the next to be theoretically more significant than Habermas does. Davidson (1984), following Quine, holds that the task and great challenge for a theory of meaning lies in reconstructing a theory of interpretation for a speaker's utterances without presupposing shared meanings. By contrast, Habermas argues that the presupposition of shared meanings is indispensable to communication and emphasizes the importance of linguistic and communicative conventions (rules) as well as that of a shared background understanding against which communication takes place.[14] Individual variations and idiosyncrasies, he believes, are the purview of *empirical* pragmatics. Where that presupposition of shared meaning turns out to be mistaken, according to Habermas, interlocutors must resort to interpretation, to "hermeneutic discourse" (2001c: 94; OPC: 80).

All of the formal-pragmatic presuppositions of communicative action are *idealizing*. They characterize what Habermas has termed the "ideal speech situation". Critics have objected that we never attain this ideal speech situation in real conversation or discourse and that, consequently, Habermas presents a hopelessly naive picture of language. But this objection disregards Habermas's thoroughgoing fallibilism. He is well aware that people have all sorts of diverging beliefs and perspectives, that they interpret their situations in different ways, and that they say things that are mistaken, inappropriate, or insincere. In this sense, the pragmatic presuppositions of communicative action are defeasible. His point, which lies at the core of his linguistic Kantianism, is that we manage to communicate successfully despite all that and that we do so, in part, because communication requires interlocutors to make these formal-pragmatic presuppositions. They function as regulative ideals in the Kantian sense and are idealizing in two regards. First, in any actual speech situation, interlocutors may use certain terms idiosyncratically or, more commonly, with difference connotations and associations; they certainly will not have all the same beliefs. If they did, there presumably would be little need to communicate. The presuppositions characterizing the ideal speech situation are therefore *counterfactual*. Second, however, from their perspective as participants in interaction, interlocutors nonetheless *must* make these presuppositions for communicative action to take place at all. They are in this sense *pragmatic* presuppositions of communication and, although counterfactual, have "a *factual* role" in structuring communication and discourse (TJ: 85–6).

A few brief remarks are in order on the role of the concept of the lifeworld relative to communicative action and formal pragmatics. Habermas has argued that the lifeworld serves as the source of justifications when interlocutors challenge each other's claims to validity. In this role, the lifeworld functions as an implicit, holistic and diffuse background of intelligibility (see OPC: 233–46). The formal-pragmatic conception of the lifeworld is a reconstruction from the perspective of the participants in interaction. The lifeworld, as distinct from system,[15] becomes visible only from the third-person perspective of the social scientist. In so far as it functions as a background of intelligibility, the lifeworld obviates the need to engage in hermeneutic discourse in order to understand what the other is saying. This opens Habermas's theory up to the objection that he fails to account for all functions of language and, in particular, that he fails to account for semantics proper, since we clearly can discuss the meaningfulness of our terms and debate the intelligibility of what we say (see e.g. Medina 2005: 8). Another way to put the objection is that one may understand an utterance *without* taking a yes or no stance towards it. One might take umbrage at the fact that Habermas claims that communication requires taking a yes or no stance toward her claims since it seems perfectly reasonable to try to understand what someone is saying without thereby *judging* whether what she is saying is true, appropriate or sincere. Following through on this objection, one might argue that the core of a theory of meaning is precisely what Habermas presupposes and is to be elucidated by focusing on hermeneutic discourse, which functions to make good on what Habermas used to call the claim to intelligibility (e.g. 1984a: 137ff.; 2001c: 90) but which he dropped from his analysis, precisely because it is assumed to be vindicated in ordinary communication.

For his part, Habermas can respond to such objections by falling back on the primacy of pragmatics over semantics. When we interact communicatively with one another, we *do* take what we say to one another to be true or appropriate. From this point of view, merely considering what someone says independently of its truth or normative rightness is a kind of abstraction that is a cognitive achievement rather than a basic building block of linguistic competence.

Critique of theories of meaning

Having identified the three types of validity claims of truth, normative rightness and sincerity as mutually irreducible, Habermas offers a schema for a critique of much of analytic philosophy of language.[16] He argues that each of its three major strands highlights aspects relating to one type of validity claim but either neglects the others entirely or seeks to explain them in terms of its privileged type of claim. Hence they are reductive in one form or another. The three types of dominant theories of meaning, corresponding to the three functions he assigns to speech, are: formal semantics (Frege, Russell and the early Wittgenstein), intentionalist semantics (Grice and Schiffer), and use theories of meaning (Wittgenstein). Habermas sees the virtue of his account in the fact that it unites these three perspectives and does justice to all three aspects: objective, subjective and intersubjective.

Formal semantics

Formal semantics aims to analyse *literal* meaning or what is said and hence focuses on the representational function and on objective truth and reference relations. As already indicated above, the insight of formal semantics is that there is an internal connection between meaning and validity. Frege argued that to know the meaning of a sentence is to know its truth conditions. But this implies that one can also know when a sentence's truth conditions are not in fact satisfied, that is, when the sentence is false. Truth is a normative notion in the broad sense that a sentence can represent states of affairs correctly or incorrectly. But we have already seen that truth conditions may be epistemically inaccessible to us. Frege also held that the referent of a sentence as a whole was either "the True" or "the False" and resorted to a form of semantic Platonism in order to ground his account of meaning. Needless to say, Habermas rejects this kind of Platonism (TJ: 111). Instead of meanings or the True/False as abstract, independently existing entities, he appeals to the practice of argumentation. On Habermas's account, the concept of the validity of a sentence cannot "be explicated independently of the *concept of redeeming the validity claim raised through the utterance of the sentence*" and hence the "very analysis of the conditions of validity of sentences *itself* compels us to analyze conditions for the intersubjective recognition of the corresponding validity claims" (OPC: 152).

As we have already seen, there are three types of validity claim, and formal semantics limits itself to an analysis of only one by focusing on the representational function of language and taking assertions to be paradigmatic speech acts. It is concerned first and foremost with the problem of reference, that is, the problem of how language connects up with the world or, rather, objects in the world, and with how sentences in a language can express *truths* about that world (OCP: 280–81). In addition, Habermas holds that the tradition from Russell and Carnap to Quine and Davidson offers an empiricist analysis of language which conceives linguistic understanding in terms of a third- rather than a second-person point of view (TJ: 69). In fact, he believes, this is a shortcoming also characteristic of intentionalist semantics.[17]

Intentionalist semantics

Intentionalist semantics focuses on speaker intentions, intended meaning, and hence on the expressive function of language. It aims to analyse meaning in terms of a speaker's intention to get the hearer to recognize her intention to make him understand what she is trying to communicate. H. P. Grice (1989) presented a complex account analysing the literal meaning of a sentence in terms of speaker meaning. On this account, a speaker *S* means something by uttering a sentence iff (a) *S* intends to make the hearer *H* believe that *p* (or believe that *S* believes that *p*); (b) *S* intends *H* to recognize that intention; and (c) *S* intends *H* to form the belief in (b) partly because *H* recognizes *S*'s intention. For example, *S* means that there is a hard winter ahead by uttering "There's a hard winter ahead" if *S* intends *H* to believe that there is a hard winter ahead (or to believe that *S* believes it); *S* intends *H* to recognize that she wants him to believe that there is a hard winter ahead; and *S* intends that *H* comes to believe that there is a hard winter ahead partly because he recognizes that *S* intends him to believe it. For *H* to understand *S*'s utterance, then, is for *H* to infer her meaning-intention. But, according to Habermas, this approach mistakenly tries to reduce the conventional meaning of linguistic expressions to non-conventional individual speaker intentions, thus setting up strategic action "as a functional equivalent for reaching mutual understanding" (OPC: 285). The result is a conception of communication as a mere transfer of information, and information in turn is understood in terms of speakers' mental contents. However, the rules of strategic action are not conventional in the way that semantic rules are, and, as we have already seen, the orientation to success characteristic of strategic action and the orientation to reaching mutual understanding characteristic of communicative action are mutually exclusive from the perspective of the actor. In this sense, we might say that, from Habermas's perspective, intentionalist semantics is guilty of a category mistake.[18]

Use theories of meaning

Use theories of meaning, finally, focus on the way in which we employ linguistic expressions. The later Wittgenstein's rejection of truth-conditional semantics in favour of use theories of meaning signified a pragmatic turn and what Habermas calls a "detranscendentalization of language" (TJ: 68). Utterance meaning, which always occurs in some context of use, takes centre stage (OPC: 280-84). Use theories highlight the social function of language and capture the fundamental dependence of semantics on pragmatics. Wittgenstein shows in *The Philosophical Investigations* (1953) that there are many different types of language use or "language games", and that such uses are inextricably intertwined with the context of interaction in which they occur. His examples of the builders, the famous rule-following discussion, and the private language argument are all designed to demonstrate the importance of intersubjectivity in linguistic communication. Where Wittgenstein erred, according to Habermas, was, first, in inferring from the multiplicity of language games that no theoretical account of meaning could be provided and, second, emphasizing the intersubjective aspects of language at the expense of its cognitive and representational aspects. Wittgenstein's rule-following discussion conceptually ties sameness of meaning to intersubjectivity: for an individual in isolation, there can be no such thing as following a rule correctly or using a word with the same meaning across instances, for that requires the presence of someone capable of assessing the rule-follower's actions. This of course raises the question of whether a linguistic *community's* actions as a whole are subject to critical assessment. Habermas argues that because the representational function of language becomes just one among many, Wittgenstein loses sight of the connection between fact-stating discourse and truth (OPC: 288).

I have focused thus far on Habermas's appropriation and critique of analytic philosophy of language, but he is just as much shaped by the linguistic turn in continental philosophy. In "Hermeneutic and Analytic Philosophy: Two Complementary Versions of the Linguistic Turn" (TJ: 51–82), he identifies the historicism inherent in the ideas of particular language games (Wittgenstein) and epochal world disclosures (Heidegger) as the inspiration for neopragmatic philosophies of language (TJ: 69). Referring to the work of his long-time colleague and friend, Karl-Otto Apel,[19] Habermas cautions that both the Wittgensteinian emphasis on habitual language games and Heideggerian world disclosure neglect the cognitive dimension of language use. Both share a transcendental conception of language in the sense that they view the world as linguistically constituted. In the case of Wittgenstein, validity is a matter of the standards of whatever language games have social currency (OPC: 288). In the case of Heidegger, truth is a function of linguistic world disclosure characteristic of a tradition (TJ: 66–9). Habermas concurs that there is no such thing as immediate access to reality for us. Yet the distinction between merely taking the sentences we utter to be true and their actually being true *matters* to us. He sides with Apel against Gadamer (as well as Rorty) that hermeneutics must hold fast to the ideal of trying to understand texts as well as other people *better*, rather than merely to understand them *differently* (TJ: 73).[20]

Coincident with publication of Robert Brandom's *Making It Explicit* (1994), Habermas revisited the topic of the theory of meaning in the mid-1990s.[21] Brandom takes up precisely the above problem of reference and objectivity in the context of a semantics based on a "normative pragmatics". The resulting inferentialist semantics seems an ideal complement to Habermas's theory of communicative action. According to Brandom, we "*treat* certain performances or behavior as correct or incorrect" (1994: 32–3), that is, we take each other to be accountable and sanction each other's behaviour. Concepts arise from *discursive* practice, namely, the giving and asking for reasons (a phrase that Brandom takes on from Sellars), which *makes explicit* the normative commitments and entitlements implicit in social practice. Brandom conceives communication as "deontic scorekeeping", as interlocutors track one another's commitments and entitlements. As the term suggests, deontic scorekeeping is a normative practice analogous to Habermas's account of interlocutors accepting or rejecting each other's validity claims. Furthermore, commitments and entitlements connect linguistic practice with other types of interactions. Agents can be called upon to make good on their commitments, to justify their entitlements, and so on, through a process of inferential articulation. Meaning, therefore, is given in terms of the inferential role of propositions in communicative practice.

Despite its many virtues, Habermas rejects several aspects of Brandom's account.[22] On the one hand, like others, he criticizes Brandom for not having a sufficiently robust notion of objectivity and trying to reduce one aspect of communication (objectivity) to another (intersubjectivity). On the other hand, Habermas charges Brandom with still being too caught up in the representationalist and objectivating frame of mind that continues to dominate analytic epistemology and philosophy of language and mind. He argues that Brandom privileges one validity claim, truth, over the others since he focuses on assertions to the exclusion of other types of speech acts and conceives of communication in terms of a third-person perspective. As a result, Brandom, according to Habermas, ultimately fails to do justice to the intersubjectivity of communicative action. Given Habermas's own cognitivism and the role discourse – that is, the articulation of reasons – plays in his own account, the force of these objections is less than damning. Reasons, after all, are generally articulated in the form of assertions. So Brandom's account seems to allow for a differentiation of different *kinds* of reasons and inferences, which seems to be just what Habermas needs. Indeed, Habermas's own differentiation between truth and normative rightness illustrates how different types of reasons operate with different conditions of justification.

Truth and rightness

Although the three types of validity claims cannot be explained in terms of one another, Habermas maintains that rightness and sincerity are analogous to truth,[23] primarily in so far as they are not *irrational* elements of speech but constitute rationally motivated and justifiable aspects of communicative action. They are claims we can make good on. But there are also significant differences between them. Truth and rightness differ from sincerity inasmuch as the former but not the latter can be "discursively redeemed", that is, justified by giving reasons, whereas the latter can be vindicated only by behaviour consistent with the sincerity claim. This raises a potential tension with Habermas's account of ethics, where he seems to allow that authenticity claims are subject to discourse, even if, perhaps, not universal consensus.[24] In "Wahrheitstheorien" (1972) Habermas articulated what he then called a "consensus theory of truth", which was very similar to Hilary Putnam's conception of truth as idealized warranted assertibility. Even this early essay, however, is best understood as a theory of the *justification* of truth claims rather than as a theory of truth *per se*. Habermas has nuanced and revised his account of truth and normative rightness in response to criticism, emphasizing that, whereas normative rightness is exhausted by rational acceptability under ideal conditions, truth exceeds rational assertibility, even under ideal conditions.[25] Whether a proposition is empirically true is, at the end of the day, independent of our ability to justify it. For the proposition "is agreed upon by all rational subjects because it is true; it is not true because it could be the content of a consensus attained under ideal conditions" (TJ: 101). It is not enough for us merely to *take* a proposition to be true; as part of our engagement in learning processes, it matters to us that it actually *be* true. And that depends on how the world is, even if our ability to claim it to be true cannot be separated from the reasons we muster in its justification. In contrast, there is no further standard for whether a given moral norm is right beyond the rational consent of all those who are potentially affected by it. That is, although truth and normative rightness claims are both fallible, how they can turn out to be false differs. Our claims to truth falter against the reality of the objective world. Our claims to normative rightness falter against the rational disagreement and the power of convincing arguments of others.

Habermas may not provide us with a fully worked-out semantics; his primary interest, after all, remains social and political theory. By the same token, the account of language he offers is clearly shaped by and dovetails with his social theory. Some have argued that he does not provide a theory of meaning at all and presupposes what he aims to explain.[26] One might also argue that he mistakenly reduces the multifarious functions of language to three types. Where do jokes, word play, and so on, fit in? Nevertheless, the goal of doing justice to the objective, intersubjective and subjective aspects of meaning and communication is a commendable and important one. It is shared by philosophers including Donald Davidson in his latest writings (Davidson 2001) (even if, as Habermas has argued, Davidson does not pull it off), and it is a goal that remains relevant today, not only with regard to philosophy of language, but also with regard to philosophy of mind and action. There is growing interest in "the second person" and in collective intentionality, in the question of the conditions of possibility of acting *together*. For these discussions, the theory of communicative action offers rich resources.[27]

Notes

1. "Reflections on the Linguistic Foundation of Sociology: The Christian Gauss Lectures", Lecture I (2001c). Habermas was not the only one to offer this diagnosis. See, for example, Bourdieu (1990). In Habermas's own theoretical framework, the dichotomy is reformulated into the division of societal structures into system and lifeworld (see Chapter 4 in this volume).
2. One might argue, of course, that in so far as one goes for a walk along a path that was constructed by others, that, too, is a social action.
3. Habermas's principal writings on language and communication have been collected by Maeve Cooke in the volume *On the Pragmatics of Communication* (1998c), which shall be my main reference.
4. *Verständigung* can also be rendered as "communication". See also note 7 below.
5. Habermas subsequently changed the name of his programme from "universal pragmatics" to "formal pragmatics". On the one hand, at the empirical level, not all speech acts satisfy the conditions of communication he outlines. On the other hand, the new name highlights the procedural nature of his account and its neutrality *vis-à-vis* any particular content of speech.
6. For an explication of the method of rational reconstruction, see Chapter 2 in this volume.
7. The *Oxford English Dictionary* distinguishes between senses of communication "relating to affinity or association" (as in "the fact of having something in common with another person or thing") and senses "relating to the imparting or transmission of something", although the latter does include the meaning of "giving something to be shared" as well as that of "transmission or exchange of information".
8. In more recent work, he traces this tripartite distinction back to Wilhelm von Humboldt's account of language (TJ: 52). See also Charles Taylor, "Language and Human Nature" and "Theories of Meaning" (1985: 215–47, 248–92).
9. In the end, Habermas does not think that Searle makes good on the promise of speech act theory, rendering it both too intentionalist and too representationalist. See his "Comments on John Searle's 'Meaning, Communication, and Representation'" (OPC: 257–76). For critical responses on Habermas's adoption of speech act theory, see Skjei (1985: 87–104); Habermas (1985a); Kujundzic & Buschert (1993).
10. The illocution/perlocution distinction is a contentious one and Habermas has modified his take on it in response to criticism of his initial account. Whereas in *The Theory of Communicative Action*, he distinguishes between "trivial" and "strategic" perlocutionary effects, he subsequently distinguishes between

perlocutionary$_1$ effects, which "arise from the meaning of the speech act" (e.g. *B* gets some money as a result of *A*'s promising to get her money), perlocutionary$_2$ effects, which "occur in a contingent way" (e.g. *B*'s friend being pleased by *A*'s giving *A* money) and perlocutionary$_3$ effects (*B*'s financing a crime with the money from *A*), which depend on the speaker hiding her (strategic) intention (OPC: 223).

11. Whether or not meanings are normative and what it means to claim that they are is the subject of a sometimes heated contemporary debate that has grown out of debate about rule-following. The catalyst for much of the current debate has been Saul A. Kripke's *Wittgenstein on Rules and Private Language: An Elementary Exposition* (1982). There is disagreement concerning the very meaning of normativity. Some authors take it to refer simply to the fact that linguistic expressions can be used correctly or incorrectly, others – usually critics of semantic normativity – claim it to be a stronger notion. For critical analyses of semantic normativity, see Hattiangadi (2007); Glüer (2001); Wikforss (2001).
12. In contrast to Dummett, Habermas retains a realist notion of truth. See *Truth and Justification* and Chapter 2 in this volume.
13. See Chapter 6 for differentiations of different types of pragmatic discourse and Chapters 5 and 6 for more detailed discussions of the discursive vindication of moral and authenticity claims.
14. For Habermas's critique of Davidson, see his "From Kant's 'Ideas' of Pure Reason to the 'Idealizing' Presuppositions of Communicative Action" (TJ: esp. 112–20). Note that while Davidson rejects the idea that meanings are in any philosophically significant sense social, his principle of charity enjoins the radical interpreter to attribute mostly true – that is, shared – *beliefs* to the interpretee in order to come up with a theory of interpretation for his utterances. In "A Nice Derangement of Epitaphs" (2005), where he argues for the primacy of idiolects over a socially shared language, he seems to allow that, unless or until we have reason to believe otherwise and adjust our theory of interpretation, the theory we apply to our interlocutor's utterances is our own. Arguably, then, Davidson does not entirely escape the need to presuppose shared meaning.
15. See Chapter 4 in this volume.
16. See "Towards a Critique of the Theory of Meaning" (OPC: 277–306). He adopts the functional analysis that follows from Bühler (1990).
17. Interestingly, Davidson draws on Grice in his defence of the primacy of the idiolect over a socially shared language. See Davidson (2005: 94).
18. For Habermas's detailed critique of intentionalism in philosophy of language as well as of mind, see his "Intentions, Conventions, and Linguistic Interactions (1976)" (2001c: 105–28).
19. Apel was one of the first to bring together continental and analytic philosophies of language and himself defends what he calls a "transcendental pragmatics". See Apel (1980, 1994).
20. Here, too, there is thus a marked difference between Habermas's position and that of someone like Richard Rorty.
21. At the same time, he turned his attention to epistemological questions he had largely set aside after *Knowledge and Human Interests*, engaging particularly with Hilary Putnam. See this volume, Chapter 2 on his formulation of "weak" naturalism, and the discussion of truth and normative rightness below.
22. See "From Kant to Hegel: On Robert Brandom's Pragmatic Philosophy of Language" (TJ: 131–74). Interestingly, Habermas's critique in various ways parallels his much earlier critique of Sellars in the Gauss lectures. See Lecture

III in *On the Pragmatics of Social Interaction: Preliminary Studies in the Theory of Communicative Action* (2001).

23. For an analysis of the notion of a validity claim, see Heath (1998).
24. This question is taken up by Joel Anderson and Bill Rehg in Chapters 5 and 6 respectively.
25. "Wahrheitstheorien" (1984a: 127–83). The essay also contains critiques of correspondence and coherence theories of truth. See also Putnam (1981). For Habermas's more recent critique of Putnam, see "Norms and Values: On Hilary Putnam's Kantian Pragmatism" and "Rightness versus Truth: On the Sense of Normative Validity in Moral Judgments and Norms" (TJ: 213–76). For an analysis of the consensus theory as a theory of justification rather than as a theory of truth, see Fultner (1996). The impetus for Habermas's revisions to his account of truth have been critiques primarily by Albrecht Wellmer and Cristina Lafont. Lafont argues that Habermas's account lacks a theory of reference and should incorporate one of the sort offered by Putnam's direct realism. See Wellmer (1992) and Lafont (1999: ch. 5).
26. A recent example of this charge is Searle (2010: 62).
27. Thanks to Jonathan Maskit for his comments on an earlier draft of this chapter.

FOUR

System and lifeworld

Joseph Heath

"Critical theory" refers to a tradition of philosophical reflection that is characterized by close engagement with the social sciences, combined with a rejection of methodological value-neutrality in favour of a style of enquiry governed by what Jürgen Habermas once referred to as the "emancipatory interest" of human reason. In Habermas's early work on historical materialism and Marxian crisis theory this emancipatory interest was not difficult to discern. However, as his work in social and legal theory became more technical, and the systematic ambitions of his project more extensive, many of his readers began to wonder what had become of these critical impulses. Particularly with the publication of *The Theory of Communicative Action*, where Habermas shifts to a set of theoretical commitments that are more Weberian than Marxist, the question began to seem increasingly pressing.

The answer, however, is not that difficult to find. While Habermas abandons his earlier claim that the class structure of capitalist societies gives rise directly to crisis tendencies, which may or may not be successfully diffused, he replaces this with the view that the pathologies of late capitalism are caused by the "colonization of the lifeworld" by "the system". Thus the distinction between system and lifeworld, which is drawn somewhat casually in earlier work such as *Legitimation Crisis*, acquires increased prominence in *The Theory of Communicative Action*. Indeed, the final three chapters of the latter work are essentially an extended reflection on the dynamics of system and lifeworld, along with the role that this distinction can play in reconceptualizing the basic terms of the Marxian and first-generation Frankfurt School critique of capitalism.

This discussion, however, has not been found entirely satisfactory by many readers. Part of the problem is that Habermas draws the system–lifeworld distinction in at least four ways, each of which is slightly different. First, he draws an action-theoretic distinction: the lifeworld is the domain of communicative action, while the system is the domain where instrumental action predominates (TCA 2:154). Second, he draws an order-level distinction, with respect to the mechanism of integration: order in the lifeworld is achieved through coordination of action orientations (social integration), while order in the system is achieved through coordination of action consequences (system integration) (TCA 2:117). Third, he distinguishes the two in terms of the media that are used to generate integration: steering media in the case of the system, natural language in the case of the lifeworld (TCA 2: 183). Finally, he describes the system as governed by a "functional" logic, and thus as comprehensible only through the objectivating lens of a non-interpretive social-scientific methodology. Thus the distinction between lifeworld and system is drawn in terms of the limits of *verstehen*, or intepretive, sociology.

These four distinctions are obviously related in some way to each other, but are not exactly the same. Thus my plan in this chapter is to present the four distinctions in sequence, in order to show why Habermas takes them to be equivalent. In the process, certain presuppositions that Habermas makes, which stand in need of further articulation and defence, will become apparent. I will conclude by showing what implications this has for the colonization thesis, and for Habermas's later critical theory.

Early formulations

Habermas's formulation of the system–lifeworld distinction, prior to *The Theory of Communicative Action*, arises out of a fairly simple modification of Talcott Parsons's structural-functionalist systems theory (LC: 5). Since the influence of Parsons is a constant in Habermas's work, it is worth summarizing briefly the various elements of Parsons's view.

The starting point for Parsons's socio-theoretic reflections was the claim that a system of purely instrumental (or strategic) action could not generate a stable social order. In this respect, he took Thomas Hobbes's characterization of the state of nature as an accurate account of what social life *would* be like, if individuals had no other resources at their disposal than those of individual utility-maximization. Furthermore, Parsons thought (in agreement with most philosophical readings) that

Hobbes had failed to show how a group of individuals could succeed in making the transition from the state of nature to that of civil society. But rather than treating this as the failure of a normative project (that of justifying the authority of the sovereign), Parsons regarded it as the source of an explanatory challenge. How does it come about, he asked, that we are currently living in a civil condition? Why are our economic interactions not characterized by a predominance of force and fraud? How is it that we are able to engage in *orderly* cooperative interactions with one another?

The answer that Parsons provided is a particularly sophisticated version of what has since become known as the cultural theory of social integration. The thought is that individuals pursue their own interests (much as the instrumental theory claims), but that the interests they have are shaped by a set of values that are culturally reproduced and widely shared. Individual pursuit of self-interest is further constrained by a set of institutional norms that generate social expectations reflecting these same values. Thus Parsons introduced the tripartite scheme of "culture, society, personality" as the basis for the explanation of social order. According to this view, values consist of a set of symbolically codified ends that are culturally reproduced. These are *internalized in personality* through socialization processes and *institutionalized in society* in the form of normative expectations (Parsons 1951: 36–45). Integration is achieved when the set of personality structures (and hence motives) of individuals in interaction are a sufficiently close match to the set of institutional expectations that the radical indeterminacy of strategic interaction can be eliminated and conflict-free cooperation can proceed.

A social system then, for Parsons, is not a spontaneous order (*ibid.*: 31). In order to persist over time, certain specific functions need to be discharged. For example, there will have to be a system of shared values, along with some mechanism that ensures the reproduction of these values. Parsons thought that with increased social complexity, specialization would arise with respect to these functions, with distinct social structures or "subsystems" developing focused on discharging each one. In his later work, he introduced the AGIL schema as a way of mapping out these structures. The letters stand for adaptation (A), goal-attainment (G), integration (I) and latent pattern-maintenance (L). The underlying idea is a relatively straightforward generalization from his action-theory. Instrumental action involves the relationship of means and ends, normative action the relationship of norms and values. Adaptation involves provision of means, goal-attainment the specification of ends, integration the enforcement of norms, and pattern-maintenance the reproduction of shared values.

The AGIL schema provides, among other things, an account of the evolution of class society that is in certain respects more compelling than the Marxian one. It generates an intuitively natural analysis, for instance, of the very standard feudal differentiation of society into peasants (A), nobles (G), soldiers (I) and priests (L). In modern societies, the four functions are discharged by the economy (A), the political system (G), the legal system (I) and various religious traditions (L). It is a consequence of this view, however, that class differentiation is not a product of distributive conflict. On the contrary, classes emerge on this view only because the division of labour they reflect allows the basic tasks required for the reproduction of the social order to be discharged in a more efficient way. There is no "fundamental contradiction" in such a society, much less any reason to expect crises or instability. Thus Parsons's analysis gave rise to the so-called "consensus" model of social order, which was taken to be in tension with the "conflict" tradition that originated in Marx (Bernard 1983).

Habermas's ambition, in *Legitimation Crisis*, was to accept the basic Parsonian architectonic, while making the modifications needed to explain how a social or economic crisis might still be possible. His central move is to deny the distinction Parsons draws between the I and L subsystems. Habermas accepts that the economy and the state can usefully be described as systems, because they are integrated through steering media (money and power), which provide self-regulating mechanisms best described in cybernetic terms. With integration and pattern-maintenance, on the other hand, integration is achieved in the medium of natural language. Natural language is, in Habermas's view, both holistic in its structure (and hence resistant to functional specialization) and constrained by norms of rationality (and hence resistant to functional adaptation). Because of this, there is no distinct "social" (I) and "cultural" (L) system, but only a shared "sociocultural system", otherwise known as a *lifeworld* (LC: 5).

Thus the best way of understanding the lifeworld, in its initial formulation at least, is to see it as an amalgamation of Parsons's I and L subsystems, corresponding to a domain of interaction integrated through natural language. Indeed, in this early work, Habermas uses the terms "lifeworld" and "sociocultural system" interchangeably. This construct serves the purpose of Habermas's crisis theory, because it provides a limit on the scope of reification and functional adaptation in society. At the time, Habermas thought the class structure of capitalist societies directly caused periodic economic crises (through overproduction and the falling rate of profit). These crises could be headed off by the welfare state, because of the functional adaptability of the medium of administrative power. Late capitalist societies were therefore characterized by a displacement of economic crises onto the state. This in turn increased the demands made by the state upon the other subsystems, including the sociocultural system (or lifeworld). The state was obliged to tap into additional reservoirs of "meaning" in the lifeworld, in order to enhance legitimation. However, because of the structural limitations of natural language as a medium of social integration, the lifeworld is not simply compliant in the face of these externally imposed demands. Thus the potential for crisis emerges, precisely because the lifeworld does not submit to the logic of functionalist modes of system integration.

Later formulations

In his early work, Habermas distinguished system from lifeworld in a highly "systems-theoretic" way, that is, in terms of the medium through which social integration is achieved. This was strongly influenced by his debate with Niklas Luhmann (Habermas & Luhmann 1971) and his desire to show that natural language could not simply be treated as a "code". The internal connection between meaning and validity, that is, the fact that every interpretation is necessarily a rational interpretation, made language non-transparent as a medium for the reproduction of social institutions and interaction patterns. In the domain of morality, in particular, Habermas was at pains to show that the use of language systematically influenced cultural reproduction in a way that disadvantaged social formations that embodied non-generalizable interests. In particular, he felt that class structures, which could easily be reproduced at the level of the system simply through manipulation of incentives, would encounter much more significant obstacles to their reproduction in the lifeworld, precisely because they were unlikely to be the object of unforced agreement.

At the time, however, Habermas had not worked out the action-theoretic "microfoundations" for this view, and so tended to formulate it strictly in terms of media. After he introduced the concept of communicative action, he reformulated the distinction in these terms (describing the lifeworld as "a concept complementary to that of communicative action" [TCA 2: 119]). As we shall see, it is the attempt to reconcile the action-theoretic and the order-level conception of the lifeworld, while at the same time trying to present the idea as a plausible successor to Edmund Husserl's phenomenological conception (see e.g. Schutz & Luckmann 1973), that is responsible for much of the confusion surrounding the concept.

Habermas's central criticism of the instrumental model of rationality, in *The Theory of Communicative Action*, is that it takes the rationality of intentional states for granted. "Action" for Habermas, as for Weber, is the subset of human behaviour that is "understandable" on the grounds that it can plausibly be explained through the ascription of motivating intentional states. All action is teleological, in the trivial sense that it can be understood as goal-directed. All action can therefore be assessed according to two criteria: in terms of the suitability of the means chosen to the goal pursued, and in terms of the justifiability of the intentional states in terms of which this choice problem is formulated. Thinking about intentional states from the perspective of the "philosophy of consciousness", however, led theorists to imagine that the intentional states might simply be taken as given, from the standpoint of practical rationality, and thus that the second component of the theory of practical rationality could be dealt with by some other, purely individualistic psychological or epistemological theory. The result was an exclusive emphasis on the appropriateness of means to ends, and hence the tendency to equate practical rationality with instrumental action.

For Habermas, the significance of the linguistic turn lies in the suggestion, not just that the content of intentional states might be given by the *semantic content* of the associated propositions, but that this semantic content might be determined by the *use* of such propositions in speech acts. It is a consequence of this view that theorists of practical rationality cannot simply treat beliefs, desires, or any other type of intentional state as explanatory primitives in the theory of practical rationality. Every rational action must be evaluated in both dimensions: in terms of the appropriateness of means to ends, and in terms of the justifiability of the associated intentional contents. In some cases, however, one or the other dimension of assessment will clearly be more important. This allows Habermas to draw an analytic distinction between two different "primitive" action types: instrumental action and speech acts (OPC: 217–20). In the simplest forms of instrumental action, what really matters is the suitability of the means chosen: the rationality of the underlying beliefs and desires is still relevant, but of secondary importance. In the case of speech acts, on the other hand, the issue of means and ends recedes in importance; what becomes essential to the rationality of the action is the justifiability of its *content*. (In the limit case, the teleological dimension becomes merely formal, equivalent to the standardized intra-communicative objective of reaching mutual understanding.)

When this model is generalized to social interaction, it provides a new set of resources to address the problem that Parsons referred to as "double contingency", or what rational choice theorists call "interdependent choice". Simply put, social interaction generates a regress of expectations. What counts as the "best" course of action for an individual will depend, typically, upon what he expects the other person to do, but what counts as "best" for this other person will depend upon what she expects the first one to do. This regress constitutes a formidable challenge to even a teleological conception of rationality, since it suggests that what counts as the "best" course of action will simply be undefined in many contexts.

Habermas's action theory suggests that individuals have two ways of resolving this dilemma (OPC: 221). They can approach the problem instrumentally, trying to establish an equilibrium using the sort of "mirror reasoning" that is familiar from game theory. This generates what Habermas refers to, following common usage, as strategic action. The alternative is that they can talk to one another, announcing intentions, issuing imperatives and making assertions. In so far as they are able to establish a set of stable mutual expectations in this way, Habermas refers to it as *communicative action* (OPC: 222). It should be noted that neither social action type is entirely "pure". Communicative action is still teleological, in the sense that individuals are each pursuing plans, trying to accomplish something through their joint action. What makes it communicative action is the fact that the double contingency problem is resolved using speech acts. What makes it non-instrumental is that agents are bound by commitments that they have undertaken in the course of reaching communicative agreement (to carry out intentions, to conform to imperatives and to treat asserted states of affairs as though they were the case). Similarly, strategic action still involves mutual ascription of intentional states, and hence deployment of essentially linguistic resources. Indeed, the type of "mirror reasoning" involved in strategic interaction requires that each player develop a very sophisticated model of what objectives the other player is pursuing, how that person will assess evidence, and so on. In this case, however, the instrumental action type is in the ascendancy, in the sense that it provides the competencies used to generate the mutual expectations that resolve the double contingency problem.

This distinction between social action types generates two parallel mechanisms of social *integration*. Integration refers to the process through which stable, cooperative patterns of interaction can emerge, despite underlying incongruity of individual preference (e.g. conflicting interests, free rider incentives, etc.). Habermas distinguishes between "mechanisms of coordinating action that harmonize the *action orientations* of participants" and "mechanisms that stabilize nonintended consequences of actions by way of functionally intermeshing *action consequences*":

> In one case, the integration of an action system is established by a normatively secured or communicatively achieved consensus, in the other case, by a nonnormative regulation of individual decisions that extends beyond the actors' consciousness. This distinction between a social integration of society, which takes effect in action orientations, and a systemic integration of society, which reaches through and beyond action orientations, calls for a corresponding differentiation in the concept of society itself. (TCA 2:117)

When Habermas talks about systemic integration "reaching through and beyond action orientations" what he has in mind are various sorts of "invisible hand" mechanisms, through which the pursuit of individual interest produces a desired pattern, even though it is no one's intention that it do so (TCA 2: 150). An example (from John Kay [2003]) would be the flow of shoppers through the checkouts at a grocery store. While the "order" of the queue is directly constrained by norms, the assignment of shoppers to queues is normatively unregulated: individuals are permitted to choose whichever queue they prefer (which results, typically, in each individual choosing the one with the shortest line-up). The collective result, however, is an optimal assignment of shoppers to checkouts, and as a result, maximization of the number of shoppers whose purchases can be processed with given resources, minimization of time spent waiting, and so on. Thus the orderliness of this aspect of the interaction is produced through a form of "system integration".

When Habermas says that this distinction between modes of integration "calls for a corresponding differentiation in the concept of society itself", what he is referring to is the distinction between system and lifeworld. The lifeworld in this sense is the domain of communicative action, where orderliness is the product of social integration (i.e. harmonization of action orientations). The system is the domain of instrumental action, where orderliness is of the product of system integration (i.e. harmonization of action consequences). Another way of putting this is to say that in the lifeworld, orderliness is brought about through preference-change, whereas in the system it is brought about through incentives. We might choose to think of this as the action-theoretic way of drawing the system–lifeworld distinction.

Unfortunately, this action-theoretical analysis fails to explain some of the other things Habermas says about the system–lifeworld distinction, and fails to map it onto the earlier, more explicitly Parsonian analysis. It is unclear from this perspective what role might be played by steering media, or why "the system" should be thought of as possessing two subsystems, the economy and the state. It is also unclear why the distinction should map onto any sort of methodological differences at the level of accessibility to social-scientific enquiry. For instance, Habermas continues the long quotation cited above by saying that "from an observer's perspective of someone not involved, society can be conceived only as a *system of actions* such that each action has a functional significance according to its contribution to the maintenance of the system" (TCA 2: 117). The connection between the coordination of action through consequences and accessibility to an observer perspective is unclear, to say the least. (Microeconomic analysis of markets – the paradigm case of system integration – is, after all, based upon a commitment to methodological individualism, and thus interpretivism, not functionalism.) And finally, it seems obvious that every domain of interaction is going to be characterized by a mixture of communicative and strategic action, and that it only encourages unwarranted hypostatization to talk about "the" system and "the" lifeworld as though they were distinct entities.

In order to sort this out, it is necessary to draw a distinction between small-s systems, that is, domains of interaction in which systemic integration is predominant, such as supermarket queues, and a capital-s System, that is, one that gets differentiated from the lifeworld over time, such as a market economy. The difference is that the latter type are self-regulating, or *cybernetic* systems. The supermarket queue, although a complex system of predominantly instrumental action, lacks a feedback mechanism. The outputs of the system are not themselves inputs, which means that it lacks the capacity for self-regulation. It does not possess homeostatic properties, and cannot usefully be described as having a goal state. It lacks, for instance, any sort of mechanism that would adjust the number of checkouts that are open in response to the average length of queues. It therefore requires constant *external* monitoring and adjustment by a manager in order to preserve its useful qualities. This is in contrast to a system like the market economy, where the primary outputs of the system (the set of prices) are also among the most important inputs.

Habermas fails to draw this distinction explicitly, for a variety of reasons, the most important being the promiscuous use of functionalist vocabulary by Luhmann and others, which led many theorists in Germany at the time to regard every regularity in human behaviour as part of a cybernetic system until proven otherwise. (By contrast, the broadside against functionalist explanation unleashed upon analytical

Marxists by Jon Elster [1985], along with the very narrow defence offered by G. A. Cohen [1982], created an intellectual environment in the anglosphere in which a "critique of functionalist reason" would seem to be about as urgent as a "critique of phlogiston theory".) Nevertheless, this distinction is essential for understanding the connection that Habermas sees between the action-level and the order-level definitions of system and lifeworld.

The classic example of a cybernetic system is that of a thermostat hooked up to a furnace regulating the temperature in a house. The thermostat takes the air temperature in its vicinity as an input, then generates an output that consists in either the completion or interruption of a circuit, resulting in the furnace being turned on or off. Feedback occurs because the heat generated by the furnace eventually changes the air temperature in the vicinity of the thermostat, resulting in a change in its output state. Because of this loop, it is not only harmless, but positively useful to describe the system in intentional terms, as having the "goal state" of maintaining a particular temperature. Furthermore, anyone who wants to change this outcome needs to be aware of the system operating in the background, in order to avoid failure and frustration. Consider the situation of someone who finds it too hot in the house, but is unable, for one reason or another, to change the setting on the thermostat. She might choose to open up some windows, in order to cool things down. But of course, the thermostat will compensate for these changes by turning on the furnace more often and for longer, resulting in failure of the plan. A more effective strategy would be the counter-intuitive one of plugging in a space heater right beneath the thermostat, which will fool it into thinking that the house is warmer than it is, causing it to leave the furnace off. The latter is what is known as a "high information" intervention, because it targets the feedback loop, as opposed to the "high energy" intervention of opening windows. It is precisely this idea of controlling system output by intervening in the feedback loop – manipulating the information it receives – that gives rise to the idea of "steering" the system (and of a "steering medium", which is simply the medium in which this system-relevant information is encoded).

It is easy to see how this model generalizes to the case of social systems. In the case of the economic system, for instance, behaviour is controlled by price signals. High energy interventions that fail to target the feedback loop are likely to be undone by "systemic imperatives," that is, the corresponding efforts of the system to maintain its goal state. Consider, for example, the issue of road pricing. Huge investments can be made in public transit, but if the effect is to make roads less congested the end result will simply be "induced traffic": people with cars will make more trips, people who move will buy homes further from work, and so on, all because travel times have declined. This will continue until the equilibrium level of congestion is re-established. The problem is that the failure to price roads sends the wrong signal, suggesting that there is a surplus of this good, or that its consumption has no social cost. The "high information" approach of tolling the roads constitutes a more effective solution, compared to the "high energy" solution of constructing alternative infrastructure, because it changes the incentives in a way that makes the "functional imperative" of the system coincide with the socially desired outcome.

The fact that direct approaches to changing outcomes are often self-defeating is one of the counter-intuitive features of cybernetic systems that reveals the limitations of an interpretivist approach to social-scientific enquiry. The "unsurveyability" of systemically integrated domains is essentially a consequence of the fact that order is achieved through external incentives, which are in turn structured by a feedback mechanism. Systemic integration of this sort permits a significant divergence to arise between the objectives that individuals pursue and the purpose that their action serves in the broader system, which has the effect of making the social order non-transparent to the individuals involved. For example, in a competitive market, each firm makes supply decisions based upon the goal of maximizing profit; the net result, however, is that profits are bid down to zero. The latter is in fact the desired outcome, since it results in marginal cost being equated to marginal revenue across the sector. An anthropologist however, constructing an ethnographic account of managerial behaviour, might easily fail to notice this, simply because none of his informants conceive of the

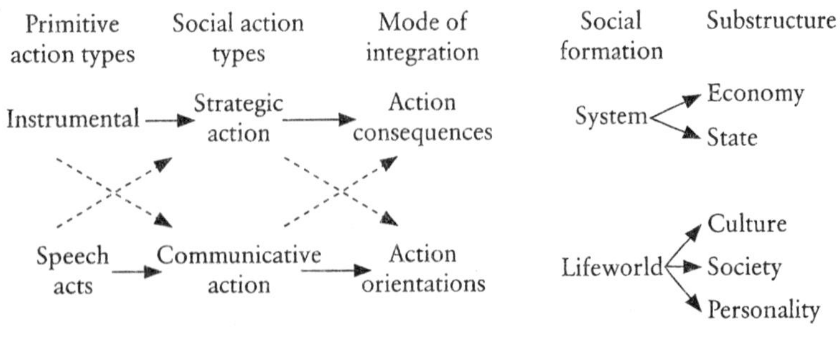

Figure 4.1 Action-theoretic foundations of the system–lifeworld distinction.

relevant set of decisions in this way. In a traditional society, interpretive methods are able to provide a perspicuous understanding of the social structure. But with the "uncoupling" of system and lifeworld over time (i.e. the introduction of self-regulation in the systemic domain), this interpretive method must be supplemented with a more objectivating, functionalist perspective, in order to provide an adequate understanding of why things turn out the way that they do.

The colonization thesis

Habermas regards the historical development and evolution of human societies as a *rationalization process* occurring in two dimensions. The rationalization of culture is a process that occurs within the lifeworld, involving increased differentiation between the three validity claims associated with every speech act: truth, rightness and sincerity. The traditional triumvirate of the true, the good and the beautiful, conceived of as a unity in premodern societies, come to be seen as subject to different criteria of evaluation (cognitive, moral and aesthetic, respectively). Thus the corresponding object domains of science, morality and art become distinct enterprises. The rationalization of society, on the other hand, involves a process of differentiation (or "uncoupling") between system and lifeworld. As truth claims become dissociated from rightness claims, there is a transition from substantive to formal moral and legal codes, which generates greater tolerance for the more consequentialist forms of reasoning required to justify the blocks of "norm-free sociality" characteristic of systemic integration (TCA 2: 171). The system in turn permits the development of far more complex and extensive forms of cooperation.

In a traditional society these systemic domains merely supplement the lifeworld, but with the transition to capitalism they begin to supplant the lifeworld, which in turn becomes dependent upon system performances in order to discharge basic functions associated with its own reproduction (LC: 24). This is why, with the transition to early capitalist societies, systemic crises are experienced, for the first time, as crises of *social* integration. It also means that the incongruity between the lifeworld and system patterns of integration becomes a source of friction, resulting in the lifeworld becoming increasingly subject to the pressure of "systemic imperatives" that lack an intuitive and immediate rationale. Furthermore, the class structure of capitalist societies generates, in Habermas's view, justificatory challenges – namely "how socially produced wealth may be inequitably, and yet legitimately, distributed"

(LC: 20) – that make them easier to reproduce through systemic means. The result is a significant bias in favour of system over lifeworld patterns of social organization and in favour of media-steered over communicative approaches to problem-solving. This generates increasing encroachment of the system upon the lifeworld, and thus an instrumentalization of social relations.

Habermas refers to the mechanism through which individuals switch over from a communicative to a predominantly instrumental action orientation in a particular domain as the *technicization* of the lifeworld (TCA 2: 263). When domains of action that are technicized become reintegrated through steering media it is referred to as *mediatization*. Again, Habermas's overly tolerant attitude toward functionalist modes of explanation leads him to treat these action-level and order-level concepts as though they were essentially equivalent (e.g. TCA 2: 180), even though the two processes can obviously come apart. Consider, for example, the problem of declining voter turn-out in Western democracies. This appears to be a consequence, at least in part, of an increasingly instrumental orientation towards the political system. Young people, in particular, are less inclined to regard voting as a civic duty and more inclined to consider it merely as an opportunity to see their preferences prevail. The result is a collective action problem, since the chances of influencing the outcome are close to zero, whereas taking the time to vote almost always entails some personal cost. Thus low voter turn-out can plausibly be described as a consequence of the technicization of the lifeworld. In some jurisdictions the state has chosen to implement a systemic solution to this problem, usually by imposing fines upon people who don't vote. This constitutes a form of mediatization of the lifeworld. But in many other jurisdictions the state has chosen to do nothing, but rather just to live with the consequences of the collective action problem. This constitutes a clear case of technicization unaccompanied by any compensating process of mediatization.

Setting aside these difficulties, however, one can see how Habermas uses the concept of mediatization to reformulate the traditional Frankfurt School concern about the possible emergence of a "totally reified society" in system–lifeworld terms. Total reification, in Habermas's view, would be equivalent to a society that was all system and no lifeworld (i.e. where the process of mediatization was so far advanced that it had squeezed out the lifeworld entirely). This possibility is already precluded, in principle, by the Parsonian analysis of the problem of order. System integration is achieved through external incentives (codified in the form of steering media). Within the system, individuals are free to adopt an instrumental orientation, but the integrity of the media is preserved only because these are "anchored" in the lifeworld, which is to say, supported by systematic patterns of non-utility maximizing behaviour (such as, for example, genuine loyalty and commitment on the part of those charged with enforcing the law) (TCA 2: 173). Thus "total systemic integration" could never occur. Society would collapse into a Hobbesian state of nature before instrumentalization went that far.

Rather than simply leaving it at that, however, Habermas develops a more careful analysis of the dynamics of this reification process. His general thought is that capitalist modernization has been characterized by a lopsided process of rationalization, one that has involved an overemphasis upon the cognitive-instrumental domain of validity in the realm of culture and an over-reliance upon systemic modes of integration at the level of society. He also thinks that the system has already gone "too far" in supplanting the lifeworld as the dominant mode of social integration. This critique is based upon the essentially functionalist claim that certain domains of action that are essential to the reproduction of society have become technicized, in our society, with increasingly pathological consequences. Hence his claim that "Only with a critique of functionalist reason can we give a plausible account of why, under the cover of a more or less successful welfare-state compromise, there should still be any conflicts breaking out at all – conflicts that do not appear primarily in class-specific form" (TCA 2: 350).

Habermas develops this analysis using the culture–society–personality framework, which he takes over from Parsons. But rather than justifying it with reference to the importance of shared values (TCA 2: 225), as Parsons does, he argues that these three symbolic orders constitute the *background* to every communicatively mediated interaction (TCA 2: 127). The cognitive demands imposed by the use of communicative action as a mechanism of social integration – the requirement that action orientations be harmonized through discursively achieved consensus – are so great that in the absence of mitigating factors it would be impossible to build stable social orders on this basis. What solves the problem is the fact that the lifeworld provides an enormous fund of taken-for-granted, shared expectations, and thus serves as a point at which demands for further justification can cease. The nature of these expectations can be analysed under three categories: first, the lifeworld provides a fund of shared knowledge (culture), second, a set of unproblematic institutional expectations (society) and finally, a standardized folk psychology (personality) that can serve as the basis for the interpretation of action and speech (TCA 2: 138).

This analysis of the role that the lifeworld plays as background to communicatively mediated exchange is the only real point of commonality between Habermas's communication-theoretic conception and the Husserlian phenomenological conception from which it gets its name. This is a fairly weak link, which is why I have suggested that the lifeworld concept is best understood as a modification of Parsons's systems theory, rather than Husserlian (or even Schutzian) phenomenology. Further confusing the issue is the fact that, in Habermas's analysis, the three structural features of the lifeworld (culture, society and personality) do not map onto the three validity-claim schema that he uses in his analysis of cultural reproduction. Habermas argues that the three lifeworld structures can be reproduced only through communicative action, but this has nothing to do with the fact that every speech act raises three validity claims. One might be inclined to think that "personality" maps onto sincerity and "society" onto rightness. "Culture", however, does not map onto truth claims. Indeed, rationalization processes within the lifeworld involve differentiation of the three different spheres of validity, that is, truth, rightness and sincerity, *within the domain of culture*. Thus the category of "culture" encompasses all three validity claims (and the rationalization of the lifeworld takes the form of a *cultural* learning process; it does not involve any sort of structural differentiation between culture, society and personality). The role that communicative action plays in reproducing the three different structures is based upon a fairly *ad hoc* analysis of the pragmatics of speech, with reference to the way that communication secures mutual understanding (thereby reproducing culture), serves to coordinate action (thereby reproducing institutional orders) and socializes individuals (thereby reproducing personality structures) (TCA 2: 137).

The functional limits on systemic expansion, in Habermas's view, are reached when mediatization begins to encroach upon domains that are essential to the reproduction of these three structures. It is at this point that "the mediatization of the lifeworld turns into its colonization" (TCA 2: 318). Thus Habermas does not view the process of mediatization as *inherently* problematic:

> It is not the uncoupling of media-steered subsystems and of their organizational forms from the lifeworld that leads to the one-sided rationalization or reification of everyday communicative practice, but only the penetration of forms of economic and administrative rationality into areas of action that resist being converted over to the media of money and power because they are specialized in cultural transmission, social integration, and child rearing, and remain dependent on mutual understanding as a mechanism for coordinating action. (TCA 2: 330)

Habermas's central objective in this analysis is to provide a retrospective interpretation of the 1960s counterculture, along with the "new social movements" that emerged during that period. The question is why major social conflict would erupt in a non-class-specific form (e.g. why Western societies shifted from having a radical working class to having a radical student population). The thought is that, while these movements seem quite disparate, what they have in common is that each is essentially a defensive reaction that arises in response to disruptions in particular domains of the lifeworld. He continues to trace this back to class conflict, although the connection is somewhat more tenuous in later work. In *The Theory of Communicative Action*, he avoids all talk of "fundamental contradictions" in the capitalist system, claiming only that the class structure generates inequality, which in turn generates a need for economic growth as a way of pacifying this latent conflict (TCA 2: 350–51). It is this need for growth that renders conformity to the functional imperatives of the system increasingly important, and thus results "in a more or less continuous increase in system complexity – which means not only an extension of formally organized domains of action, but an increase in their internal density as well" (TCA 2: 351).

Conclusion

While the second volume of *The Theory of Communicative Action* is billed as a "critique of functionalist reason", it is fairly clear from Habermas's analysis of system and lifeworld that he gives "functionalist reason" somewhat more credit than it deserves. Having provided action-theoretic foundations for the system–lifeworld distinction, Habermas proceeds to ignore several of the steps that must be taken to bridge the gap between the action-level concept of communicative action and the order-level concept of integration through steering media. He does so, I have suggested, because of certain functionalist presuppositions, which prevent him from contemplating seriously the thought that instrumentalization of social relations may generate straightforward lapses of orderliness, as opposed to renewed orderliness through steering media (i.e. that the world may become more Hobbesian, rather than more Kafkaesque).[1] It is possible to repair this deficit, I have suggested, by paying greater attention to the role that feedback mechanisms play in distinguishing forms of order that are merely produced through alignment of incentives from those that are supplemented by an additional mechanism that gives them self-regulating properties. This might also help remedy some of the loose talk that one encounters in Habermas's analysis about "functional imperatives" (e.g. What are these imperatives? In what sense is mediatization a response to them?).

With respect to the colonization thesis, Habermas's analysis is guided by the desire to explain two things: first, why the welfare state has failed to pacify all social conflict, and second, why the social conflicts that do erupt take a non-class-specific form. Again, in the absence of functionalist presuppositions, it is unclear why either question should be considered troubling. It is one thing to grant that capitalism does not contain fundamental contradictions that guarantee a constant succession of economic crises; it is quite another to assume that the welfare state generates a presumption against the emergence of any form of social conflict. One can see how deeply embedded Habermas is in the Parsonian "consensus" tradition by reconsidering these two guiding questions from the perspective of the social ontology laid out by John Rawls at the beginning of *A Theory of Justice*:

> Although society is a cooperative venture for mutual advantage, it is typically marked by a conflict as well as by an identity of interests. There is an identity of interests since social cooperation makes possible a better life for all than any would have if each were to live solely by his own efforts. There is a conflict of interests since persons are not indifferent as to how the greater benefits produced by their collaboration are distributed.
> (1971: 4).

The scope of this claim – the fact that it ranges over all social institutions, not just the state – along with the suggestion that cooperation necessarily generates conflict, suggests a somewhat deflationary answer to Habermas's two questions, and constitutes therefore a significant challenge to the thought that a critical theory of society should be organized around the system–lifeworld architectonic.

Note

1. For more detailed discussion, see Heath (1996).

FIVE

Autonomy, agency and the self

Joel Anderson

Autonomy and authenticity are usually seen as largely individual matters. It is often thought that, in trying to understand what it means genuinely to lead one's own life, we start by trying to get a handle on what individuals *themselves* want, and then examine the ways in which social pressures, political domination, material deprivation and so on interfere with them in ways that threaten or distort the self. This is the picture we encounter in Locke and Hobbes, right on through to contemporary liberalism. And, with some exceptions, it remains the dominant view.

It is decidedly *not* Jürgen Habermas's view. He takes autonomy, agency, identity, authenticity and the self to be fundamentally intersubjective phenomena. Moreover, even in comparison with relational or social approaches to autonomy, he conceptualizes this social dimension differently and in ways that cut deeper than the now widely accepted idea that our identity is shaped by our surroundings or that many of our deepest convictions can be realized only together with others. As he remarked in recent autobiographical reflections, his early childhood experiences with surgery on his cleft palate, and the frustrating, humiliating difficulties in making himself understood through his speech impediment, "opened [his] eyes to the intersubjective constitution of the human mind and the social core of our subjectivity, as well as to the fragility of communicative forms of life and the fact that socialized individuals are in need of special protection" (BNR: 17). If, like Habermas, one is convinced that our fundamental vulnerability lies in the possibility of being excluded from the protective and enabling forms of social cooperation and mutuality (or of having them break down), it will seem very strange to take the perspective of an independent individual as the self-evident starting point for reflection on autonomy and the self.

At the same time, Habermas has a deep distrust of groupthink or collectivism and stands squarely in the Enlightenment tradition that defends individual freedoms against domination.[1] Again, his personal experience is relevant, specifically, of seeing how Nazi ideologues and post-war German conservatives have sought support for their policies in philosophical theories that treat the individual as a mere "effect" of social or cultural forces, or as an expression of tradition, Spirit, language or Being.

This dual emphasis on the social (or "intersubjective") and the individual makes for a rich conception of autonomy: Habermas is a staunch defender of individual autonomy, authenticity and self-determination, but not on the basis of the standard liberal empiricist understanding of the self-sovereign self. To appreciate the complexity without getting lost in the complications, it will be useful to start out with a few distinctions, to which I now turn.

Fives senses of autonomy in the wake of Habermas's rejection of philosophy of consciousness

Habermas's views on the self and autonomy are not as widely discussed as many other aspects of his philosophy, in part because there is no specific terminology he uses for the cluster of related positions he takes.[2] One can, however, distinguish five distinct theoretical contexts in which Habermas discusses autonomous agency and authentic identity: deliberative democracy, moral philosophy, free will, social theory and personal identity. One way to get a first approximation of these different dimensions is by contrasting them with states of persons who lack these dimensions of autonomy. To lack *political autonomy* is to be subjected to illegitimate domination by others, specifically by not being integrated in an appropriate way in processes of collective self-determination. To lack *moral autonomy* is to be incapable of letting intersubjectively shared reasons determine one's will. To lack *accountable agency* is to behave as the result of compelling forces rather than to act for reasons. To lack *personal autonomy* is to be unable to engage in critical reflection about what to do with one's life. And to lack *authentic identity* is to have one's claim to recognition *vis-à-vis* others get no uptake.

Each of these senses of autonomy contribute to the overall conception of autonomy in Habermas's work, but the relations between them are complex. My aim here is to show how they all illustrate several consistent Habermasian themes – intersubjectivity, performativity and historicity – all of which are key components of Habermas's project of developing an account of autonomous agency that moves behind the limits of what he calls the "philosophy of consciousness".

Moving beyond "philosophy of consciousness" (or, as he sometimes says, taking a "postmetaphysical" approach)[3] is not a matter of dismissing subjectivity and consciousness as legitimate topics of philosophical investigation. What Habermas is rejecting, rather, is a broad philosophical approach that first emerged prominently with Descartes, an approach that considers the key philosophical questions, such as how we ought to relate to others, what really exists and how we can know anything, to be best answered by focusing on how one's mind and will grasp the world. The paradigm example of this is Descartes's discovery that the one thing that he could not doubt was the idea that there existed, at a very minimum, some subject who was doing the doubting (*Cogito ergo sum*: I think, therefore I am). Habermas has written extensively on why this approach leads to various philosophical dead ends, how the so-called "linguistic turn" undermined the fundamental premises of the approach, and what the implications are of rejecting the philosophy of consciousness. For our purposes, the key idea is this. In analysing our practical dealings with the world, philosophy of consciousness (and most mainstream analytic philosophy today) tends to focus on understanding how an individual's mental states (beliefs and desires) generate effects according to general causal mechanisms and do so in a way that can be fully grasped from the point of view of an outside observer. According to Habermas, this way of framing the task of understanding autonomous agents and their actions is still stuck in "philosophy of consciousness" in overlooking three key aspects of autonomous agency: intersubjectivity, performativity and historicity.

Intersubjectivity

Intersubjectivity is perhaps the most central component of overcoming philosophy of consciousness and especially the guiding assumption that there is something located in the individual – motivation, reflection, desires, conscience, subjective experience and so on – that is prior to and ultimately independent of the social world it affects. This "subject–object dichotomy" is precisely what Habermas targets, as presupposing that there is an inside and an outside: an inside source that we can know from a "first-person" perspective and an outside world of effects, *including other subjects*, that we can study from the third-person perspective of the outside observer. Habermas's alternative takes intersubjectivity to be basic, in the sense that agency, critical reflection, motivation and so on are what they are in virtue of being elements of our interactions with others. For Habermas, the starting point for philosophical investigation of autonomous agency in particular is to be located in communicative interactions, democratic institutions, practices of giving and asking for reasons, and the informal background "lifeworld". Consider a case I take up in the discussion of free will: when one acts for reasons, a full explanation of what one is doing must make reference to the cultural and linguistic background in virtue of which certain noises count as giving reasons. But this cannot be adequately grasped, according to Habermas, on the model of causal interactions among physical events, since reasons, objections, counterarguments and the rest are phenomena that, although perfectly real, come into view only within the "space of reasons", to use the Wilfrid Sellars phrase that Habermas has taken up recently, especially in his debates with Robert Brandom.[4] Thus, just as a "three-point basket" only exists within the meaningful space opened up by the game of basketball (and, in the US, only since 1979), "autonomy" is something that comes into view only once we take on certain attitudes in our interactions.

Performativity

Talk of attitudes is widespread, of course, within philosophy of consciousness, as elements in how an individual subject represents the world. In Habermas's postmetaphysical approach, attitudes play a markedly different role, as *performatively undertaken presuppositions*. On this view, taking something to be a three-point basket, for example, is not best understood in terms of my pretending something because I predict that you will pretend it too. Rather, my taking something to be a three-point basket is an aspect of the engaged perspective of participants in the game of basketball. To be able to see a three-point basket, one has to be an "insider" to the game of basketball, even if one is participating only as a spectator. This perspective or attitude is not so much a way of *thinking* about the world as a way of *doing* something in the world, hence something "performatively undertaken". The idea that certain phenomena have their reality as part of social practices conflicts with the influential physicalistic assumption that the only things that are real are those things that can be perceived from the detached ("third-personal") perspective of the natural sciences. And, indeed, Habermas's rejection of philosophy of consciousness is linked to his defence of an inclusive alternative to "hard", eliminativist naturalism.[5] For our purposes, it is important that this move to inclusive naturalism allows room for situating ideals and counterfactual presuppositions as part of the reality that shapes agents and actions. In particular, even though we all know about one another that we are not fully rational or autonomous, it is nonetheless an unavoidable part of the practices within which autonomy is central that, in so far as we are engaged in those practices, we must presuppose one another's autonomy. But this "*factual* role of performatively presupposed *counterfactual* assumptions"[6] is something that can be grasped only once one moves from a philosophy of consciousness to the social pragmatism Habermas defends.

Historicity

Once our grasp of reality is understood not primarily as a matter of mental representation but of practical engagement, it becomes "detranscendentalized" and thus something with a history. Habermas here stands in the tradition of Hegel and Marx (and, to some extent, Nietzsche and Foucault) in treating familiar topics of metaphysical philosophy, such as reason, morality or the mind, as real-world phenomena that emerge in particular social and historical contexts, rather than as timeless facts, relations or essences. This historicity occurs at two levels. First, these phenomena (including autonomy) are what they are now because of how they emerged, as part of complex real-world processes. In the case of autonomy, as we shall see, these developments are bound up with processes of modernization, involving changes in interpersonal relations, social institutions and material conditions. The second dimension of development occurs in the context of "life history", that is, our *individual* biographical development, in which each of us acquires the know-how to be autonomous, or to reason, or to act morally. Since this individual process is deeply dependent on supportive social conditions, the historical character of an individual's autonomy is further intertwined with autonomy's intersubjectivity.

Private autonomy, public autonomy and democratic self-governance

The tension between individualistic and social understandings of autonomy is particularly clear in the context of political philosophy, and that makes political autonomy a good topic to take up first. On the one hand, there is the familiar sense of autonomy as a matter of being free from illegitimate interference in one's choosing what to do. This is what Habermas calls "private autonomy", which he sees as an indisputably important principle. But it is complemented by "public autonomy", the form of self-governance that one exercises together with others in authorizing laws and other forms of collective action. Ensuring public autonomy is a matter of ensuring that those subject to collective decisions, laws and so on can see themselves as its authors, as in the case of democratically adopted laws. Importantly, this is not about getting one's way or not being interfered with. If I participate in a fair and inclusive debate, but the vote at the end goes the other way, I may be unhappy about my position not winning out, but my overall political autonomy is still preserved, unless there are grounds for criticizing the procedures. Traditionally, public and private autonomy have been seen as opposed. Habermas see them as not only important and compatible but as actually presupposing one another and emerging jointly. Neither can be assumed to have primacy over the other; they are "equally basic" [*gleichursprünglich*].[7] Public and private autonomy come into existence and develop only by *dovetailing*. Without a legitimate political order that guarantees individual rights and liberties, private autonomy simply does not exist. To sum up a complex argument, autonomy is something that emerges together with social practices, political institutions, legal rights and so on, but this is not merely a point about circumstances that are favourable for its development. It is not that autonomy becomes *difficult* without the framework of rights or the institutions of democratic decision-making; it ceases to exist. Autonomy is thus a social construction to the very core.

Here, again, we see the implications of rejecting the individualistic metaphysics of philosophy of consciousness. I will mention two. First, the emphasis on the intersubjectivity of political autonomy underscores the importance of maintaining those social, cultural and material conditions that make it possible. As Habermas regularly emphasizes, when social trends and public policies undermine those conditions (roughly, what he terms "lifeworld resources"), they cut deep into the very possibility of autonomy. Second, as a social construction, political autonomy is thus always caught up in ongoing processes of historical transformation. For example, as members of modern societies come to view one another as entitled to welfare rights, the substance of autonomy shifts as well. Looking forward, one can then ask, as Habermas does, what changes in these conditions are necessary for ensuring that both autonomy and democracy can develop in ways that make them able to handle the new challenges served up by a globalizing and increasingly complex world (PDM: 344).[8]

Moral autonomy, reason and the will

Even this brief treatment of democratic self-governance highlights Habermas's emphasis on the interdependence of individual and collective self-determination. Moral autonomy is distinctive, however, in being the context in which the egoistic desire to do what one feels like is expected to submit most unconditionally to the demands of the universalistic point of view. And, indeed, on Habermas's approach, moral self-determination becomes indistinguishable from determination by *reason*. In order to remain focused on issues of autonomy and the self, I will limit myself to highlighting briefly this notion of autonomy as alignment with reason and then go on to discuss two of Habermas's particularly interesting claims on the scope of morality and on moral motivation.

Habermas is keen to emphasize the Kantian point that moral autonomy is a matter of bringing what one *wills* in line with what one sees oneself as having reasons to do. The morally autonomous agent is self-determining because she is not subjected to any alien force, including desires or passions that we find ourselves having but wish we did not have. Moral autonomy, then, is a matter of desiring, choosing and acting in the way that one has reason to do. "In Kantian terms, the [morally] autonomous will is *entirely* imbued with practical reason" (BFN: 164). For the fully morally autonomous agent, it will be irrelevant that she strongly desires to do something that she knows to be wrong. But having one's will determined by reason does not undermine one's self-authorship, especially once it is clear that "listening to reason" is a matter of engaging, as a full and equal participant, in the ongoing process of giving and asking for reasons. Because of this, moral autonomy is not merely *compatible* with being responsive to relevant considerations raised by others. It requires it.

In linking moral self-determination with determination by reason, Habermas again illustrates how far he is from approaches that link autonomy to empirical influence and effective control. But this move also raises the concern that Habermas's theory is far from empirical human lives as well. To address this concern, two aspects of Habermas's approach to morally autonomous agency are worth highlighting.

Ethical-existential autonomy

Soon after first developing (with Karl-Otto Apel) his discourse ethics in the 1980s, Habermas came to revise the initial dichotomy between the moral will (guided by reason) and the strategic will (driven by preferences and assisted by means-ends reasoning). He now distinguishes an "ethical" form of reasoning and autonomy in which neither reason nor will has the upper hand (JA: 12; Habermas 2003b: 1–15).[9] In this domain of significant personal choices, an individual ultimately appeals to some sense of what she just finds herself caring about and what sort of person she herself wants to be (rather than what all rational agents must want, as is the case with moral autonomy), and at least as long as moral norms are not being violated, it makes no sense to require agents to step back from their deep personal commitments and consider their merit from the moral point of view. At the same time, Habermas emphasizes, there is also room for progress in understanding what one really cares about; sometimes we discover that we were mistaken about what is important to us; not that we change our mind, but that we correct ourselves, often in response to our exchanges with others. This possibility for error opens up the possibility for rational insight, which Habermas, in typical intersubjectivist fashion, understands as a form of dialogue. In this "ethical-existential discourse" (as he calls it) one engages in an open-minded give-and-take about what one really cares about and finds important and tries to make sense of one's personal commitments and values by fitting them into a larger sense of broader values, personal relationships, life history and so on. The capacity, then, to engage in this process in a fruitful way is what one could call personal autonomy, in a sense I return to below.

The growth of autonomy

It is also key to Habermas's approach that autonomy in the domain of morality and ethics is a real-world phenomenon resulting from ongoing historical processes. Here again we see the dovetailing of individual development ("ontogeny") and social evolution ("phylogeny"). As a matter in individual development, moral autonomy requires that an individual advance successfully through processes of cognitive development, psychological maturation, interactive competences and individual socialization (MCCA). At the phylogenetic level of the moral community, development also takes place, and in two quite different regards.

First, what morality demands of us is not something fixed but something that evolves over time. Despite Habermas's emphasis on moral universalism, consensus and objectivity, he draws a clear distinction between claims to truth (which refer to a reality that transcends the reach of human knowledge) and claims to moral rightness (which refer to the set of norms for governing our interactions that is best justified in moral discourse). From inside the performative perspective of participants trying to figure out jointly what norms are justified, moral debates feel like debates over truth, according to Habermas. But this does not change the fact that morality is ultimately a human social construction (TJ: ch. 6). The valid moral norms legislated and internalized by morally autonomous agents thus represent our current best efforts in the ongoing process of learning to solve the moral challenges continually posed by life and raised in discourse.

The second point has to do with the context-dependent development of motivational resources and supports for moral agents. The basic claim is that my effective ability to act morally involves having access to various "lifeworld resources" that support us when sheer insight and willpower aren't enough, and as a tough-minded sociologist, Habermas knows that it would be naive and unrealistic to expect them to be enough. As "lifeworld" resources, these supports are part of the implicit background of our actions, and they are a remarkably diverse bunch.[10] They include what Habermas calls "personality": character traits such as self-restraint or considerateness, as well as good habits that have become "second nature", all of which make it decidedly easier to be morally autonomous. The same can also be said for customs and taboos, which also relieve individuals of the burden of having to motivate themselves morally all the time. The comfortable ease of traditional, conventional mores comes at a price, however, for they function as they do only as long as they are uncontestable. With the shift to a modern "postconventional" social order, customs and habits lose their unquestioned authority and can motivate only if they are taken to be legitimate. In modern societies, enforceable law, justified in a way that fits with individuals' political autonomy, comes to provide a primary mechanism for ensuring that people do the right thing.[11] Of course, if you live in a society that has bad laws or were raised with bad habits, it will still be harder for you to act morally. This is why Habermas puts so much emphasis on the importance of developments not only at the level of laws but also at the informal level of culture and personality – on what he calls a "rationalization of the lifeworld". In this sense, improvements in socio-psycho-political structures constitute improvements in one's moral autonomy.

Accountable agency, free will and the space of reasons

We have already seen how Habermas's rejection of philosophy of consciousness shapes his views on moral and political autonomy. But the implications are perhaps most striking in his recent interventions in free will debates, particularly in his recent efforts to counter the increasingly widespread talk of neuroscience and psychology "proving" that free will is an "illusion".[12]

In debates over free will, the central issue is whether what we do is ever truly up to us, given that everything that happens in the universe, including movements of our bodies or changes in brain states, is determined by prior states of the world in accordance with deterministic laws of nature. As it is typically framed, the question of autonomous agency is a matter of having a certain sort of causal efficacy, and we seem to be faced with a nasty dilemma: give up the idea that we cause our actions (as distinct from our brains causing our actions) or presuppose some sort of alternative form of causation in which agency operates outside the laws of nature. Since the latter amounts to something like voodoo, it is argued, autonomy and the conscious will turn out to be illusions.

As mentioned earlier with the example of three-pointers in basketball, Habermas's proposed solution centres on what it means to do something as a participant within a social practice. Consider now chess. Everything that happens in a chess match could ultimately be explained in terms of microphysical causal chains. If we do that, then there are no pawns or knights or rooks, only bits of wood. Clearly, however, chess players are not suffering from an illusion or pretending in thinking that a bit of wood is a pawn. They're not *pretending* it is a pawn; it *is* a pawn. Imagine someone grabbing the microphone at a chess tournament and dramatically announcing that the game of chess is a fraud, because "pawns *don't exist*!" Such a person would be, as the saying goes, unclear on the concept. Like pawns, reasons for acting are perfectly real, even though (like pawns) they exist only as part of social practices in which we give and ask for reasons. But, assuming that free will is a matter of being able to respond to reasons, then there are few good reasons to doubt whether autonomous agency is a natural part of the (social) world.

That, in a nutshell, is Habermas's view on free will, although there are many further details, complexities and implications that could be discussed.[13] Here I shall focus on three aspects that are relevant for understanding Habermas's core claim regarding the intersubjectivity of autonomy.

First, as he did with regard to democratic self-governance and moral autonomy, Habermas links free, autonomous agency to rationality and justification. This move places Habermas with Plato, Kant and others on one side of perhaps the most fundamental controversy regarding free action and autonomous agency. The other side is occupied by empiricists (from Hobbes and Locke to Russell and contemporary neuroscientists), who connect autonomy and freedom with a causal power to make events happen. Habermas's basic intuition is that this causal efficacy is not really the freedom we care about. Indeed, such a view seems unavoidably to make the causation of arbitrary bodily movement – "Lift your arm intentionally and spontaneously, at exactly the moment you feel like doing it" – into the defining case of free action. But these are, almost by definition, trivial cases, because they are supposed to be done for no reason at all. The freedom and agency we really care about, by contrast, are better typified by actions in which we believe that our choices matter to us, that we have reasons for them, and that they make sense to us. And that puts free agency squarely in the domain of aligning oneself with reasons.

Second, Habermas sees neuro-sceptics about free will as failing to appreciate its historical nature. From the standpoint of natural *science*, "acting for reasons" might not seem like a respectable element in a scientific explanation; but it is clearly part of the natural *history* of our species. Like the existence of language centres in the human brain or "Sicilian Defences" in the game of chess, acting for reasons is something that has emerged in an ongoing process of historical development. Indeed, on Habermas's view, the real challenge for empirical research regarding free will is to explain, in detail, the co-evolution of the space of reasons and the human brain's capacity to engage with the cultural artifacts we refer to as reasons. Like the historical linguistics of, say, the Frisian language, understanding the evolutionary emergence of "acting freely for reasons" would involve exploring causal, developmental processes of a peculiar sort of entity, namely, something that can be studied only in so far as we have already acquired it. After all, just as you cannot study the evolution of Frisian without having mastered the language, you cannot study the evolution of the space of reasons unless you know how to make moves in the game of giving and asking for reasons. Thus a really serious science of free will would also have to account for *itself*: "The natural genealogy of the mind is a self-referential project; the human mind tries to capture itself [*sich einholen*] in comprehending itself as a product of nature" (Habermas 2007b: 42).[14] Indeed, by denying that reasons are part of the natural world, physicalistic forms of naturalism have difficulty viewing their own accomplishments as part of the real world.

Third, and perhaps most important, Habermas views the reality of free will as bound up with the reality of our social practices of holding one another accountable, taking each other to be praiseworthy or blameworthy, and expecting that others view us capable of justifying (usually) what we do. Like the assumption that the person on the other side of the chess board knows the rules of chess, our belief in one another's free will is part of the game, in this case, "the language game of responsible agency" (Habermas 2007b).[15] This presupposition may be defeated, for example, in cases of mental disorders or compulsion, but the process of identifying nonautonomy can be undertaken only by those who are part of the practice of distinguishing cases of acting responsibly from cases of being unable to appreciate what one is doing. Since there is no way to determine whether someone can respond to reasons except from the standpoint of other reason-users (just as there is no way to determine whether someone can speak Frisian without appealing to the judgement of Frisian-speakers), autonomous agency is something that emerges only in the mutual attribution and contestation of that status.[16]

Habermas's discussion of autonomous agency (in the sense of free will) is also important in bringing out links with his understanding of science, humanity and the natural world. But, among his discussions of various senses of autonomy, it is an outlier in having little to do with the notion of gaining critical distance on one's reasons and challenging, as it were, the rules of the language game. Habermas's key idea in the discussion of free will is that the contrast with determinism lies in the ability to respond to reasons rather than physical forces. The link between autonomy and the power of critique is more central in his discussions of other senses of autonomy.

Personal autonomy, social integration and modernization

Alongside political self-determination, moral autonomy and accountable agency, we can also distinguish a form of autonomy usually referred to as "personal autonomy". This has to do with the capacity to lead one's own life, to determine what to do with the freedom one has. This is what we strive for with our children, that they acquire the capacity, in the process of maturation, to navigate the choice-situations that give shape to their lives: whom to love, where to live, how to contribute productively to society and so on.

Most contemporary theories of autonomy attempt to specify general criteria for what autonomy is, in terms of timeless and universal standards of reasons-responsiveness, internal cohesiveness, and so on. Habermas's approach differs from these in emphasizing the socio-historical development of personal autonomy as a real social phenomenon. Autonomy, in this sense, is to be specified in terms of competencies that one needs for finding one's way in an increasingly complex world. As a real-world social phenomenon, autonomy emerges as a result of contingent historical processes, both within the life history of the individual and within the development of societies, particularly in processes of modernization.

Habermas takes his cue from Émile Durkheim, who linked the obligation to be a "person" – that is, "an autonomous source of action" – to processes of differentiation in society, whereby individuals increasingly get different roles that they must fulfil, in coordination with others:

> Thus the advance of the individual personality and that of the division of labor depend on one and the same cause. Thus also it is impossible to will the one without willing the other. Nowadays no one questions the obligatory nature of the rule that ordains that we should exist as a person, and this increasingly so.
>
> (Durkheim 1984: 336)[17]

Habermas ties this point about the contingency and historical specificity of the imperative to be autonomous to the development of social structures. Because personal autonomy initially has its value and function in the context of navigating choices, the more complex a society becomes and the more choices individuals must face, the richer and more developed their autonomy has to be in order to be able to fulfil that function successfully. The upshot is that in more complex societies, not only must one (as Durkheim argued) be autonomous; there is also an expansion in what being autonomous involves.

This process of modernization continues in the form of what Ulrich Beck (1992) and others have termed "individualization".[18] As traditional restrictions have loosened regarding choices of occupation, marriage partners, religion, lifestyle and so on, contemporary individuals must make dramatically more decisions than their grandparents. The expansion in possibilities for choice brings with it an expansion in the responsibilities for choosing well. If one grows up in a highly conventional social world where one's choice of occupation, spouse, religious affiliation and so on is set at birth by one's place in society, there is not much autonomy to exercise and not much to be blamed for in terms of career planning. As these matters all become the responsibility of individuals throughout society, everyone needs to become autonomous, in this sense of developing the skills to make complex choices, guided by a clear understanding of what one really cares about.

Here again we see familiar themes in Habermas's approach: personal autonomy is a real phenomenon that has emerged historically as a feature of the intersubjective world. In this dynamic process of societal evolution, individuals need to develop certain autonomy competencies, which in turn facilitate a further growth in social complexity, leading to yet greater demands on individuals to orient their lives autonomously and to navigate this increasingly complex social world.

Two further dimensions of Habermas's analysis of personal autonomy are crucial to his overall view: the idea that autonomy involves the capacity for relating *critically* to the demands placed on one and the idea that, as in the case of moral autonomy, social structures (the "lifeworld") provide *enabling support* for the exercise of personal autonomy.

From conventional accountability to critical autonomy

For Habermas, autonomy is *critical* autonomy, which he understands as a radicalization of the ability to explain one's choices to others. What we have seen so far is that social transformations require one to make more decisions and that one is held accountable for making good decisions. This accountability is not just a matter of cleaning up your own mess when you make bad decisions, it is also a matter of being accountable to others for justifying your choices. Although Habermas acknowledges that people grant each other a degree of "private autonomy" (legally guaranteed leeway to do as they please), he emphasizes that cooperating with others and seeing ourselves as autonomous requires being able to justify one's choices. In one sense, one can do so by appealing to conventions (as when one decides to get married or go to church just because "that's what one does") or to one's preferences (as in, "I've always pictured myself as the breadwinner for a family"). For complicated reasons, Habermas believes that this conventional form of accountability is inadequate:

> The independent performances that are here demanded from the subjects consist of something different from rational choices steered by one's own preferences; what these subjects must perform is the kind of moral and existential self-reflection that is not possible without the one taking up the perspective of the other. (PMT: 199; see also TCA 2:91)

The basic intuition is that there is a kind of expansion of one's perspective required in coordinating one's action communicatively with others, since everyone then has to be attuned to how their verbal behaviour will be understood. This role-taking ability is already required for conventional interaction. As the horizon of who can challenge the view is extended beyond one's parochial community and beyond the present time, the requisite interactive competence becomes one that incorporates a reflexive and critical attitude. Individuals must understand their choices as able to stand up to challenges from others. Habermas argues that the demand for postconventional personality structures ("ego-identity") coincides with a demand for certain competencies for interaction.[19]

The growth of autonomy

This is a lot to expect from people, as Habermas is fully aware. And this leads to the second point: autonomy is not something we can pull off by ourselves. Our ability to be personally autonomous in Habermas's sense depends on how we are raised, on the culture that frames our choices, and the institutional guarantees that facilitate choosing and leading an autonomous life. With regard to all these developments, however, societal pressure and demands will simply overwhelm individuals who are not able to respond effectively. As we saw in the case of moral motivation, the development of postconventional personality structures and full autonomy-competence also requires what Habermas refers to as a supportive "lifeworld that meets us halfway" [*entgegenkommende Lebenswelt*] (e.g. MCCA: 207). In this sense, what is required is not just any lifeworld but rather a rational lifeworld, where "rational" is understood in terms of what it is that enables agents to navigate these learning processes and maintain what they have accomplished.[20] This a further reason why, as a social critic, he is very concerned about cultural trends, social transformations and (especially in his work in the 1970s) the psycho-social developments that affect childhood socialization.

In sum, we can say that there are three ways in which the autonomy of someone can be affected by societal transformations: processes of individual development (education, upbringing, material resources), demands from social institutions that burden capacities for self-steering and social processes that encourage (or discourage) critical reflection (often by providing contexts for critical reflection). As a result, "respecting the autonomy" of others becomes decidedly not a matter of getting out of the way. Here again we see Habermas's conception of the intersubjectivity of autonomy.

Self-realization, identity and authentic selfhood

In turning now to discussions of authenticity, it is time to say something about the widespread objection that Habermas's emphasis on the intersubjectivity and agreement goes wrong in rendering autonomy a matter of agreement and fitting in with others, whereas it ought to be about listening to the beat of a *different* drummer, and swimming *against* the tide. Where, it might well be asked, is the unique, individual self in all this? In responding, Habermas needs to find a way to accommodate our intuitions about autonomy and authenticity being emphatically about individuality and particularity. The basic (modern) aspiration at issue here is *a desire to be recognized for who one is*; not for some rational, idealized version of who one ought to be, and certainly not for being what others want one to be.

It will come as no surprise that Habermas insists, even here, on an intersubjectivist account. For, although he shares the intuition about the importance of particularity, he does not share the commonly held idea that authentic individuality is somehow about *uniqueness*, about being different from everyone else who exists or has existed. In this section, I start out from Habermas's rejection of uniqueness, and then reconstruct three steps in his alternative view: (i) that meaningful and authentic life choices must be criticizable, (ii) that denying the truth about one's life history undermines the basis for recognition for who one is, and (iii) that the most fundamental mode of identity we claim from each other is that we claim to have a point of view in dialogue.[21]

So what exactly is wrong with thinking of authentic, individual identity in terms of being uniquely distinct from others? Indeed, according to Durkheim (in the same work quoted above), what we expect of an autonomous individual is that there is "something within him that is his and his alone, that makes him an individual" (1984: 335). There are several problems with defining oneself in terms of uniqueness. Aside from making one's own identity hostage to the fickle choices of others (to imitate one, for example), being a bundle of properties that happened to depart from others is clearly not what we are after. After all, as Charles Taylor writes, "Defining myself means finding what is significant in my difference from others. I may be the only person with exactly 3,732 hairs on my head, or be exactly the same height as some tree on the Siberian plain, but so what?" (1992: 36). These uniquely distinguishing facts lack any personal significance for me, they are not aspects of who I am that I take ownership of in the relevant sense. Moreover, it is not really clear what it could even *mean* to build my sense of who I am around either of those facts. And in the absence of it being at least intelligible how that can be something that has significance for my self-understanding, it cannot play that role.

The intersubjective language of value-clarification

This brings me now to the first positive claim in Habermas's intersubjectivist account of authentic identity and autonomous selfhood: that understanding oneself in one's own individuality is not a matter of trying to ascertain the descriptive facts; rather, it is a matter of making sense of the significance of one's actions, feelings, thoughts, desires, experiences and so on. But if there is to be the requisite difference between making sense and merely *having the feeling that one is making sense*, there must be a possibility for going wrong here. That is, when working out who one is, one is actually always doing two things: one is making the case for a particular understanding of what one feels, does, thinks and so on, but one is also trying to figure out whether that account makes sense. But intelligibility is not something I can just decide. Striving for authentic individuality (which is no guarantee for *attaining* it) requires striving to make sense of oneself in terms that are intelligible, and this necessarily links one to public language.[22]

So, one's sense of "who-one-is-and-wants-to-be" is criticizable. It can fail to make sense. When such unintelligibility threatens, disputes can arise. These disputes are resolved, according to Habermas, neither through the agent's resolute self-assertion nor by the community's majority vote but rather in an open and dialogical process. As is the case for "discourse" generally, participants in ethical-existential discourse aim to figure something out jointly and in a manner that is maximally open to relevant considerations. Habermas describes this as follows:

> In this context the critique of self-deceptions and of symptoms of a compulsive or alienated mode of life takes its yardstick from the idea of a conscious and coherent mode of life, where the authenticity of a life-project can be understood as a higher-level validity claim analogous with the claim to truthfulness of expressive speech acts. (IO: 27)

As he clarifies in a footnote, higher-level or "more complex" validity claims such as theories are not true or false in the way that individual sentences are true or false.[23] The notion of incorrectness in the domain of authentic identity is thus unusual in two ways. First, authenticity must be assessed on the basis of how acts fit into an overall life, which explains why isolated out-of-character acts do not show someone to be inauthentic. Second, like the question of whether someone is being truthful about her expression of feelings, claims to authenticity can really only be made good on by actually living one's life in a way that supports it. You are not the only one who can raise critical questions about whether your actions do, in fact, support your claim to really care about something; but ultimately, you *are* the only one who can ensure that the evidence obtains, by living your life authentically.

The inauthenticity of selective self-examination

What is particularly important in assessing authenticity is an agent's willingness to face the facts about himself. No matter how clear, appealing and coherent one's sense of who one is, if it can be maintained only by suppressing key facts about what one has done or deceiving oneself about one's deep motives, then one lacks authenticity.[24] Partly, this is for the same reason that "massaging the data" undermines findings in science. But furthermore, someone who presents a selective picture of his past or refuses to take responsibility for past actions – something Habermas famously accused Martin Heidegger of doing regarding his Nazi past[25] – is presenting a self for recognition to which he cannot actually lay legitimate claim. It is not simply the self-*portrait* itself that is flawed; it is the mode of self-*portrayal*. A faulty portrait can be filled in or corrected by others; but no one else can take over the task of presenting oneself, and no amount of information presented by others can rectify the failure of authenticity found in a distorting self-presentation.

In analysing this deeply *performative* dimension of authenticity, Habermas takes his cue from Kierkegaard's image of voluntarily and courageously facing judgement by an omniscient God. He takes this "vertical axis of the prayer" and uses the example of Rousseau's *Confessions* to "tip this into the horizontal axis of interhuman communication" (PMT: 167). Kierkegaard's model of radically honest self-presentation thus gets transformed into Rousseau's model of self-portrayal to the unrestricted audience of the book's readers. (The contemporary parallel would be a highly personal blog with unrestricted access.) Once this shift is made, "the individual can no longer redeem the emphatic claim to individuality solely through the reconstructive appropriation of his life history; now the positions taken by others decide whether this reconstruction succeeds" (PMT: 167). This dramatically intersubjectivist account of authenticity is remarkably radical. Most of us are accustomed to picking rather carefully those to whom we tell all, and few of us actually want to hear everyone's tell-all tales. Habermas is not advocating wholesale autobiographical exhibitionism but rather articulating the ideal to which a fully authentic individual can be held. It is a stance or attitude rather than behaviour that is mutually expected here. And it is not just about getting the facts right. As Habermas says about the case of Rousseau:

> These confessions belong to a different genre than the descriptions that a historian could give of Rousseau's life. They are not measured against the truth of historical statements, but against the authenticity of the presentation of self. They are exposed, as Rousseau knows, to accusations of *mauvaise foi* [Sartre's term for "bad faith"] and of self-deception, not simply to that of being untrue. (PMT: 168)

In other words, there is a *performative* dimension to Rousseau's confessions and, by extension, all claims to authenticity of the form, "This is who I am."

The performativity of claims to self-authenticity

This performative dimension – a dimension that is tied to the act of asserting a claim to being who one is – brings me to the third, and perhaps most elusive, piece of Habermas's intersubjectivist account of personal identity and authentic selfhood, the idea of vouching for oneself and being recognized by others for so doing. On Habermas's interpretation, what we do in making these claims is to vouch for ourselves, and this is something fundamentally different from raising "validity claims" to truth or even rightness (PMT: 190). Vouching is a matter of issuing to others a guarantee that one can make good on (or fail to make good on) by living up to one's claim. And this is something that one must do oneself. Alongside this existential significance of vouching for oneself, there is nevertheless something intersubjective about it, for one can only undertake it *vis-à-vis* others. Vouching for oneself is always an appeal for recognition from others (which is not to deny that their failure to recognise one may turn out to reflect *their* narrow-mindedness). We can aspire, in private, to live up to certain goals, but we can vouch for ourselves only to others.

What is particularly striking about this notion of *securing confirmation from others with regard to one's vouching for oneself* (for which Habermas invents the term "*Selbstvergewisserung*"), is that Habermas rejects the idea that this involves others agreeing with one on one's choices or self-understanding. Rather, what matters is that one is recognized as willing and able to try: "the meaning of this guarantee has been *completely* grasped by the addressee as soon as he knows that the other is vouching for his ability to be himself" (PMT: 169). The assertion I make performatively to all is that I am the one who is ultimately accountable for leading my life. Paradoxically, however, that very reality is not an assertion of an independent metaphysical claim; rather, its reality is partly constituted in the space of intersubjective recognition.

In sum, Habermas's theory of the intersubjectivity of authentic individuality has three elements. The first element relates to the intersubjectivity of value-clarification and the publicly evaluative language employed there. The second element articulates the inauthenticity of suppressing facts about one's past or surrounding oneself with flatterers.[26] And the third element has to do with the performative character of claims to authenticity, as a matter of vouching for oneself to others. Ultimately, these points are related: if we want to understand what it means to get beyond lazy self-characterization and conventional labels and to really answer the question of who one *really* is, we need some way of capturing the radical depth with which this question can be asked. And engaging as co-participants in ethical-existential discourse requires recognizing one another as willing to take responsibility for how one lives one's life.

Conclusion

The foregoing overview is intended to provide a sense of the richness of Habermas's wide-ranging discussions of various usages of "autonomy" as well as a sense of the consistent themes that cut across these individual discussions. There are, of course, numerous points on which Habermas could be criticized or, at the very least, where the argument could be more fully developed. One task yet to be done, however, is to explain exactly what the interconnections are between these different usages of autonomy. What, for example, is the relationship between political and personal autonomy, particularly with regard to private autonomy? To what extent does moral autonomy presuppose free will, and vice versa? And what is the precise relationship between authenticity and ethical-existential autonomy? These are important interconnections to work out, but they will have to be left for another day. What is clear, in any case, is that Habermas sees the deep interconnections as coming properly into view only once one moves away from the traditional oppositions between the individual and the social – typically based on a philosophy of consciousness – and makes the turn to an intersubjectivist approach.[27]

Notes

1. I recall Habermas, just before the start of a weekly seminar meeting in 1988, remarking on his just-completed first official visit to the DDR: "There really is such a thing as a pathological society" ["*Es gibt doch so etwas wie eine pathologische Gesellschaft*"].
2. Indeed, although the title of Peter Dews's collection of Habermas interviews, *Autonomy and Solidarity: Interviews* (1996), captures two centrally motivating themes in Habermas's work, the word "autonomy" is to be found on only two pages. Important discussions of Habermas's views on autonomy can be found in Kevin Olson and William Rehg's Chapters 7 and 6 in this volume, and in Allen (2008); Baynes (1992); Warren (1995); Forst (2002); Cooke (1992).
3. See especially PDM, PMT, TJ and Chapter 3 in this volume.
4. See Sellars (1956) and Brandom (1994). See also Barbara Fultner's discussion in Chapter 3 in this volume.
5. TJ; Habermas (2007b: 13–50); see also Searle (1995).
6. Jürgen Habermas, "From Kant's 'Ideas' of Pure Reason to the 'Idealizing' Presuppositions of Communicative Action: Reflections on the Detranscendentalized 'Use of Reason'" (TJ: 83–130). See, again, Fultner's analysis of the pragmatic presuppositions of communicative action in Chapter 3.
7. For a full discussion of Habermas's account of political autonomy, see Chapter 7 in this volume.
8. See also Cronin's discussion of how the increasing complexities associated with globalization call for a cosmopolitan expansion of democratic institutions, in Chapter 10 of this volume.
9. For a discussion, see William Rehg's contribution to this volume, also for a discussion of Habermas's view that moral insight is realized through participation in moral discourse.
10. On the lifeworld, see Joseph Heath's Chapter 4 in this volume.
11. See Christopher Zurn's Chapter 8 in this volume, Habermas (1988b) and BFN. See also Heath (2008); Heath & Anderson (2010).
12. Habermas's arguments – and references to his opponents – can be found in "Freedom and Determinism" (BNR: 151–80) and "The Language Game of Responsible Agency and the Problem of Free Will" (2007b).
13. For a full discussion, see Anderson (2007).
14. This argument, which has its roots in critical theory's longstanding commitment to the reflexivity of science, is developed in the rather speculative final section of that essay.
15. Habermas is drawing here especially on the seminal work by P. F. Strawson, "Freedom and Resentment" (1974).
16. This is a central theme in recent work in the tradition of Wilfrid Sellars (esp. *Empiricism and the Philosophy of Mind*). For further elaborations, see Brandom (1994); Anderson (2008); Lance & Heath White (2007); Habermas, "From Kant to Hegel: On Robert Brandom's Pragmatic Philosophy of Language" (TJ: 131–73).
17. See also Habermas's discussion of Durkheim in TCA 2: 43–111.
18. Habermas discusses this in "Individuation through Socialization: On George Herbert Mead's Theory of Subjectivity" (PMT: 193–200).
19. Thomas McCarthy nicely summarizes the contrast between conventional and critical reason-giving in terms of Habermas's notion of discourse: "Accountable agents are able to provide publicly defensible … accounts of their actions and

beliefs, that is, to satisfy interaction partners that their beliefs and actions are backed by good reasons. Autonomous agents are able to do so also at a critical-reflective level of discourse" (1994: 44).

20. For an excellent discussion of these issues, see Offe (1992).
21. The most important text by Habermas on this topic is the rich and complex essay, "Individuation through Socialization," (PMT: 193–200), which also contains an extensive discussion of George Herbert Mead's theory of subjectivity. Other important texts are "A Genealogical Analysis of the Cognitive Content of Morality" (IO: 3–46); "Employments of Practical Reason" (JA: 1–17); and "Historical Consciousness and Post-Traditional Identity: The Federal Republic's Orientation to the West" (1989a: 249–68). For excellent discussions of these issues, see Cooke (1991, 1994a).
22. This idea that meaning is not something "at our disposal" is a central theme in Habermas, one that is strongly influenced by Ludwig Wittgenstein's argument for the impossibility of a "private language".
23. IO: 273, fn. 37. See also the final section of Rehg's contribution in this volume.
24. There are very complex issues of the continuity of personal identity over time that could be raised here, as has been done especially by Derek Parfit (1986). Habermas does not discuss them, however.
25. See Max Pensky's discussion in Chapter 1.
26. For a discussion of when it might not be actually appropriate to require others to account for themselves, see my discussion of the "ethics of accounting practices" in Anderson (1996: ch. 7.2).
27. I would like to thank Thomas Fossen, Barbara Fultner, Antti Kauppinen, Lillian O'Brien, Tom Bates, Markus Schlosser and Christopher Parr for feedback on earlier drafts. Thanks also to Bas Kops for research assistance.

PART II

Moral and political theory

SIX

Discourse ethics

William Rehg

Habermas's moral theory goes by the name of "discourse ethics". The name itself is potentially misleading, given developments in Habermas's position since he first unveiled his discourse ethics in 1983. Many philosophers understand ethics as broadly equivalent to moral theory, the normative study of moral practices, and discourse ethics is one such theory. But Habermas also uses the term "ethical" in a narrow sense, to refer to issues having to do with personal fulfilment and political self-determination, which he distinguishes from questions of *moral* right and wrong. This distinction has antecedents in German thought. Rejecting the Aristotelian amalgamation of moral virtue and happiness, Kant insisted that morality had to do with obligations that were unconditionally binding on all rational agents, whereas the constituents of happiness varied from person to person, time to time, and culture to culture. Today this basic contrast between morality and ethics tends to appear as the difference between the "right" and the "good", or justice and the good life. In the context of such a distinction, discourse ethics is more accurately designated as a "discourse theory of morality" or a theory of justice.

A number of key concepts undergird Habermas's discourse theory of morality. To avoid misunderstanding at the outset, it helps to begin with two concepts that help us situate his approach to morality. First, as the opening paragraph implies, discourse ethics presupposes a particular conception of the *moral domain*, as distinct from other areas of practical reason. Second, Habermas first elaborated discourse ethics as a form of *metaethical cognitivism*, in response to moral scepticism. At the heart of that response there lies a conception of moral justification, spelled out in two central principles, the *discourse principle* (D) and *universalization principle* (U). These principles have a neo-Kantian character, which marks discourse ethics as *deontological*, *impartialist*, *proceduralist* and *dialogical*. After reviewing these concepts, we delve more deeply into the (U)-principle by examining the basic assumptions on which it rests. Although (U) presents a highly idealized model of moral consensus, Habermas holds that it nonetheless guides real moral discourse. To understand this claim, we must examine the concepts of *conscience*, *application* and *motivation*, which in turn lead into Habermas's moral psychology and theory of law.

Although Habermas sharply distinguishes morality from questions of the good life, he is not unaware of the importance of such traditional ideas as flourishing, well-being and the common good. The chapter thus closes with a discussion of Habermas's treatment of *ethical authenticity*, followed by a brief remark on the link between *autonomy* and *solidarity*.

The moral domain

In ancient Greek and medieval thought, moral virtue generally played a leading role in accounts of human flourishing and happiness. By contrast, Habermas distinguishes the domain of moral questions from issues connected with the pursuit of happiness and the good life. This is not to deny the importance of morality for the good life, but to recognize the challenges posed by cultural pluralism, which calls for a differentiated analysis of the distinct "employments of practical reason". To understand Habermas's conception of the moral domain, and thus the scope of discourse ethics, we must see how he distinguishes morality from two other areas of practical reason, which he labels "pragmatic" and "ethical-existential" (see JA: 1–17).

The *pragmatic* use of practical reason is familiar from rational choice theory. In pragmatic reasoning, we calculate the means to some given end or we assess and specify particular goals and preferences in light of our values. In distinguishing pragmatic reasoning from moral discourse, Habermas rejects attempts to reduce unconditionally binding moral obligations to rational choice considerations. He thus aligns his understanding of pragmatic reasoning with what Kant called rules of skill and counsels of prudence, both of which involve "hypothetical imperatives", statements of what one ought to do, *if* one seeks to satisfy some preference or realize some value (JA: 3).[1]

Habermas draws the distinction between *ethical-existential* reasoning and the moral domain along a number of lines. Although his differentiation of morality and ethics remains controversial,[2] four contrasts suffice for an initial sense of his approach to morality. First, the moral domain has to do with general norms or rules of action (e.g. "help the needy", "do not steal") and particular judgements that apply such norms to concrete situations ("I ought to help this panhandler"). Moral norms and judgements are either intersubjectively valid or not, whereas ethics is concerned with goods and values that must be weighed against each other, and thus can come in degrees of importance, inasmuch as one can speak of greater and lesser goods. Second, the two domains differ in the questions they address. Moral norms and judgements answer questions about how we ought to treat each other as persons: what behaviours are obligatory, prohibited or permissible in view of their effects on persons. Ethical value judgements answer questions about the good life or the good society; at the personal level, ethical questions have an existentialist quality, as questions about who I am and who I want to be. Third, the content of deliberation and argument differs in the two cases. Moral deliberation requires an impartial point of view that takes into account the interests and values of all those affected by a prospective rule of action or individual choice, whereas ethical deliberation draws on the individual's (or group's) particular traditions, history and values with the aim of making personally (or collectively) authentic decisions. Fourth, the expected scope of reasonable consensus differs for the two kinds of question. In Habermas's view, answers to moral questions should command universal agreement, at least in principle, among all reasonable persons. At first glance, it seems we should not expect the answers to ethical questions to win assent beyond the circle of people who share the relevant tradition and values.

These contrasts notwithstanding, some important relations link morality and ethics. In line with many neo-Kantians, Habermas insists on the *priority* of moral norms over the individual's or group's pursuit of the good: ethical and pragmatic reasoning should move within the boundaries set by our moral duties towards others. Otherwise moral norms cannot bind all persons unconditionally (IO: 27–30). At the same time, ethics enjoys a kind of existential priority: the personal choice to live one's life morally is not itself a moral issue, but an ethical one. To that extent, the question of why you or I, or we human beings in general, should *value* a life regulated by moral norms and respect for autonomous persons, is a matter for ethical discourse.[3]

Metaethical cognitivism

One can see elements of Habermas's discourse ethics in his early work on the public sphere and truth (STPS; "Wahrheitstheorien" [1984a: 127–83]). But he first explicitly articulated a "discourse ethics" in response to metaethical issues that had emerged in the first half of the twentieth century. For present purposes, metaethics has to do with second-order questions in moral theory. Whereas *normative ethics* addresses first-order questions about which moral principles and norms are right, *metaethics* studies the nature of the moral domain, that is, questions concerning the fundamental semantics of moral claims, whether they prescribe, state moral facts and so on; their ontology, whether or not they refer to an objective moral reality; their justifiability; and their practical character, how they are linked with motivation. In his 1983 article on discourse ethics (MCCA: 43ff.), Habermas focused above all on the metaethical topic of the objectivity of moral statements.

By the mid-twentieth century, two basic positions on moral objectivity dominated the metaethical landscape. At one end of the spectrum, subjectivists, for example, emotivists in Anglo-American thought and Nietzscheans in continental philosophy, held that moral claims merely express the speaker's wishes, feelings or will to power. Subjectivists thus took a sceptical view of moral claims: although statements like "lying is wrong" appear to express a kind of objective knowledge, ascribing properties to behaviour in a manner similar to statements about the external world, their depth semantics is non-cognitive. In fact, the speaker is simply saying something like "I dislike lying", or "I want to discourage you from lying". At the objectivist or realist end, intuitionists took the surface grammar of moral statements more or less at face value. In attributing moral properties (goodness, rightness) to actions, persons and states of affairs, the speaker makes a claim about an objective moral reality that in some sense is accessible to direct perception, analogous to the perception of the properties of physical objects. Moral statements are thus true or false depending on their conformity with moral facts that obtain whether we know them or not.

Each side emphasized different surface features of moral practice and discourse, albeit at the cost of other features. For example, intuitionists pointed to the fact that we talk as though moral statements have an objective character, whereas subjectivists emphasized the practical (motivating) force of moral feelings and the interminable character of many moral debates. In this context, J. L. Mackie's "error theory" represented an advance for the sceptical camp. Mackie accepted the fact-stating (cognitivist) grammar of moral claims, but he rejected their putative object on ontological grounds: there are no objective moral properties to which such statements can successfully refer, so all moral statements are false (Mackie 1977). This sceptical approach seemed to do justice to both sets of surface features: yes, we talk as though there are moral facts, and yes, it is no surprise that we cannot resolve many moral disputes, for our talk answers to no objective reality.

We can read Habermas's discourse ethics as a metaethical attempt to save objective morality from scepticism (MCCA: 43ff.). The key to Habermas's solution lay in his pragmatic approach to language, on the one hand, and his longstanding critique of naive-realist models of objectivity and truth, on the other hand (see KHI). As a pragmatist, Habermas insists that moral theorists must adopt the "performative perspective" of engaged participants and take the objective character of moral discourse seriously rather than explain it away as subjectivists do. To that extent, he sides with intuitionists in adopting a cognitivist analysis of moral discourse: moral statements involve claims to objective knowledge in some sense. However, both error theorists and intuitionists make a common mistake in modelling moral objectivity on the objectivity of knowledge-independent facts (to which true statements, it seems, must somehow correspond).[4] But how else are we to think of moral objectivity? Habermas's pragmatic analysis of language answers this question without positing the "queer" ontology that Mackie attributed to moral realists.

Specifically, Habermas draws on his theory of communicative action with its system of validity claims (see Chapter 3 in this volume). In a manner analogous to empirical claims about the external world (e.g. "exposure to second-hand smoke contributes to lung disease"), moral judgements and norms regarding right action (e.g. "those able to do so should help the needy") raise claims to intersubjective validity. As stances on matters that admit of objectively correct and incorrect answers, validity claims are inherently open to potential criticism and public justification. Just as one can contest and defend the *empirical truth* of the claim about second-hand smoke by referring to good reasons (i.e. experimental and epidemiological evidence), so it should be possible to contest and defend the *moral rightness* of the norm of helping the needy by the appropriate sort of reasons. For both types of claims, then, one can speak of a kind of objectivity that resides in *rational intersubjective justifiability*, that is, the capacity of validity claims to be publicly defended with good reasons against criticism. However, unlike truth, which depends on an external world that ultimately transcends the justifications of empirical claims, rightness depends entirely on the quality of the justifying reasons.[5] We next consider what kind of reasons those are.

The (D) and (U) principles

Habermas's discourse ethics links the objective validity of moral statements – and thus the cognitive character of morality, or morality as a form of knowledge – with their public justifiability. Specifically, a moral norm or judgement is valid only if one could, if necessary, offer convincing reasons in its defence. But reasons convincing to whom? And what kind of reasons? If we focus for now on the justification of norms, we find that Habermas gives us two principles. The more general "discourse principle" (D) states the conditions for impartially justifying norms of action in general, that is, not only moral norms but also legal-political norms and other sorts of institutional and culture-specific rules and obligations:

> (D) Just those norms are valid to which all those possibly affected could agree as participants in rational discourses.
>
> (BFN: 107; trans. mod.)[6]

Notice that (D) answers the question of audience, those to whom good reasons must be convincing: "all those possibly affected" by the norm in question. But (D) does not say what count as good reasons, beyond the condition that they be convincing in rational discourses. The reason is that (D) covers all types of social norms, and the content of good reasons varies by norm-type.

For the justification of moral norms, which potentially bind all persons and not merely members of a particular polity or group, Habermas proposes a universalization principle (U):

> (U) A [moral] norm is valid just in case the foreseeable consequences and side-effects of its general observance for the interests and value-orientations of *each individual* could be *jointly* accepted by *all* those affected without coercion.
>
> (IO: 42; trans. mod.; cf. MCCA: 65)

Here we have the answer to both of our questions. Moral norms must be justified to those whose "interests and value-orientations" are foreseeably affected by the norm in question. Thus (U) further specifies the audience of affected persons. (U) also answers the second question: the appropriate kind of reasons are arguments for the general acceptability of the foreseeable consequences and side-effects of a norm for each affected person's interests and values.

(U) involves a rich set of assumptions, not all of them obvious in the formulation above. Before examining those assumptions, we should notice how (U) rests on four concepts that place discourse ethics firmly in the neo-Kantian tradition. First, Habermas takes a *deontological* approach to the moral domain, focusing on unconditionally binding obligations and prohibitions. These take the form of general norms that spell out the mutual concern and respect we owe to each other as persons, thereby setting limits on the pursuit of particular aims. Hence (U) assumes that a moral norm, once adopted and generally observed, has foreseeable impacts on the pursuit of goods by individuals and groups – their "interests and value-orientations" – in the typical situations governed by the norm. For example, a norm such as "one may freely use one's cell phone for purposes of communication" directly regulates action that aims at communication, clearly a widely shared value or good, which individuals have an interest in pursuing. The cell-phone norm in effect codifies the interest in a particular means to realizing that good, and should the norm be adopted, it would have "consequences" for practices of communication in so far as it would govern those practices. However, the general adoption of such a norm also has "side-effects" on other interests and values that are not directly at issue in (or intended by) the norm, such as enjoying a quiet meal in a restaurant, or driving safely in heavy traffic. According to (U), then, when we accept a moral norm, we accept the foreseeable ways in which that norm governs and affects the pursuit of goods, whether by individuals or groups.

Second, like Kant, Habermas identifies the "moral point of view" with an *impartial perspective*. Unlike Kant, however, Habermas does not associate impartiality with a realm of freedom that lies beyond, or abstracts from, empirical differences among persons: their particular interests, inclinations and circumstances. Rather, (U) makes explicit provision for a process of perspective-taking in which participants take account of the consequences, interests, needs and particular values at stake for each affected party (person or subgroup). Justifying a norm thus requires a *joint* acceptance of the foreseeable impacts of the norm on *each* party's pursuit of goods. Impartiality is achieved precisely by developing arguments that forge common ground among differences, transforming interests and values into reasons that make a claim on all persons and thus deserve consideration.

Third, like Kant, Habermas takes a *procedural* approach to morality. This means that discourse ethics, when read as a normative ethics, does not provide a particular set of substantive norms or inviolable values (as in natural law theory), but rather a procedure or method for testing substantive norms for their moral acceptability. The (U)-principle, in other words, represents Habermas's version of Kant's moral principle, the Categorical Imperative. However, a fourth concept differentiates Habermas's approach: whereas Kant's principle is apparently designed to guide the solitary ("monological") moral deliberation of the mature individual, (U) is *dialogical*, calling for a real discourse (i.e. a process of argumentation) in which the involved persons set aside the pressures of everyday life and take a "hypothetical attitude" towards the moral claim at issue, testing it for its justifiability on the basis of good reasons that everyone involved could accept. In so far as such a discourse is sufficiently reasonable, that is, free of coercion and inclusive, it warrants a provisional confidence in its outcome.[7]

Three assumptions behind the (U)-principle

Habermas proposed (U) as a moral principle for pluralist societies that could no longer count on a single religion or worldview as a basis for resolving moral conflicts. He thus considered it important to "derive" (U), that is, to show that it logically follows from some non-contentious premises (IO: ch. 1; DE: 78ff.). Although the derivation of (U) remains a matter of scholarly controversy,[8] the premises at issue suggest that three basic assumptions underlie (U). By examining these assumptions, we obtain a more precise understanding of what "rational intersubjective justifiability" means.

Topical Assumption: the concept of a moral norm

To begin with, Habermas assumes a particular kind of social context in which discourse ethics becomes relevant, namely one in which actors want to resolve conflicts by reaching agreement on a *moral norm*. He also assumes they understand just what kind of norm they accept when they reach such agreement.[9] This assumption about the topic of moral discourse has implications for what count as relevant reasons in moral justification, as well as for who is "possibly affected". Recognizing the deontological character of discourse ethics, we might spell out this assumption thus:

> Topical Assumption: a moral discourse concerns a general rule that (a) states unconditionally binding requirements for treating persons with due concern and respect, and (b) accordingly governs and affects the pursuit of goods (by persons and groups).

Clause (a) makes explicit the deontological aspect of moral norms that (U) presupposes, and clause (b) restates the earlier point that norms have consequences and side-effects for interests and value-orientations, and thus affects anyone pursuing those interests and values. Taken together, these clauses capture important semantic and social-functional features of moral norms.

To say that moral norms are "general" is to make a claim about their semantics, namely that they are formulated in general categories, and thus do not use proper nouns referring to particular individuals, do not explicitly allow for personal exemptions, and so on. Thus we would object to the norm "No one ought to lie, except of course me, Pinocchio, when it is in my interest". To say that moral norms are "unconditionally binding" means that they obligate us even when it is inconvenient. In other words, they constrain the pursuit of goods – particular interests and shared value-orientations – on the part of individuals and groups, so that such pursuit is consistent with "concern and respect" for persons. The latter two terms are a shorthand for the moral purposes behind positive and negative obligations. An obligation to help the needy, for example, constrains the pursuit of personal goods by requiring some degree of active concern for others' welfare, whereas the prohibition against theft constrains the pursuit of property, so that one demonstrates respect for owners.

Generality and unconditionality allow moral norms to serve a social function, namely to regulate potential (and actual) conflicts of interest by holding all parties, whether individuals or groups, to common rules that bind them regardless of their particular interests, goals and values. Because this governance regulates interpersonal relations, moral norms do important work in sustaining the web of mutual recognition: they set down baseline requirements about how to treat persons with the kind of respect and concern that recognizes their status as persons.

The primary question for discourse, then, is just what those requirements ought to be, and how much they depend on further role specifications. For example, does the moral treatment of children differ in some ways from that of adults? Or does gender sometimes make a moral difference? To answer such questions, participants must agree that the foreseeable ways a prospective norm would govern (and affect) the pursuit of goods are consistent with concern and respect for persons. The content of the Topical Assumption thus points to the kind of reasons or arguments that count as relevant in moral discourse, namely considerations that elucidate the value of the goods at issue, conditions of respect, ideals of personal dignity, likely social effects of a norm and so on. Such arguments often attempt to interpret shared ends or values and social practices in the light of moral emotions, experiences of disrespect and the like. To go back to our earlier example: one might argue for a limitation on cell phones in restaurants by linking mutual respect among diners with the value of intimate conversation that ought not to be interrupted by outside parties.

Consensus Assumption: specifying (D) for morality

Habermas assumes that actors facing moral conflicts want to arrive at *consensus* on an acceptable moral norm via rational discourse, that is, through a dialogical process of argumentation. The participants thereby commit themselves to a dialogical, impartial justification on the basis of reasons acceptable to all those affected, the basic idea contained in the discourse principle. In assuming (D), Habermas puts two ideas on the table: the idea that good reasons require consensus, and the idea that such consensus must issue from a reasonable discourse. Call this the "Consensus Assumption".

Given that the context is moral discourse, we can state the Consensus Assumption as a more precise version of (D) by appropriately specifying the phrase "all those affected". The Topical Assumption implies that one is affected by a moral norm N_M if (a) one's social role falls under the requirements set by N_M, or (b) one's pursuit of goods would be governed or affected by N_M. For example, if Mary is materially needy, then her "social role" as a needy person would fall under a moral requirement that obligates the well-off to help the needy, as a way of showing due concern; thus she would count as an affected party. The well-off would also fall under such a requirement in virtue of their role, and their pursuit of goods would be partly governed by such a norm. Such a norm might also have side-effects, such as instilling feelings of humiliation or inferiority in the needy (one of Kant's worries).

If we specify the affected parties in (D) for moral discourse, then the Consensus Assumption takes the following form:

> A moral norm N_M is justifiable on the basis of good reasons only if all those (a) whose social role falls under the requirements set by N_M, or (b) whose pursuit of goods would be governed or affected by N_M could accept N_M in a reasonable discourse about it.

This assumption is probably the most ambitious move in Habermas's argument for (U). Although some level of consensus on basic moral norms is a prerequisite of social stability, (D) seems to presuppose a modern context in which the individual's responsibility for the *justification* of moral expectations has been "radicalized".[10] In other words, discourse ethics presupposes a distinctly modern idea of moral autonomy, the idea that valid normative expectations must be those that each reasonable person could accept in good conscience, through his or her own insight, and not simply on the basis of authority or social convention. So understood, autonomy has the status of an "idea of reason", an idealization that is largely counterfactual: we cannot demonstrate it empirically and perhaps rarely achieve it. Yet we must presuppose some degree of autonomy when we hold each other accountable for our choices and actions.

Process Assumption: pragmatic presuppositions of argumentation

Even when specified as above, (D) leaves open the conditions that make a discourse reasonable. Habermas's third assumption spells out these conditions by referring us to some basic "pragmatic presuppositions" of argumentation in general: conditions that arguers must presuppose if they are to consider their discourse reasonable. Here he draws on a multi-dimensional theory of argumentation that has been widely accepted by argumentation theorists (see especially Wenzel 1990). According to that theory, the conditions of a good or cogent argument include not only the logical properties of the argument *product* – the premise–conclusion package; they also include the dialectical *procedures* of criticism and reply, in which arguers test the adequacy of the argument, and the rhetorical *process* of arguing – the social conditions under which arguers conduct their dialectical criticism and strive to persuade each other.

The third assumption articulates the crucial standards that govern argumentation as a social process of persuasion. The most important such standards call for the inclusion and equal voice of relevant contributors, absence of (self-)deception and freedom from coercion (IO: 44; MCCA: 87–9). Such idealizations have some intuitive plausibility as conditions on a fully adequate dialogical justification, in which participants examine all the available information and arguments to the point where further scrutiny of that input would not alter the outcome.[11]

Habermas considers these pragmatic presuppositions to hold for argumentation in general: they apply not only to reasonable moral discourse, but also to scientific discourses, legal discourse, and so on. In a moral discourse, the relevant contributions or reasons would be those that bear on the topic at issue, as stated in the Topical Assumption, namely reasons bearing on the acceptability of (a) rules governing concern and respect for persons, and (b) their likely effects on the pursuit of goods. We may thus formulate this assumption about process as follows:

> Process Assumption: a discourse on a moral norm is reasonable only if it satisfies these conditions: (R_1) everyone capable of making a relevant contribution (i.e. considerations bearing on the moral question at issue) has been included and given equal voice, (R_2) the participants have not been deceived or self-deceived about the reasons, but understand the relevant reasons and their import, and (R_3) the participants are free to consider all the relevant reasons and potential defeaters and judge them on their merits.

Like the idea of autonomy, the standards in this Process Assumption function as counterfactual idealizations that can never be fully realized or guaranteed by institutional procedures. Nonetheless, arguers must presuppose they have "sufficiently approximated" these idealizations if they are to regard their dialectical testing of arguments as adequate. Habermas now seems to regard the judgement of "approximation" as a kind of negation: in scrutinizing our process, we do not see any obvious violations of the most important standards (TJ: 108; cf. JA: 41–57).

If we think of (U) as simply pulling together these three basic assumptions, then we can explicate its complex structure as follows:

> A moral norm N_M is justifiable on the basis of good reasons only if:
> (i) everyone whose social role falls under N_M, or whose pursuit of goods would be governed or affected by N_M,
> (ii) could accept N_M as an unconditionally binding requirement for treating persons with concern and respect, and as foreseeably governing and affecting each person's/group's pursuit of goods,
> (iii) after taking part in a discourse that satisfies these conditions: (R_1) everyone capable of making a relevant contribution (i.e. reasons that bear on [ii] above) has been included and given equal voice, (R_2) the participants have not been deceived or self-deceived about the relevant reasons, but understand their import, and (R_3) the participants are free to consider all the relevant reasons and potential defeaters and judge them on their merits.[12]

The three clauses above lay out the core dimensions of moral discourse: (i) the *participants* whose agreement or collective acceptance is necessary for the public justification of a norm, (ii) the *content* of collective acceptance, precisely what they must accept about the norm, and (iii) the *conditions* under which their acceptance counts as reasonable. Dialogical perspective-taking emerges from the combination of clauses: (i) everyone affected must be able (ii) to accept the likely effects for each person/group (iii) after listening to everyone's input in a reasonable discourse. This mutual testing of arguments forces participants "to adopt a self-critical stance towards their own interests and evaluations of situations and to take into account others' interests from the perspectives of the others' self-understandings and worldviews" (BNR: 86–7; trans. mod.).

In line with the idealized character of the Consensus and Process Assumptions, (U) is stated above as a counterfactual: (U) does not require that everyone affected must *actually* accept a valid moral norm after contributing to a reasonable discourse. Rather, it requires only that those affected *could* accept a valid norm, *were* they capable of participating in a sufficiently reasonable discourse. So one might interpret discourse ethics as advancing a merely hypothetical thesis: whenever we accept a moral norm as part of our everyday social practices, we presuppose that it could be justified under idealized conditions of discourse, although we do not expect the norm ever will be so justified. Habermas, however, has something more ambitious in view: he regards (U) as operative in real moral discourses. This suggests that discourse ethics should somehow guide actual discourses. To see how, we must move from metaethics to normative ethics.

Real discourses of justification

Habermas's discourse ethics has a number of resources for bringing idealizations like (U) down to earth. A crucial distinction here is that between "justification discourses", which focus on justifying general norms for all those affected, and "application discourses", in which the group of persons immediately involved in some situations strive to identify which norm is appropriate for their particular circumstances. Since the latter process also involves justification (namely of a situated judgement), we can avoid confusion by distinguishing when necessary between "general justification" and "justification in context". I begin with the former.

Real moral discourses over the validity of general norms have become a familiar part of contemporary culture and politics. One need only recall the ongoing debates about capital punishment, abortion and physician-assisted suicide (PAS), to name three issues in the United

States. Its idealized character notwithstanding, discourse ethics can inform our participation in such debates at two levels: at the personal level, and at the public political level.

At the personal level of moral conscience,[13] these debates confront individuals with serious moral questions that affect decisions of different kinds: how to vote on a law or political candidate, how to counsel a friend, or simply how to form a responsible opinion. In considering a referendum that would legalize PAS, for example, the morally conscientious voter must ask whether or not PAS is morally permissible in general. Discourse ethics implies that in making up my mind about such questions, I am responsible for informing my conscience in view of the arguments and counterarguments, and when I believe the arguments to be stronger on one side of the issue, I presume that my assessment of the arguments would hold up, were all the affected persons able to scrutinize the available arguments as reasonably as possible. Given that I cannot actually consult all those affected, I must make a prudential judgement about the appropriate dialogue partners: not only immediately involved persons but also sources of wisdom and diverse perspectives that are available through texts and other media. And when I encounter objections to my view, I am responsible for meeting them or else changing my position. If I find myself unable to agree with others, and if none of us exhibit evident failures of reasonableness (e.g. bias or prejudice, unwillingness to consider relevant considerations or viewpoints, etc.), then neither I nor my interlocutors may regard our respective views as fully (objectively) justified for all persons. We have at best partial justifications that have not been conclusively defeated.

At the level of public deliberation, discourse ethics becomes part of a theory of legitimate lawmaking (see Chapters 7 and 8 of this volume). Briefly, Habermas's democratic theory holds that laws are legitimate in so far as they issue from a process of public deliberation and lawmaking whose organization and execution warrant a presumption that the outcome is reasonable. If the law at stake regulates a moral question such as those above, then the legitimacy of that law would partly depend on whether the deliberation, both at the broad public level and in the legislature, displayed features that warrant confidence that it was conducted under sufficiently reasonable conditions for moral discourse. This does not mean that discourse-ethical principles like (U) provide a blueprint for the design of deliberative processes, but rather that (U) can inform our assessment of legitimacy by having us scrutinize the process for its inclusiveness of perspectives, freedom from coercive pressures and so on.

Both levels, the personal and the political, are situated in broader historical processes in which personal reflection, public debate and social-political developments come together in collective learning processes. This suggests that we do best to regard real discourses of general justification as temporally-spatially de-centred: as taking place over great lengths of time and across a great variety of social contexts. The discourse on slavery, for example, goes back at least to ancient Greece, and reached its conclusion only in the last two centuries. Although slavery is still a social reality, attempts to defend slavery in the public sphere have essentially disappeared, and it is now difficult to imagine how any reasonable person could seriously entertain its defence. From a discourse-ethical perspective, to accept that slavery is wrong means to believe that this historical process of discourse, despite all its flaws, eventually generated a sufficiently thorough and conclusive scrutiny of the relevant considerations for evaluating the morality of slavery, considerations that include not only intellectual arguments but also the historical record of human suffering and struggle.

Discourses of application

So far we have focused on general moral norms. But for most of us the moral life primarily concerns making judgements of right and wrong in concrete circumstances, either prospectively (e.g. how ought I morally to handle this conflict with my business partner?) or retrospectively (e.g. did I do wrong last night in breaking my dinner engagement?). Such questions demand situated judgements about what you or I, as unique human beings, ought or ought not to do here and now (or ought to have done then and there). In other words, the answer must include precisely those semantic features that general norms exclude, the proper names of individual actors in concrete situations, which are often complex and develop out of unique local histories. The (U)-principle, by contrast, only provides for the justification of general norms in light of foreseeable, that is, *typical* circumstances of possible application; thus (U) does not anticipate the myriad complications that can arise in everyday life. In some situations, conflicting norms might seem to apply, so that one is unsure which norm to obey (e.g. may I lie if that is the only way to keep a promise of confidentiality?); in others we might confront unusual circumstantial contingencies. Drawing on work by Klaus Günther, Habermas treats such judgements as *applications* of general norms in particular circumstances (JA: 13–14, 35–9; see also Günther 1993).

The primary task of a discourse of application is to judge whether or not a generally valid norm is appropriate for a particular situation in the light of the concrete circumstances and alternative normative possibilities, that is, the other norms that might plausibly apply. This often involves a specification or qualification of the norm (e.g. lying is normally wrong, unless there is no other way to preserve a promise of confidentiality) (see Richardson 1990). In qualifying a norm for contextual sensitivity, one recognizes that general norms have an abstract character qualified by a *ceteris paribus* proviso: norm N is valid, other things being equal. Philosophers sometimes say that general norms have a "prima facie" or "*pro tanto*" validity: they hold *in so far as* other aspects of the concrete situation do not justify an exception or compliance with a different norm. Thus, when other things are not equal, one must make the exceptional situational features explicit in an "all-things-considered" judgement.

If we approach such situated judgements dialogically, then they count as justified in context, and thus appropriate, in so far as they are reached under conditions formally similar to those in (U), that is, conditions that specify the group of affected persons, the content of what they accept and the kind of discourse in which that acceptance qualifies as reasonable. However, the substance of these conditions shifts in view of the fact that the issue concerns the appropriate application of a presumptively valid general norm, rather than its general justification. We can spell out these conditions in a "principle of appropriateness", according to which the application of a generally valid norm N in situation S is justifiable in context on the basis of good reasons only if:

(i) everyone affected by the judgement, that is, everyone involved in S and directly affected by the execution of the judgement,
(ii) could accept the appropriateness of the norm N for S, in view of the relevant concrete features of S, the foreseeable effects on those affected, and the alternative normative possibilities in S,
(iii) after taking part in a discourse in which all those capable of making a relevant contribution – that is, all those familiar with S and its features, who are able to speak to the issues in (ii) – have, in a manner free of (self-)deception and any coercive pressures, considered the relevant reasons and judged them on their merits.[14]

Notice here that the relevant reasons differ significantly from those in a discourse of general justification. Although the principle of appropriateness, similar to (U), calls for reasons touching on the foreseeable effects of the judgement, it also demands close scrutiny of the particular features of the situation and the alternative norms that might appear relevant. The participants must describe and interpret the situation in a way that captures the full range of alternative normative possibilities, and then evaluate these alternative interpretations as adequate or inadequate, with a view to the likely effects on the people involved and coherence with other valid norms. The better arguments would be those that included a more complete description of the situation and more coherent interpretation of its normative requirements, in light of the various norms that might apply and the likely effects of each alternative.

Like (U), this principle of appropriateness involves counterfactual idealizations, and hence is formulated in terms of what those involved *could accept* in a discourse, were they able to assess the available information and arguments so thoroughly that any further scrutiny would not overturn their conclusion. However, given the situated character of applications, and assuming the decision at issue has limited repercussions, the circle of affected persons is likely to be small enough to make real discourses of application possible in which all of those affected are actually included. One can also consider some institutionally structured procedures as cases of real discourses of application, or as subject to critical scrutiny from the standpoint of a principle of appropriateness. Habermas cites legal adjudication as an example of real application discourse (BFN: 109, 172, 217ff.). At the level of application, then, discourse ethics has the potential to inform deliberation and decision-making in such areas as law, environmental dispute resolution, health-care ethics committees, urban planning and the like.[15]

The analysis of appropriate application also allows Habermas to respond, at least to some extent, to criticisms that proponents of an "ethics of care" levelled against Kantian morality.[16] The critics argued that Kantian approaches, with their fixation on impartial, universally valid norms, had overlooked the moral significance of particular interpersonal relationships. The moral features of a parent's relationship with her children, for example, cannot be fully captured in general rules that cover any parent–offspring relationship in general; rather, the parent must be sensitive to the unique needs of *this particular* child, which may be somewhat different from the needs of its siblings. Habermas's concept of application responds to this critique by recognizing the fact that each person, taken as an individual, is "absolutely different from all others" (IO: 40).

The problem of motivation

The foregoing remarks aim to show how discourse-ethical idealizations, although largely counterfactual, can still inform real moral discourse. The feasibility of discourse ethics, however, also hangs on a solution to the problem of motivation. In the Aristotelian tradition, this problem has been connected with weakness of the will, and its solution lay in the development of virtue. The virtuous person is precisely the one who is motivated to act morally, for that is just what virtue consists of: a stable disposition to do the right thing readily, consistently and with pleasure.

Discourse ethics must deal with the problem of motivation at two levels (at the least): the motivation to enter (and stay with) a moral discourse, and the motivation to adhere in practice to the norms one believes have been (or could be) justified in discourse.[17] The first problem poses the question, what grounds do we have for thinking people will bother with moral discourse? In reply, Habermas appeals to the work of developmental psychologists such as Lawrence Kohlberg and Robert Selman (MCCA: 116ff.). According to Kohlberg, children's moral development advances through three levels of moral judgement, designated as the preconventional, conventional and postconventional levels. As children mature through these levels, they develop increasingly powerful capacities for solving sociomoral problems. Starting with the self-interested viewpoint of the preconventional level, they advance through the social-conformist conventional level with its "law-and-order" mentality, to arrive finally at the postconventional level, where they realize that existing laws and social conventions must be justified in relation to universal principles of justice.

In citing moral psychology, Habermas does not claim that the empirical psychological research uniquely selects discourse ethics as the correct theory of justice; that remains a matter for philosophy. The point, rather, is that the feasibility of discourse ethics depends on a particular familial and educational culture, one whose typical socialization processes foster the development of postconventional dispositions in the members of a society (BFN: 113–14). Unlike the conventional-level personality, which adheres to established social norms and laws just because the group approves them, the postconventional personality is able to critically scrutinize the status quo in light of universal principles of justice. In other words, one is ready for moral reflection. Habermas proposes his discourse ethics as the proper method of such reflection.

However, the widespread development of postconventional attitudes does not suffice to make discourse ethics socially feasible. In fact, compared to conventional morality, postconventional morality is at a disadvantage when it comes to motivation: the critical postconventional attitude often cannot compete with the emotion-laden traditions, solidarities and habitual attachments that support established norms, customs and practices with which one has become familiar. In addition to postconventional personality structures, therefore, a socially motivated discourse ethics also depends on social and institutional structures that (a) encourage, or even require, discursive methods of problem-solving, and (b) remove obstacles to complying with justified norms or discourage noncompliance (see BFN: 114–16). Assuming that a sufficient number of people are capable of a postconventional attitude, these two sorts of institutional structure help solve the two motivation problems described above. For example, policy-making procedures can help motivate participation in discourse by requiring bureaucrats to hold public hearings as a step in decision-making. And regulatory oversight mechanisms can discourage morally questionable behaviour in a given sector of society, thereby helping its members comply with moral norms.

Ethical authenticity and the good life

As a moral theory, Habermas's discourse ethics is predicated on a conviction shared by many moral philosophers today, namely that philosophy is no longer in the position to dictate a comprehensive theory of the good life that is both informative and universally valid (see IO: 3–46; Habermas 2003b: 1–15). Habermas thus carves out the moral domain from its traditional setting, the encompassing set of issues that have to do with flourishing, happiness and the good life, and restricts the task of moral theory to the reconstruction of the "moral point of view" from which we can impartially justify (and apply) norms for the treatment of persons in general. This modern approach to morality has not gone unchallenged, particularly by feminists and thinkers influenced by Aristotle and Hegel. In response, Habermas has developed an account of the "ethical employment of practical reason" that, though context-bound, is not entirely at the mercy of subjective preferences.[18] Indeed, to appreciate Habermas's discourse ethics as a moral theory, it helps to have some sense of his treatment of the "ethical" questions that once constituted an important dimension of moral philosophy, and that still trouble it today.

Ethical questions about the good life arise not only for individuals but also for groups. For groups, ethical questions "refer to a shared ethos: what is at issue is how we understand ourselves as members of our community, how we should orient our lives, or what is best for us in the long run and all things considered". Our focus here, however, is on "ethical-existential" questions that arise for the individual, that is, questions about who one is and wants to be, or how one should lead one's life so that it is "not misspent" (IO: 26, 27). Unlike moral questions, ethical questions do not yield universally binding answers. But neither do they merely yield the hypothetical imperatives of pragmatic reasoning, which have only a conditional validity that depends on the individual's existing preferences, values and goals. Rather, ethical deliberation can lead to answers that are "absolute" or unconditional *for an individual*, as, for example, when one confirms a compelling call to some vocation, such as medicine (JA: 5). And unlike pragmatic reasoning, where each individual has "final epistemic authority" to identify his or her preferences, ethical reasons are open to intersubjective testing in discourse (IO: 25–7). To see how, we must start with the validity claim at issue in ethical discourse. We can then specify the appropriate audience and reasons.

The clearest examples of ethical-existential questions concern major decisions about the direction of one's life, for example, decisions about marriage and career. At issue in such decisions are "authenticity claims". As Habermas puts it, "the authenticity of a life-project can be understood as a higher-level validity claim analogous with the claim to truthfulness of expressive speech-acts" (IO: 27). More precisely, authenticity claims are complex validity claims that combine truthfulness (i.e. sincerity) with evaluative claims, that is, claims about the values and goods realized by one's life choices.[19] For example, a decision to become a doctor involves a claim that such a career genuinely fits with who one is and wants to be, on the one hand, and realizes goods that deserve our approval, on the other.

The first side of this claim presupposes a truthful relation to oneself; thus the authenticity of one's decision can be challenged for its truthfulness or sincerity. In general, sincerity claims are exemplified by simple first-person statements about one's subjective experience or attitudes ("I feel at ease with Mary", "I enjoy playing rugby"). In classifying such statements as validity claims, Habermas highlights their inherent relation to potential criticism and vindication, which normally involves testing such statements for consistency with the speaker's behaviour ("But you appear very nervous whenever Mary is present"). Such criticism does not necessarily charge the speaker with lying; he or she could be self-deceived or simply lack self-knowledge. The matter is somewhat more complicated in assessing the sincerity dimension of an authenticity claim. Consider an applicant to medical school, for example. She might display behavioural inconsistencies (e.g. her contentious behaviour in groups belies her claim to enjoy working with others) or pursue incompatible goals (medicine and a demanding sports career). But she also might lack the necessary talent or temperament, or knowledge of her deeper desires or real motivation (e.g. she is subconsciously responding to parental expectations). Each of these incongruities casts doubt on something like her sincerity, that is, on whether her goal *fits* with who she is and can become.

The evaluative side of our applicant's claim – the affirmation of genuine goods or values that are internal to the practice of medicine[20] – is widely acknowledged, and so our would-be doctor is unlikely to be challenged on evaluative grounds. However, she might misinterpret or fail to appreciate the goods of medicine (e.g. she sees its value solely in terms of personal financial gain, or dismisses the importance of the doctor–patient relationship). Accordingly, applicants to medical school are screened along a number of dimensions, which in effect cover both sides of authenticity: both the applicant's personal fit with the medical profession (academic competence, sources of motivation in the candidate's life history) and her understanding of its value, thus her previous exposure to the profession and her awareness of its demands and rewards (through volunteer work in health care, "shadowing" of physicians, etc.).

This analysis shows that authentic personal choices involve validity claims that can be challenged and defended with objectively good reasons, that is, reasons that can hold up in rational discourse. The relevant reasons for ethical-existential discourse include, on the one hand, personal narratives and information about one's talents, psychology, temperament, behaviour and the like; on the other hand, narratives and arguments that interpret or articulate the merit-worthy values that one hopes to realize by pursuing some significant life-project. The better applications to medical school display all of these elements; understood as part of an ethical discourse, such applications attempt to justify the authenticity of a life decision.

What the medical-school applicant carries out in a rather formal process occurs informally for many important life decisions. Such processes represent the site for ethical-existential discourse. But discourse with whom? In many cases, we simply consult our friends and more experienced elders. And this seems appropriate, given that an authentic choice must suit the individual as someone with a unique personal history and identity: the most obvious participants in an ethical-existential discourse belong to the circle of persons who are familiar with the chooser or share the chooser's lifeworld (JA: 11). However, as a species of reasonable discourse, ethical discourses must satisfy the process assumptions described earlier. Such discourses thus remain open in principle to anyone who can make a relevant contribution to the matter at hand, that is, anyone who can testify to the behaviour, history, temperament or talents of the person whose authentic choice is at issue, or who can speak to that person's understanding of the values at issue (Anderson 1996: ch. 6.3 [i.a, ii.a]). Again, the health-care example is instructive: the committees that review applications to medical school draw on multiple sources of information, and include members with little or no direct (face-to-face) knowledge of applicants. Forms of autobiographical literature further buttress this point. In confessional first-personal narratives, authors like Rousseau present their life choices and self-understanding to the "universal public of a justly judging posterity" (PMT: 166; cf. 149ff.).[21]

In holding personal judgements about the good life accountable to ethical-existential discourses, Habermas insists that such judgements involve validity claims whose objectivity is measured by their public justifiability before reasonable audiences. According to the analysis above, an authenticity claim is valid only if the appropriate audience could rationally agree that (a) nothing they know about the speaker's life history and concurrent commitments, talents, motives, temperament and behaviour defeats her authenticity claim as a claim about what is good for *her*, and (b) the speaker's interpretation of the relevant values at issue, that is, the claim that her choice pursues a significant *good*, is understandable. A speaker's ethical justification can meet these two standards without everyone agreeing that her choice is the best one available to her (cf. Anderson 1996: ch. 6.3 [ii.b], 6.4).

But an important question still remains: exactly what audience must agree that an authenticity claim meets the two standards above? Although ethical discourse must admit anyone who can supply at least one piece of relevant information, not every such contributor is in a position to assess the authenticity claim at issue. Assessment requires an adequate grasp of all the relevant considerations, hence considerable knowledge of the person and the interpretive context and background of relevant values. However, a precise definition of the epistemic position that satisfies this "adequate knowledge" condition remains elusive. On the one hand, some features of Habermas's view suggest that this audience of judges is limited to those with intimate knowledge of the subject who makes the claim. On the other hand, Habermas's treatment of autobiographical literature suggests a potentially unlimited audience. Biographical studies, which sometimes bring more information to light than was available to contemporaries of the subject, also support the latter view. Indeed, close acquaintances and friends are sometimes those least prepared to judge an authenticity claim, particularly one that revolutionizes conventional values. Consequently, the appropriate scope of the judging audience, as opposed to the contributors to an ethical discourse, probably does not admit of a single clear determination, but rather must be answered on a case-by-case basis.

Conclusion: dialogical autonomy and solidarity

Two values lie at the core of Habermas's discourse ethics: autonomy and solidarity. As should be clear, discourse ethics develops the Kantian notion of autonomy in a more explicitly dialogical direction. This dialogical turn has implications for the idea of moral solidarity (Habermas 1990b; MCCA: 195ff.). Kant's notion of the kingdom of ends – the idea of a moral community of autonomous agents – in effect assumes a pre-established moral solidarity at the level of pure reason. Guided by the Categorical Imperative, the mature, autonomous individual can discern the demands of solidarity through private reflection. For Habermas, by contrast, what solidarity requires of us depends on the outcome of a real intersubjective engagement with others. That engagement is itself both autonomy-preserving and solidaristic: in moral discourse, on the one hand, each participant receives the respect due to an autonomous person as a source of relevant contributions; on the other hand, participants bond together in solidarity with others, namely in the common enterprise of testing contributions for their merit in the justification of moral norms and judgements that all those affected can accept. The norms that issue from such discourse serve the common good, for they protect the web of relationships in which persons treat each other with concern and respect. If moral discourse has this internal structure and social effect, then discourse ethics provides an apt approach to moral questions in modern societies that emphasize the value of individual freedom, yet yearn for solidarity.

Notes

1. Cf. Kant (1993: §2); for a rational choice model of morality, see Gauthier (1986); for Habermas's criticism of moral theories based on pragmatic reason, see IO: 12–16.
2. If Habermas cannot maintain the separation between ethics and morality (and the priority of morality), then his conceptions of moral obligation, consensus and political legitimacy appear in doubt; for a criticism of this separation in political discourse, see McCarthy (1998).

3. See Habermas (2004); in his *Future of Human Nature* (2003b: 16ff.), Habermas argues for a universal "ethical self-understanding" of the human species, rooted in the value of moral autonomy.
4. Today, moral realists are apt to understand moral truth not as correspondence but in minimalist terms; for further discussion, see Thomas (2006).
5. See TJ; Habermas's moral theory, though cognitivist, counts as anti-realist, whereas his theory of truth remains realist: good reasons justify our taking a claim as true, but truth itself is a matter of adequately representing a mind-independent world. For criticisms of his moral anti-realism, see Lafont (1999: ch. 7).
6. Habermas (MCCA: 66) initially understood (D) as a moral principle, but he later revised this view, so that it functions as a principle for the impartial justification of social norms in general (BFN: 107).
7. In aligning his moral theory with the Kantian tradition, Habermas sides with the liberal side of the liberal–communitarian debate, giving the right priority over the good. But his insistence on real discourse that takes account of particular values and interests meets at least some communitarian concerns; see Rehg (1994).
8. For important criticisms, see Benhabib (1986: 306–9, 325–6); Wellmer (1991); Heath (1995); for positive attempts to explicate the derivation, see Rehg (1994: ch. 3); Ott (2004); for a careful overview of the debates over (U), see Gottschalk-Mazouz (2000).
9. Habermas has not been very clear about this, although he does assume that participants understand "the concept of a moral norm" (IO: 42) and "what it means to justify actions in moral terms" (BNR: 87, 88).
10. See Wingert (1993: 237–52); in line with other theorists, Habermas also accepts this point (IO: 45).
11. Habermas attempted to justify these idealizations by sketching transcendental arguments based on performative self-contradictions in the attempt to deny them; such arguments depend on the self-contradictory nature of statements such as "using lies, I convinced everyone that norm N is right" (MCCA: 89–91).
12. This reconstruction presents (U) as a conditional, whereas Habermas has presented (U) in both conditional and biconditional forms. But the conditional formulation fits better with his formulations of (D) as a conditional; cf. MCCA: 65–6, 93, 197; IO: 41–2; BFN: 107.
13. For a discourse-ethical account of conscience-formation, see Rehg (2004); for the moral aspects of political deliberation, see Chapter 7 of this volume.
14. Quoting Günther, JA: 37–8 provides a loose statement of this principle, which presupposes an ideal of the coherence of norms; see Günther (1993: 243). Victor Peterson, "A Discourse Theory of the Appropriateness of Moral Norms" (ms.) has proposed an alternative formulation of the principle.
15. On law, see Chapter 8 in this volume; broad features of Habermas's discourse ethics have been influential in studies of participatory policy-making, for example Webler & Tuler (2004).
16. A prime mover in this critique was Carol Gilligan's *In a Different Voice* ([1982] 1993); for broader discussion, see Kittay & Meyers (1987); Rehg (1994: ch. 7); Meehan (1995).
17. For a discussion of the types of motivation problems in discourse ethics, see Christmann (2004: ch. 1, §V).
18. Important critiques include Benhabib (1992); MacIntyre (2007); and Taylor (1989). Habermas's response draws not only on Taylor but also on Kierkegaard's existentialism (Habermas 2003b: 1–15).

19. See PMT: 167, also 77. For a lucid critical exposition of ethical-existential reasoning, see Anderson (1996: ch. 6).
20. The idea of goods internal to a practice is found in MacIntyre (1984: 187).
21. Third-personal biographies also seem to play a role in a wider ethical discourse in so far as they present the subject's life for public evaluation of its authenticity. Note that Habermas's treatment of autobiographical literature is more concerned with claims to individuality, or "identity claims", than with ethical-existential validity claims. With the former, a speaker makes a claim to be recognized by others as a unique individual who can take responsibility for her beliefs and choices. Consequently, identity claims are tacitly presupposed in all communicative interaction, and when one criticizes someone's ethical self-understanding or choices in an ethical discourse, one tacitly accepts that person's identity claim; see Habermas's "Individuation through Socialization" (PMT: 149ff., esp. 188–91).

SEVEN

Deliberative democracy

Kevin Olson

Discourse and democracy

Jürgen Habermas refers to his democratic theory as a "discourse theory of democracy". He starts from the idea that politics allows people to organize their lives together and decide what common rules they will live by. To do this, it must accord a prominent place to political argumentation and justification. Because these practices are inherently communicative ones, they bear the same implicit presuppositions as any other forms of communication. On this basis, it is possible to discern various norms, attitudes and assumptions that people must make in order to engage in political argumentation.

In Habermas's analysis, these features of political practice form a set of "pragmatic presuppositions" that people make when engaging in political communication. Most crucially, deliberative participants have to presuppose that anyone can take part in discourse and anyone can introduce and challenge claims that are made there. They must also see one another as equals, reciprocally granting one another equal status in deliberation. Further, they must assume that others are under no compulsion while they are participating, by either the direct or implied force of others. Participants must "presuppose" these features in the sense that they wouldn't think of a political argument as truly justified if some people, who may have important things to say about it, have been excluded from the discussion, or if the participants don't see one another as equals who needed to be persuaded to agree to the claims being made. Political interaction can count as deliberative only when participants approach it with these presuppositions in the background of their acts (OPC: 367; see also Alexy 1989: 193).

Habermas builds a democratic theory around these insights about political communication. At the heart of modern politics, he claims, are discursive processes of lawmaking. They create legal norms by allowing each person affected by a given norm to agree to the norm itself. This is a version of a more general principle of universalization that Habermas calls the discourse principle, or "D". It states that "Just those action norms are valid to which all possibly affected persons could agree as participants in rational discourses" (BFN: 107; cf. MCCA: 66). Here the basic character of political argumentation is the same as other processes of arriving at understanding. People advance validity claims, take a positive or negative position towards those advanced by others and make presuppositions about the character of the practice they are engaged in. In Habermas's analysis even political forms of communication have this familiar character.

The most distinctive difference between communication in the general sense and its specifically political forms, according to Habermas, is the legal character of the latter. Political argumentation is structured by legal norms, and the implicit presuppositions of communication take a more specific form when they operate within this context. They are based on the idea that people living under a system of laws must agree to the laws they live under. Their agreement is communicative in character. Because political communication is legally constituted, however, Habermas does not apply the discourse principle "D" directly to it. Rather, he describes political discourse as taking a new form in legal-political contexts, the "democratic principle". It states that "Only those statutes may claim legitimacy that can meet with the assent of all citizens in a discursive process of legislation that in turn has been legally constituted" (BFN: 110). It describes the form of generalizability required to make sure that all those affected by a law are able to agree to it. This principle expresses the cooperative orientation of people communicating with one another in politics, especially the fact that they recognize one another as "free and equal members of an association that they have joined voluntarily" (BFN: 110).

It is important to qualify the sense in which Habermas sees idealized notions of equality, reciprocity, inclusion and generalizability as "pragmatically presupposed" by participants. From a theorist's perspective one can see these presuppositions operating in the background of actual democratic practices; actual citizens may or may not be aware of them. On Habermas's account, though, citizens will "intuitively" discover the need for such presuppositions as they try to reach agreement about matters of common concern through legally structured political processes. This is an important innovation in democratic theory. By interpreting the implicit presuppositions of practices that people already engage in, a theorist can identify implicit norms and commitments in those practices. This is an interpretive enterprise: a matter of tracing the generalized structure of a practice, the typical ways it is performed, and speculating about the kinds of attitudes and commitments needed to perform it consistently.

In this sense, Habermas's democratic theory is a "rationally reconstructive" one. It tries to produce an interpretive, fallible account of practice, but one that does not simply describe what is most obviously visible. Rather, Habermas's interpretations are designed to reconstruct the inner rationality of practices, showing what participants would implicitly presuppose if they were to have a full, complete understanding of what is needed to accomplish the goals they set themselves. This requires one to trace out the pragmatic presuppositions of a person's actions if they were to carry them out in a consistent, non-contradictory manner. Those findings can then be shown to the person as a kind of critical mirror, one that illuminates unseen aspects of tasks that they have already set themselves.

Such an interpretation is fallible because it can be shown to be wrong. It is not a matter of occupying an ideal philosophical viewpoint for assessing people's actions, but rather of conducting a sensitive dissection of their practices to show them things they may not themselves understand about those practices. There is no privileged standpoint in this process and no *a priori* right answer. Rather, it gives the theorist an interpretive role in clarifying the functional requirements of democracy, at the same time providing grounds for criticizing political regimes that don't match up to the presuppositions of their own practices.

Habermas is often misunderstood as calling for an "ideal speech situation" to be realized as a *precondition* of democracy. From this point of view, the implicit presuppositions of democracy would actually need to exist in full-blown form for legitimate deliberation to occur. For example, people would need to be actually equal in the most substantial ways for their political practices to count as real examples of deliberative democracy. Proceeding from this misinterpretation, Habermas's critics then charge that his view is so hopelessly idealized that it could never be realized in practice. What is worse, they claim that Habermas thereby ignores actual inequalities and forms of power that disadvantage some people in real politics.

The "ideal speech situation" is a phrase that Habermas used in a 1972 essay, "Wahrheitstheorien" (1984a: 174–83). It has caused widespread misunderstanding of his ideas and a great deal of mistaken criticism, leading him to distance himself from the essay and use the term only with heavy qualification. Habermas does not believe that the presuppositions of communication need be fully or perfectly realized in speech or democratic practice.[1] His point is much more subtle: that people make such presuppositions themselves in communication and democracy. These idealizations are an implicit part of communication, but only as idealizations that constitute the practice itself. They are, in this sense, counterfactual assumptions that people try to realize in practice, partly succeeding and partly failing. This gives practices like deliberative democracy an open-ended, ongoing character. To the extent that communication and argumentation fail – that they result in misunderstandings, are plagued by power or inequality – people must make further attempts to clarify their intentions and communicate across differences of power and inequality. Such practices always fall short of their aims to some extent. To say that they nonetheless contain idealized presuppositions is not to impose moral principles on them, nor is it to constrain, channel or narrow them, but simply to trace out the attitudes that people already take in performing them.

Autonomy, citizenship, rights

The status of "free and equal members" takes a particular form in contemporary societies. According to Habermas, it is expressed in the autonomy that citizens have to form mutually acceptable laws and live under them. Citizens see one another both as addressees of the law and as its authors (BFN: 104). Their freedom as addressees of the law is expressed as "private autonomy". Symmetrically, Habermas refers to citizens' freedom as authors of the law as "public autonomy". These two forms are interlocking and mutually supporting in the sense that each presupposes the other. A secure status as a private individual is needed to participate in public political processes. It is a form of private freedom that gives people the security and material capabilities to engage as an equal in politics. At the same time, public autonomy is needed as participatory freedom to spell out the details of private life and protect it. Political participation allows citizens to specify the concrete protections they need from the legal system. Recognizing the deep, mutual implication of public and private autonomy, Habermas refers to them as "co-original". Each one is needed for the other, and neither would be possible without the other.

Habermas notes that these dual forms of autonomy are coded as rights in the liberal democratic tradition. Rights anchor the status of "free and equal members" of the polity by simultaneously guaranteeing public and private autonomy. They also institutionalize the ideals of equality, reciprocity and inclusion that are implicit in communication. These legal measures form a system of rights that establish the communicative conditions for creating legitimate law (BFN: 104).

In Habermas's account, these include three functionally defined categories of rights that specify the status of a participant in deliberation: (1) rights to equal liberties as a subject of the law, enjoying the greatest possible liberty that is compatible with the same liberty for others; (2) rights defining membership in a political community, typically the status of a citizen; (3) rights to assert claims that one's rights have been violated and to have these violations remedied. These rights establish a functioning system of law in which people are recognized as legal subjects, granted freedoms of various kinds and have legal recourse when those freedoms are not respected. They supply the bases for the legal system by specifying the sense in which citizens are subjects of the law.

The first three categories of rights are not in themselves democratic, however. Citizens are established as particular kinds of legal subjects and granted rights, but not yet enfranchised as democratic citizens. To breathe democracy into the system of laws, the rights defining it must be interpreted as elements of democratic lawmaking. This requires a further category focused on the political capabilities of citizens. The citizens constituted by the first three categories must have (4) rights giving them equal opportunities to participate in the political processes that create law. This allows them to participate in formulating the laws they live under, including the details of the rights of citizenship outlined in categories 1–3. Finally, citizens must also have (5) rights to the material circumstances needed to have equal opportunities to use their rights. This acknowledges that democratic politics often occurs in social and economic conditions that provide some people with better opportunities to participate than others. The fifth category is designed to redress this problem by equalizing differences in material circumstances that interfere with people's political participation or civil freedom.

All of these categories of rights are theorized in discourse-theoretic terms by Habermas. The first three are defined as protections needed by people who are organizing a legally structured system of cooperation through discursive means. The fourth institutionalizes discursive forms of politics, ones providing for public communication and argumentation. The fifth acknowledges the materiality of discursive participation: the fact that individual differences and material circumstances have an important bearing on political agency.

Because rights must arise out of actual democratic practice, Habermas outlines these categories in only the most schematic terms. He identifies key functions that a legal system would have to fulfil but leaves the details unspecified. In so doing, however, he also describes the self-referential, cyclical political dynamics that would make a more detailed specification possible. By first outlining the general form of democratic law (1–3), then identifying the conditions under which citizens could author such laws (4–5), this scheme describes an internally self-generating political system. The first three categories describe the form of a system of laws needed to institutionalize public and private autonomy. The fourth details the political processes that would make this scheme a reality. It identifies actual practices of democracy needed to make this scheme an autonomous creation of the people who live under it, rather than a theorist's abstract schema. As such, this system of rights self-referentially creates the grounds for its own legitimation. It makes possible the actual political processes that in turn develop and refine it.

Habermas says that the first four categories of rights are "absolutely justified" as presuppositions of constitutional democracy, but the fifth category is only conditionally justified (BFN: 123). In his view the formal, legal entitlements that provide people with civil protections and participatory membership are necessarily presupposed in discursive lawmaking, while the kinds of social rights typically associated with social policy are not. This treatment of social rights is far too weak, however. To give them a weaker justification than the other four groups involves the theory in a set of vicious paradoxes, where the political system cannot legitimate itself precisely because of its incomplete attention to material inequalities (Olson 2006: 101–106, 115–30). These problems show that politics and discourse are material to their very core, and social rights must stand on the same grounds as civil and political ones.

Ironically, Habermas may not even need the fifth category of rights. He derives it from the others, in effect, by reconsidering them a second time from a "conditional", material point of view. He asks what citizens would need as participants in a legally structured democratic system if we consider them not simply as discursive agents in the abstract, but as materially unequal in various ways. This extra reconsideration is necessary only if one first interprets the other four categories in a strictly formal sense, however, artificially bracketing their inherently material character.[2] A strictly formal, immaterial reading of these categories is unwarranted, though, because the presuppositions Habermas traces in discursive lawmaking come out of the real, embodied practices of real people in complexly unequal societies. The presuppositions of discursive democracy must always be assessed against the background of material inequalities. Thus each of the categories of rights would aim at forms of equal opportunity in which the old Weberian distinction between "formal" and "substantive" law does not apply. Each aims at actual equality in its particular domain: forms of equality that cannot be considered purely formal or purely substantive. Material equality is not an additional consideration, then, but one already lying at the heart of equality between democratic citizens. Citizens could not treat one another as equals if they did not see each other as real, embodied – that is to say, material – people. Strictly speaking, then, thinking about material inequality is not separate from thinking about the rights needed to create discursive democracy. Rather, it is a central part of citizens' efforts to devise these first four categories of rights.

In this abstract, reconstructive account of deliberative democracy, Habermas's reliance on familiar ideas like rights, citizenship and autonomy might draw some attention. From one perspective this could seem like a failure to think outside of the status quo, privileging already familiar ideas and legal devices rather than searching for new possibilities. This is not an oversight on Habermas's part, however, but a deliberate piece of sociological and historical realism. His account is based on the insight that our current legal framework evolved in complex ways under contextually specific pressures. These elements of our political imaginary are somewhat arbitrary from a philosophical perspective, then, and they could well have turned differently. Having acknowledged that abstract point, Habermas notes that we currently use the institutions of Western liberal democracy to coordinate our cooperative behaviour. These particular legal devices are social and historical facts for us; our lifeworld has already been rationalized in specific ways that can be redirected but not ignored. Habermas's reliance on specific forms of law is not an abstract commitment, then, so much as an acknowledgement that he is working within a particular Western legal and political tradition. Legally structured forms of argumentation are our currently favoured mode of organizing our life together. This form of law is not necessary in any philosophical sense; it is merely the historically specific organizational schema that we have inherited from several centuries of experimentation.[3] It draws on cultural resources immanent in the Western legal tradition to constitute and channel deliberative politics.

In sum, Habermas's conception of deliberative democracy is built on three different ideas: the idea that discourse is basic to politics; the idea that political discourse is organized through legal means; and the idea that the legal institutionalization of political discourse tells us a lot about how democracy should be organized, if we assume that it relies on legal devices already known to us. Thus we go from the assertion that communication is fundamental to political processes organizing cooperative interaction to a system of rights for establishing such political processes.

Structures of democratic deliberation

The most important thing about discursive democracy from Habermas's perspective is the way it forms a normative basis for popular sovereignty. Following in the footsteps of republicans like Emmanuel Sieyès and Hannah Arendt, Habermas describes this as a form of "communicative power".[4] He arrives at this idea by interpreting popular sovereignty through the lens of discourse theory. From that perspective all political legitimacy comes from the communicative power of citizens. Communicative power is generated through public discourse. It is based in the homegrown formation of ideas and opinions that occurs when people talk to one another. This routine communication has the vital function, for Habermas, of public opinion formation. It represents shared ideas about matters of common concern in a raw, unfiltered form.

To base popular sovereignty on public communication, Habermas has to explain how diffuse public opinion can be transformed into a more general, universally acceptable form. It must become truly popular: the "will of the people" in a more cohesive and literal sense, rather than a chaotic aggregation of subjective, individual opinions. For Habermas this wide variety of ideas, suggestions and partly self-interested, partly communally oriented individual viewpoints can be transformed into ideas of common concern through discourse. Public opinion is "processed" through public argumentation to produce norms "to which all possibly affected persons could agree as participants in rational discourses" (BFN: 107). Here the rich communication of everyday life becomes source material for procedurally regulated public discourse, transforming it from loose talk into discursively generalized norms. It takes on the generalized form specified in the discourse principle: normative reasons that would be acceptable to all affected.[5] This reworking of public opinion through argumentation transforms it into what Habermas calls communicative power (BFN: 371).

Communicative power is a discourse-theoretic equivalent of the will of the people. It takes the idea of popular sovereignty through a linguistic turn, functioning as what Sieyès called constituent power by constituting a sovereign basis for governments and states (Sieyès 2003: 136). Communicative power constitutes sovereignty by synthesizi[ng] social agreement for such regimes and ensuring that this agreem[ent] expresses generalizable interests (BFN: 153–4). It thus constitutes a unified popular will in an abstract, postconventional sense.

To encourage the generation of communicative power, Habermas maintains a clear distinction between two different discursive domains. These two spheres are organized along different lines and perform different functions. The greatest amount of communication occurs in the interstices of daily life. It is diffuse, unregulated, open, chaotic and "autochthonous". This is the domain of multiple, overlapping, "weak" public spheres that discuss topics and form opinions about them (BFN: 307–8, 360–65). It represents a discourse-theoretic view of the political in the broadest sense: subjectless public opinion formation that is the product of open-ended, ongoing communication.

This form of public opinion is long on sovereignty but short on effectiveness. It carries the force of its popular origins but cannot coalesce into binding legal decisions. For this task Habermas theorizes a second domain of publicity, connected with the first but different from it in character. It is a domain of official lawmaking, a parliamentary body structured around ideals of public argumentation. This "strong" public sphere is procedurally regulated to require generalized forms of justification along the lines of the principle of democracy. It lacks the contextual immediacy of weak public spheres, but compensates for this by drawing the themes and contents of weak publics together into forms of communicative power.

Habermas characterizes these domains as "core" and "periphery" (BFN: 298, 354–8, 380–83, 442). Weak public spheres constitute the periphery; they are domains of open-ended, contextual discourse animated by citizens' problems and concerns. Strong public spheres sit at the core of this scheme. As domains of parliamentary argumentation, they provide a centre for interpreting diffuse public opinion, expressing it as the unified will of the people and writing it into law.

Habermas uses various metaphors to describe how these qualitatively separate domains might be connected. He writes of "sluices", "transformers" and "sensors in the lifeworld" to indicate how inchoate, colloquially articulated public opinion might be taken up and translated into binding law (BFN: 300, 354, 356, 358, 359). While this language is poetically suggestive, it does not actually explain how public opinion and law would be connected. To see this connection, we need to consider in more detail what is being described. Habermas often advertises his discursive turn in democratic theory as relying on "subjectless" forms of communication (BFN: 184, 299, 361, 486). This allows him to put a great deal of distance between himself and a stricter republican like Jean-Jacques Rousseau. Rousseau must rely on the face-to-face presence of the people because he lacks a way to render their agreement intangible (BFN: 300–301). Habermas's discourse theory gives him this means, allowing him to shift focus from a populace collectively assembled to a populace dispersed yet connected through abstract, "subjectless" flows of communication.

From this perspective, Habermas's talk of "sluices" and "sensors" evokes processes through which diverse public opinions can be translated into generalizable reasons for binding laws. This occurs, according to Habermas, when the loose discourse of informal public spheres is taken up into parliamentary decision-making. Legislators are thus tasked with bridging the gap between informal, weak public spheres and formal, strong ones. They must be able to reconceptualize and translate the content of popular opinions into generalizable reasons that could be acceptable to all possibly affected by them. One might imagine public opinion about nuclear reactors, for instance, as taking the form "I don't want that thing in my back yard". The translation of such an idea into parliamentary argumentation, as seen from Habermas's perspective, might be something more akin to "Siting nuclear power plants near residential areas poses unacceptable risks".

By maintaining two deliberative domains while connecting them, Habermas takes full advantage of their relative strengths. Weak public spheres permit flexible consideration of a wide variety of ideas and viewpoints without prejudice to their origin or the identity of the person expressing them. This form of discussion is "subjectless" and diverse, deliberative in the very broadest sense of inclusion and openness. Strong public spheres have symmetrical and synergistic strengths. They require generalizability in public justification, ensuring that deliberation produces laws acceptable to all who might be affected by them.

By knitting together the dual strengths of these two domains, Habermas avoids many of the criticisms typically levelled against deliberative democracy. Deliberative theories are often criticized for being impossibly demanding of their citizens. Because most citizens engage in normal, everyday communication in Habermas's theory, while the burden of deliberating along the strictest lines of equality, reciprocity and generality is limited to the "official" public sphere of legislative decision-making, the burdens placed on normal citizens are relatively light.

Another charge often levelled against deliberative theories, particularly those of a neo-Kantian bent, is that they constrain the wild, ungovernable energies of the people in narrowly procedural form (Wolin 1994a, 1994b). "The political" is thus narrowed and tamed, removing important considerations and important modalities of politics from the public sphere. Again, this charge goes somewhat wide when levelled against Habermas's theory. His description of weak public spheres allows for broad diversity of viewpoints and political modalities without any particular constraints. Thus it accommodates a wide array of activities and expression that might count as political. Problems could potentially occur, however, when the contents of weak public spheres are taken up into the proceduralized debates of strong publics. Here we might ask whether anything is lost in translation. In principle the "sluices" connecting the two domains should be able to preserve the contents of public opinion in its wildest form. However, the form of law and procedural limits on discourse do impose limitations on the kinds of things that can be codified and the form that politics can take. Whether this is ultimately a problem awaits further discussion between Habermas and his critics.

Political culture and constitutional patriotism

By conducting a subtle analysis of the implicit presuppositions of deliberative democracy, Habermas raises some important issues in new and interesting ways. Chief among these is the cultural character of democratic norms. Habermas notes that the democratic framework he describes is not a purely voluntaristic, contractarian one. Rather, it must be "embedded in the context of a liberal political culture"[6] or "nourished by the 'democratic *Sittlichkeit*' of enfranchised citizens and a liberal political culture that meets it halfway".[7] Here he focuses in particular on the ways in which democratic norms arise out of cultural traditions. Democratic ideals of equal voice, openness, inclusion and so on do not merely fall from the sky, nor can they be imposed on a free populace by political theorists. Rather, these ideas must originate organically within the societies that adopt them, either through long processes of historical development or by borrowing from other traditions. For Habermas, the West's particular versions of these ideals are exemplified by the heritage of the French and American revolutions.[8] They are specific inventions with long histories of their own.

While Habermas sees our democratic ideals as developing within specific historical traditions, he does not see their contents as accidental. The particular details of these traditions may be contingent – different schemes of rights, different emphases on republican or liberal elements[9] – but Habermas views their overall shape as driven by deeper pressures. These are the functional requirements of generating systems of legal cooperation through public argumentation. As a matter of historical record, then, Habermas is prepared to claim that democratic lawmaking cultivates political traditions "from within", shaping their essential features in a slow but implacable way. Norms of communication, developed and used to facilitate political argumentation, will in time become sedimented in political culture. What first starts as a creative solution to functional problems is eventually embedded in collective memory and collective identity.

Thus, for instance, the American guarantee of free political speech, ratified as a constitutional amendment in 1791, has established a cultural template for subsequent political traditions and acts of legislation. Habermas would acknowledge the contingency of this innovation as a specific act while also claiming that it satisfies deep functional needs of public discourse, providing people with forms of private autonomy that safeguard their use of public autonomy. While individual historical traditions might meet a democratic regime "halfway", the nature of their interaction is a complex one. According to Habermas, it reveals the extent to which communication can generate democratic norms and shape political traditions from within such regimes themselves.

With this kind of process in mind, Habermas sees public discourse as having an ability to rectify undemocratic regimes.[10] It can purge such regimes of illiberal norms and sectarian forms of identity by subjecting them to public argumentation. Non-generalizable norms and inegalitarian, exclusionistic identities do not survive this scrutiny, leaving only thin forms of identification around core principles of the constitution. This "constitutional patriotism" is developed through discourse, building a culture around communicative norms that are realized in law. It is a form of post-traditional political culture that combines unique, identitarian aspects of one's own culture with more generalized norms that reflect the quiet, functional needs of public argumentation.[11]

This is a bold claim about the cultural character of democracy. Habermas believes that culture formation is shaped by communication itself. Since communicative practice is in turn moulded from within by implicit presuppositions of equality, reciprocity and inclusion, Habermas argues that this influence would spread from the immediate sphere of public argumentation to the broader, more free-floating and anonymous domain of culture. Moreover, the effect would work in reverse as well: a culture of equal and inclusive communication would socialize the people who write laws, resulting in legal codes that in turn promote such practices.

Whether political traditions are in fact shaped from within by communication is an important and interesting question. On one hand, the inner pressure that communication exerts on political practice could explain the growing world tendency towards democratic forms of government. Even states that are not politically open or democratic seem increasingly unable to constrain the political discourse of their citizens.[12] Free speech breaks out in ways difficult to contain, in turn providing a forum for its own legitimation. Claims to other liberties quickly follow suit. This spread of democracy seems to continue the direction of Euro-American historical development over the past several centuries. Its seeming teleology could be explained by Habermas's thesis that politics involves communicative claims-making.

On the other hand, political traditions are multiple and varied, containing norms with many different and conflicting implications. It is not clear exactly how political cultures would be shaped from within by implicit norms of communication. It is certainly true that culture is linguistically reproduced, and we would therefore expect culture formation to depend on norms of equality and reciprocity inherent in communication. However, culture formation is a diffuse, anonymous, largely "subjectless" process which is only partly communicative. It is shaped in other ways by material practices, institutions and laws that have an extra-discursive facticity of their own. While individual acts of communication are governed by the implicit norms of language, there is no guarantee that culture formation as a whole would be characterized by any sort of broader norms. There is, then, much more to be said about the relation between democracy and culture, and the role of communicative norms in mediating that relationship.

Innovations and limitations

Habermas's democratic theory is not simply a theory of deliberative democracy, but one that ties together micro- and macrolevels of analysis into a comprehensive account of democratic constitutional development. Here communication is the normative pacemaker for legally constituted public argumentation, constitutional lawmaking and the development of political cultures in dynamic relation with democratic regimes. The sweep of this theory and its complex references to many areas of research make it more robust while also expanding the number of moving parts that must mesh effectively with one another.

A principal strength of Habermas's democratic theory is the way it combines idealization and interpretation. The theory is built on an interpretive analysis of actual political practices that allows one to trace the presuppositions that people make in performing those practices. It derives considerable normative leverage by being rooted in the practices it aims to criticize. This theory can thus exercise a kind of moral suasion to reform democratic practices "from within". Unlike theories that seek to impose a morally or theoretically based vision of democracy on actually existing politics, Habermas works immanently within the Western democratic tradition to explore normative resources that are already implicit there. His work combines fallible social-scientific interpretation with philosophical reconstruction, developing an amalgam of the two. The fallible, interpretive character of this investigation allows the theory to draw its normativity out of actual practices, rather than imposing foreign philosophical norms upon them. This tension between facts and norms produces an account of democracy that is empirically and historically rooted, yet critically insightful. Moreover, the theory acquires its critical bite specifically by interpreting real practices: actual citizens could be persuaded to see such an analysis as a description of their own goals and the means needed to achieve them.

Habermas's democratic theory has this normative leverage only to the extent that it portrays democratic practice accurately, however. Theory and practice must come together in a way that the theoretical reconstruction accurately identifies norms and attitudes that people really do presuppose.

Obviously Habermas puts great weight on the communicative character of democracy. His theory is built on a linguistic turn: a fertile innovation in democratic theory by any account. The question, though, is whether actual politics are linguistic in the ways described by the theory, or whether it amounts more to a kind of theoretical vanguardism. Modern politics rest to some extent on the processes of communication portrayed by Habermas's theory, to be sure. To some extent political claims are raised and resolved as validity claims on which one can take a yes or no position: characteristics of argumentation in the most strictly rational sense. Habermas thinks that this mode of communication will become even more important as societies shift away from older forms of identity and solidarity, and need to synthesize new ones under post-traditional conditions.[13] Furthermore, he sees communicative content as deposited in constitutions from the beginning, by virtue of the communicative character of their founding acts: constitutional conventions and the formation of new, revolutionary identities. Political traditions gradually solidify as present generations discover the normative residues of these founding acts in the original document, rendering that meaning more explicit through subsequent acts of legislation and adjudication.[14]

Although modern politics are partly communicative, a great deal of political action occurs through other means: forms of symbolization and non-verbal representation, vote aggregation, influence peddling and self-interested compromise negotiation. Discursive democracy has less interpretive purchase here. It seems less to reflect the implicit character of these political practices because they are not based on asserting and redeeming validity claims about generalizable interests.

Just as Habermas makes large gains by playing off the tensions between idealization and actual practice, this method also poses certain risks. Chief among these is the danger of poorly drawn connections between idealization and practice. Indeed, this sometimes seems the case in Habermas's political writings. At times his interpretations of actual politics are startlingly illuminating. This is often aided by Habermas's linguistic turn, which allows him to see things in contemporary politics that are obscure to others. Particularly in his engaged writings as a public intellectual, Habermas proves to be a perceptive observer of contemporary politics, keenly aware of its ambiguities, tensions, conflicts and impasses. At other times, however, he seems to err on the side of idealization rather than interpretation. In these moments he focuses more on constructing an idealized vision of democracy that draws heavily on contractarian notions of constitutional liberalism, rather than tracing the fine-grained details of particular practices. In these cases it is unclear how fully norms of equality, reciprocity, inclusion, generalizability, non-contradiction or reason reconstruct actual practice.

From this perspective, one might see Habermas as following two lines of research that sometimes meet in powerful ways and sometimes travel separate paths. On one hand, there is a rational-reconstructive project that describes a self-consistent theory of discursive democracy; on the other, an interpretively subtle reading of the strains, impasses and complexities of contemporary politics.[15] Ideally these two moments would come together seamlessly, so that the interpretive, fallible character of Habermas's democratic theory would be substantiated by his subtle reading of actual politics. Whether this is the case is at times hotly debated by his critics as well as those who have benefited from his keen insights into contemporary democratic practice.

Notes

1. See BFN: 322–3; OPC: 365–8; JA: 54–9; "The New Obscurity: The Crisis of the Welfare State and the Exhaustion of Utopian Energies" (Habermas 1989a: 69).
2. This modifies my earlier criticisms, noted above, in certain ways.
3. Habermas, "Remarks on Legitimation through Human Rights" (PNC: 118–22); BFN: 111–12.

4. Habermas, "Hannah Arendt: On the Concept of Power" [1976] (1983: 171–87); BFN: 147–50.
5. Habermas, "Popular Sovereignty as Procedure" [1988] (BFN: 484).
6. Habermas, "Citizenship and National Identity" [1990] (BFN: 499).
7. Habermas, "Postscript" [1994] (BFN: 461). Cf. BFN: 184, 358; "Popular Sovereignty as Procedure" (BFN: 471, 487).
8. Habermas, "Popular Sovereignty as Procedure" (BFN: 463–74); Habermas (2001é: 774).
9. Habermas, "Popular Sovereignty as Procedure" (BFN: 465).
10. Habermas, "Apologetic Tendencies" (1989a: 226–7).
11. Habermas, "Historical Consciousness and Post-Traditional Identity" (1989a: 261–2).
12. Cf. Habermas, "Remarks on Legitimation through Human Rights" (PNC: 113–29).
13. Habermas, "Does Europe Need a Constitution? Response to Dieter Grimm" (IO: 159–61); "1989 in the Shadow of 1945: On the Normality of a Future Berlin Republic" (1997: 175–6).
14. Habermas (2001e: 775–6; 2003c: 193–4).
15. Patchen Markell (2000) characterizes this double-stranded tendency perceptively.

EIGHT

Discourse theory of law

Christopher Zurn

This chapter focuses on Jürgen Habermas's multifaceted, wide-ranging account of law in his 1992 *Between Facts and Norms.*[1] Habermas's "discourse theory of law" is one of the most capacious and fruitful theoretical paradigms for the study of modern law and legal phenomena available today. This theory, moreover, systematically links up with the other elements of Habermas's philosophy surveyed elsewhere in this volume. Habermas's philosophical method and ambitions are analogous to those of Aristotle and Hegel (although he rejects their metaphysical, ahistorical and essentialist goals).[2] That is, he aims to integrate the partial insights of other theories of law into a systematic account reflecting the complexity of law, while overcoming any partiality, one-sidedness or weaknesses of the other theories. The range of theories considered is very broad, encompassing not only traditional philosophical analyses of law but also perspectives on law from moral philosophy, political philosophy, argumentation theory, philosophy of the social sciences, political science, sociology, international relations theory, comparative constitutionalism, legal dogmatics, theories of legal adjudication and theoretical issues raised by various topics in private law, public law and international law. Thus, any brief survey of Habermas's philosophy of law must be selective and abridge some of the theory's range and complexity.[3] At the risk of over-simplification, this survey of main theses is organized according to three broad perspectives on law: history and sociology; philosophy; and legal adjudication.

Historical and sociological perspectives on modern law

Habermas's legal theory starts from a focus on *modern* legal systems. Hence, the ambitions of the theory differ from those of "analytic jurisprudence", which aims at a trans-historical account of the nature of law that would explain why it makes sense to apply the concept "law" to all manner of apparently different practices in diverse societies. In contrast, because the discourse theory of law limits its purview to legal phenomena characteristic of Western societies of the past three or four centuries, it takes a more sociological and historical approach to law, focusing on the questions of what roles law plays in modern societies and how positive legal orders structure domains of social action and life.

We can get an inroad to Habermas's thought here by turning to two central themes of his sociological theory of modernity.[4] The first theme is the idea that modernization processes in the West break down previously established habits, traditions and taken-for-granted understandings. The authorities of the Church and encompassing religious doctrines are no longer taken as sufficient backing for claims about the world, humans and norms of social interaction. Increasing religious diversity is the wedge that opens the door to recognizing the pluralism of worldviews, values and forms of life. Increasing travel, communication and commerce force a widening awareness of the number and diversity of different groups and societies, both across the world and within Europe. As "eternal verities" lose their sacred status in the face of value pluralism and cultural diversity, ever more areas of social life and social interaction also lose their automatic and smooth coordination through shared hierarchies of authority and taken-for-granted norms, values and orientations. Without a stable and common lifeworld background of shared understandings, individuals must increasingly resort to explicitly thematizing and negotiating the terms of their interactions. That is, they must rely on communicative action, rather than shared and authoritative background values and norms, to coordinate their interactions. Communicative action is, however, both burdensome and risky: not only does it require collective effort and time, but because it can only work when interaction partners voluntarily give their assent, it does not guarantee success in the way that eternal verities and settled hierarchies of authority do. In the absence of a commonly recognized authority, when communicative action coordination fails, the only resort is to forms of direct coercion. Even when successful, face-to-face interactions do not have the organizational power needed to develop large complex networks of social action that can effect social integration across large distances of space, time and social divisions.

Thus modern forms of *cultural rationalization* – value pluralization, group diversification and the loss of the shared sacred canopy and its attendant clerical authority – increase individuals' reliance on burdensome and risky forms of communicative action in order to coordinate their lives together, even though such forms of interaction lack the organizational capacities of previous authorities.

A second theme of Habermas's social history is that modernization also involves *functional differentiation*: a decoupling of economic and bureaucratic systems from the lifeworld they were previously embedded within. More and more domains of economic activity are released from direct political and clerical control, as well as from the traditional norms and values according to which such control operated. In the economic sphere at least, persons' individual actions are oriented solely by the incentives of profit and loss, and these actions are anonymously coordinated through market mechanisms, "behind the backs" of the actors themselves. In a "functionally differentiated subsystem of purposive-rational action" such as the economy, individuals take up a self-interested strategic stance towards other persons, calculating whether the actions of others will help or hinder their own pursuits in much the same way that they might calculate the likely effects of the weather on their monetary interests. In a similar way, rationalized bureaucracies develop in which individuals orient their actions according to anonymous rules and procedures, and functional mechanisms effect the coordination of action. As another subsystem of purposive-rational action, rationalized bureaucracies structure the use of power through abstract functional mechanisms. Systems of power, like economic systems, also become separated from lifeworld forms of action coordination and decoupled from constraint by everyday meanings, values and norms.

One central thesis of Habermas's legal philosophy is that *law*, specifically modern positive law, is increasingly required for social integration in the face of the disruptive effects of modern processes of cultural rationalization and functional differentiation. To understand how legal systems foster social integration in the face of the disruptions of modernization, we need to look at a few of modern law's features. First, positive law operates through general, publicly promulgated norms that apply across various domains of social life. Such legal rules form a stable social environment by setting default rules for interactions, which in turn generates a context of reliable expectations against which individual actors may plan their activities and coordinate them with other persons. In this way, law compensates for the cognitive loss of a lifeworld background of stable, shared and certain meanings and values. Positive laws need neither a society-wide consensus on substantive values nor explicit communicative action in order to achieve social integration. Legal rules also create entitlements – rights – which attach to individuals and are guaranteed to be enforced through the state's monopoly on the legitimate use of force. In this way, law compensates for the motivational deficits of a modernized lifeworld: even though different individuals may subscribe to different value systems and have diverse action orientations, social actors under a modern legal system can count on the material incentives of the law – largely the threat of punishments and penalties – to underwrite expectations of more or less reliable, legally compliant behaviour on the part of other individuals. By structuring organized forms of cooperation through secondary rules that determine how primary rules governing conduct are produced, by defining jurisdictional powers and by making it possible to form legal entities such as corporations and associations, law relieves actors of the organizational demands that communicative action cannot fulfil, while enabling large-scale action coordination and regulation across complex and far-flung social institutions.

Furthermore, the very structure of rights allows for a specifically modern kind of individual freedom: persons may act according to their own volition from either moral, strategic or other reasons, provided only that they not infringe others' rights in legally delimited contexts. And they may express this freedom in creative and unique ways since, under a system of purely secular positive law, whatever is not explicitly prohibited by law is permitted. This type of freedom is presupposed by systems steered by money and power, for markets and bureaucracies are domains where individuals are free to act strategically, openly pursuing their own self-interest without regard for the welfare or concerns of others. In such domains, actors are free, within legal constraints, to treat others as mere means to their own ends, allowing the anonymous functional mechanisms of the system to provide for the goods and services needed for others to realize their ends. These anonymous functional mechanisms work only if legal systems enforce the basic building blocks of markets and administrations: property rights, non-fraudulent and enforceable contracts, including agreements authorizing specific power hierarchies such as businesses and other organizations, and so on. One way to see law's central role in organizing subsystems is according to the main division of a legal system: private law structures the economy through contracts, torts and other private obligations, whereas public law structures state bureaucracies through constitutions, statutes and regulations, including criminal laws. Law delimits the boundaries of such subsystems: for instance, allowing land but not kidneys to be bought and sold, or allowing private arbitration institutions but not private militaries. Law, then, both structures and delimits functional systems, even as those systems presuppose the freedom of strategic action made possible only through individual, legally enforceable rights.

Legal systems implicitly raise claims not only to being effective but also to being legitimate (indeed, without the perception of legitimacy, law loses a good degree of its effectiveness). However, modern legal systems cannot rely on older, "metasocial" sources of legitimation such as God, divine ancestors, sacred rulers, heavenly institutions and the like, nor can they be legitimated simply through the state's monopoly on the coercive use of force. On the contrary, social actors demand that law effect a normatively correct structuring of social interaction that is rationally justifiable to those who are subject to its imperatives.

Hence idealizing pressures for the legitimation of law through reason and collective civic self-determination find increasing expression in modernity, whether theoretically articulated in the seventeenth- and eighteenth-century social contract and republican political philosophies, practically demanded in the American and French revolutions, or institutionally anchored in the new bourgeois representative democracies structured through legal constitutions from the late eighteenth through the twentieth centuries. Much of Habermas's theoretical work on law analyses the meaning, sources and justification of such legitimacy claims for governments and legal systems, but these questions of normative political philosophy cannot be discussed further here.[5] Most important here is the sociological claim: modern legal systems must generate norms which are both *effective* and *legitimate* in order to structure diverse domains of society reliably.

The key insight is that modern legal systems can fulfil these two criteria only if law simultaneously interacts with systems and the lifeworld. According to Habermas's normative political theory, the legitimacy of a system of collectively binding positive laws can be generated only through the "communicative power" of individuals acting together communicatively in intersubjective relations of mutual recognition and giving themselves the laws they agree to be bound by. The solidarity realized by communicative forms of association represents for Habermas one of the three main sources for social integration in modern societies, along with money and power, as discussed above. According to Habermas's sociological theory, functional media must be responsive to legal imperatives if law is to be an effective mechanism of social coordination in modern complex societies. In order to be both legitimate and effective, law somehow must be able to connect communicative and functional forms of social integration: solidarity, money and power.

We have already seen how this is possible, for law "talks" both in the ordinary, lifeworld language of norms and values, by incorporating communicatively generated moral norms, collective values and policy priorities, and in the specialized codes of markets and administrations, which operate within legal frameworks. Thus, a central metaphor in Habermas's theory is that law acts as a *transmission belt* that transforms the communicative power generated by forms of mutual recognition into binding legal programmes that organize and regulate administrative agencies and economic markets. Law is the way in which political solidarity legitimately controls systems of power and money, even as it allows those functional systems leeway to integrate their social domains through anonymous mechanisms.[6] And the constitutional state provides the parliamentary, judicial and bureaucratic institutions and mechanisms for this transformation of communicative into administrative power, even as all of these institutions and mechanisms are themselves established and regulated by law.[7]

This transmission belt thesis and focus on the constitutional state are remarkable developments in Habermas's critical social theory, for law now occupies pride of place as a potential emancipatory mechanism. Through law, communicative action can "counter-steer" functional subsystems run amok, yet without losing the apparently irreplaceable efficiencies of capitalism and rationalized bureaucracy for material reproduction. Law, then, harbours perhaps the most significant emancipatory potential available in modern societies, for it makes possible "the conditions for constitutionally domesticating the circulation of power in complex societies" (BFN: xl). This potential can be realized only when the power of solidarity, through legitimate mechanisms of constitutional democracy, controls the political state, which in turn regulates the major sources of functional social power. When, however, as is all too common, major social powers nevertheless steer the constitutional mechanisms, for instance by pressuring the state to legislate and regulate in the interests of certain industries instead of the interests of all affected, then law can end up instead as a *de facto* bulwark against progressive social change. Because law responds to diverse imperatives, illegitimate power can also employ the cloak of formal legality to dress itself up with the mere semblance of legitimacy. Hence modern law is normatively ambiguous: a potential resource for both legitimate emancipatory social action and unjustified use of state power to the unequal benefit of powerful interests. Habermas labels this ambiguity of law the "external tension" between validity and facticity: law in modern, complex societies can institutionally enforce both valid social norms and unjustified power relations.

Philosophical issues in modern law

Distinguishing this external tension in law between facts and norms from the tension Habermas labels "internal" will help to change our perspective from the sociology of modern law to the philosophy of modern law. For while the external tension exists only because of contingent facts about modern law's place among a particular set of social arrangements, the internal tension is intrinsic to positive law itself. Individuals encounter modern positive law as a Janus-faced phenomenon. On the one hand, laws demand obedience simply through the threat of a coercive sanction for disobedience, through the mere facts that a particular legal rule exists and that the state will use its actual monopoly on coercive means to ensure compliance. On the other, law also claims to present reasonable demands to autonomous individuals, that is, legitimate demands for forms of action that free and reasonable individuals should be able to accept, since they make everyone's equal autonomy possible. So law is both coercive and freedom-guaranteeing: a social fact that is nevertheless responsive to normative idealizations. Law is *factical* – generated, administered and enforced by actual social institutions beyond the control of any individual – yet claims normative validity – deserving of the reasoned recognition of each because it makes possible the equal freedom of all in society. This internal tension can also be seen in the different orientations actors may take towards the law. Individuals may approach a legal system as purely strategic actors, attempting, like Holmes' "bad man", to predict the risks and potential benefits from the probability of the state's use of force, and aiming to manipulate the social environment, including the law and other persons, in order to secure instrumentally their own private interests (Holmes 1879: 478). Alternatively, individuals may approach a legal system from a moral point of view, seeking to understand individual legal rules and the system as a whole as a legitimate and reasonable scheme of social norms that ought to obeyed simply because it commands what is right, regardless of the law's likely impact on their own particular interests.

Hart (1994) famously captured this dualistic character of law in his insistence that any adequate philosophy of law must incorporate both the external, observers' point of view and the internal, participants' point of view. Habermas's diagnosis of the problems of analytic jurisprudence similarly claims that, in attempting to avoid law's internal tension between facticity and validity, various theories exaggerate truthful insights, ensuing in one-sided accounts of law. Legal positivism is correct that modern positive law artificially constructs an order of social reality, but it carries this voluntarism too far. It ignores the fact that law cannot achieve social integration exclusively through commands backed by coercive threats, but also must be able to claim legitimacy in order to have binding force for its addressees. In a parallel manner, natural law theory correctly sees that many laws have quite similar content to independently correct moral duties, but it gets carried away by the overlap of law and morality and thereby ignores much of the voluntaristic positivity of modern law. For many legal duties have no intrinsic moral content: think of the legal duties to drive on a specified side of the road or to attach one's signature to contracts. In addition, much of law does not concern the enforcement of duties, but rather the establishment of enabling rules that allow social actors to form their own relations with and obligations to others – think of the laws of contracts and corporations – and these arrangements are neither moral nor immoral, but rather merely instrumentally useful or useless, efficient or inefficient, and so on. Only a legal philosophy with a perspective situated "between facts and norms" – and this means also between the extremes of legal positivism and natural law theory – can make proper sense of the complex phenomena of modern legal systems.

So what is the relationship between law and morality?[8] Habermas claims that: (i) legal norms and moral norms are different kinds of action norms, and (ii) the basic principles of legal legitimacy and moral validity are two different specifications of one more general and basic principle for the validity of action norms. To begin with the differences between legal and moral norms, recall that law relieves socially interacting agents of the high cognitive, motivational and organizational burdens of social action coordinated through face-to-face communicative interactions relying only on the actors' moral competences. Following Kant (1999), Habermas insists that modern law can accomplish this because, unlike morality, law abstracts from the reasons that motivate actors, demanding only that, for whatever reasons, they comply. Further, law relates only to the external relations between social actors, rather than the internal structure of relationships that morality concerns. The weakly motivating force of good moral reasons is replaced in law by the coercive threat of sanction. Because individuals can take a strategic stance to one another through the law, in many legally delimited domains individuals may treat others as mere means, whereas it is immoral to do so in unstructured communicative interactions. In addition, the basic element of modern law is the legal right: it is a legal status, established through some positive legislative, administrative or judicial act, attached to legally recognized persons (including artificial persons like corporations), adjudicable through the courts and providing individuals with a claim on the enforcement powers of the state. Moral rights, by contrast, are a moral status, established through the intersubjective use of moral reason, attached to moral persons, adjudicable only through collective moral deliberation, and with only a claim upon moral duties of enforcement. Justified moral norms are universally valid for all moral agents, whereas justified legal norms claim validity only for the subjects of a particular positive legal system. Moral norms are narrowly tailored to what can be regulated in the equal interest of all affected, whereas legal norms relate not only to the analogous impartial domain of what is equally just to all legal subjects, but also to ethical questions of what is good for us, to prudential questions about the best means to realize politically selected goals, and to questions concerning fair terms for strategic bargaining. In short, legal norms incorporate a full range of different types of normative content, concerning justice, ethics, prudence and bargaining, whereas moral norms concern only impartial issues of the right. Finally, legal norms, unlike moral norms, are used to programme political power in order to solve collective action and coordination problems across large, complex and far-flung institutions of social life, particularly through the use of enabling rules for the establishment of corporations, associations, states and state agencies, and other collective entities.

Regarding the second claim concerning the principles for justifying legal and moral norms, Habermas has changed his position. In the 1980s Habermas, like Kant, saw legitimate legal norms as derived from moral norms either directly or indirectly, whereas since *Between Facts and Norms* he has insisted that law must not be thought of as derived from, subordinate to, or in any way an imitation of morality. His claim now is that there is one very general and basic principle specifying how any kind of action norm, whether a moral or legal norm, might be justified: namely, the principle of discourse (D). The basic moral principle (U) – the principle of universalization – is then to be conceived of as a specification of (D) tailored to the distinct domain of moral norms. The basic legal principle – the principle of democracy – is to be conceived of as a specification of (D) tailored to the domain of legal norms.[9] Principle (U) for justifying moral norms and the principle of democracy for justifying legal norms are then conceived of as *equiprimordial* specifications of the same more general normative principle of discourse (D); the mistaken subordination of law to morality is thereby avoided. In practical terms, this means that laws gain their legitimacy precisely through the active processes of democratic discussion and decision, where those democratic procedures are themselves legally constituted. Legal norms are justified through the legally structured procedures of constitutional democracy.

Why does Habermas insist on the equiprimordiality of law and morality? Recall that, unlike morality, which is mainly a system of knowledge concerning individuals' duties to others, law is a practical system internally connected to political power. Modern law both structures political power through establishing the institutions of the constitutional state and uses political power in order to administer and enforce legally enacted policies. But in order to structure and employ political power *legitimately*, modern legal systems must make it possible for those subject to the law to understand themselves simultaneously as the authors of that law. Because the rule of law requires the political use of the coercive power of the state, and because we can no longer rely upon "metasocial" guarantees for the rightness of legal programmes, the only way to ensure that all affected by the exercise of political power have an equal opportunity to participate in the collective determination of the nature and direction of that political power is through the procedures of deliberative democratic self-determination. Hence, one of the central theses of Habermas's political philosophy, that there is a deep, internal relation between the rule of law and democracy, is also one of the motivating intuitions behind the thesis that law cannot be subordinate to morality. If law were simply derivative of morality, then a democratically constituted political community would not be able to express popular sovereignty, at least with respect to the specific legal norms that morality simply dictated the content of. To be sure, legitimate laws may not contradict morality: for instance, the law may not violate morality by arbitrarily treating women worse than men. But there are multiple and critical questions about how extremely general and abstract norms of interpersonal conduct are to be precisely reflected in a system of determinate legal rights and enforced through the varied instruments of political power. For instance, would a law banning women capable of becoming pregnant from working with materials hazardous to fetal health, say in a lead-acid battery factory, arbitrarily discriminate on the basis of sex? Such questions can only, in the end, be determined through legally constituted democratic procedures, as those procedures provide the only warrant for legal legitimacy under "postmetaphysical" conditions. But if law were subordinate to morality, all such questions would be beyond the control of democratic processes.

Habermas diagnoses precisely this error in the tradition of natural law liberalism: in understanding the fundamental rights of individuals as pre-political dictates of morality, it subordinates popular sovereignty to a moralized conception of the rule of law. Rather, subjects of modern law must themselves determine together, through collective public reasoning and decision, the legal contours of the fundamental individual rights that are to be granted to each: "they themselves must agree on the relevant aspects under which equals should be treated equally and unequals unequally" (BFN: xlii). Said another way, securing individual private autonomy through law presupposes a collective use of public, political autonomy to determine the exact contours of individual rights. Of course, legal and political theory must also avoid a parallel error of taking any and every exercise of collective political agency as sufficient for legitimating the use of state power. For democracy is itself only justified to the extent to which we can expect that following a set of specific procedures for collective decision-making will warrant the expectation of better, more rational and reasonable outcomes than would ensue from not following those procedures. That means that the procedures of democracy are in fact rather exacting, which is why they are spelled out in and institutionalized by a legal constitution. Legitimate democracy requires, among other things, a stably institutionalized and reflexively developing system of fundamental rights of individual liberty, equality and political participation, and a separation of governmental powers, all of which must be developed and maintained through the mechanisms of modern law. In short, legitimate democratic procedures require constitutionalization; and constitutional government must in turn be democratic. Hence the central thesis of *Between Facts and Norms* – "the rule of law cannot be had or maintained without radical democracy" (BFN: xlii) – is systematically connected to other fundamental and distinctively Habermasian theses: the equiprimordiality of private and public autonomy, and the mutual presuppositionality between democracy and constitutionalism.[10]

The discourse theory of legal adjudication

Turning finally to a perspective attuned to the work of judges, it helps to review Habermas's discourse theoretic account of the separation of governmental powers.[11] Instead of endorsing the classical idea that the three main branches of government – legislative, executive and judicial – are each designed to exclusively fulfil their own unique functions – making, implementing and applying laws, respectively – he argues that, under contemporary conditions, each of the three branches in fact often takes on certain functions classically restricted to other branches. Consider, for instance, the ways in which administrative agencies in developing regulations, or judiciaries in employing common law techniques, each take on essentially legislative tasks. Habermas argues that the separation of powers is better understood in terms of the distinctive ways in which reasons and arguments are employed for each function, that is, in terms of the different kinds of communicative discourse appropriate to each function. The process of making laws is grasped in terms of the logic of justification discourses, where the full panoply of reasons and arguments – not only issues of justice, but also consideration of ethical-political values, prudential considerations, the results of fairly achieved bargains, and relevant empirical data – may be brought to bear in a constructive consideration of which general legal norms are acceptable to all citizens in an open and democratic process of opinion and will formation. The process of implementing laws is grasped in terms of limited pragmatic discourses, where agencies are restricted to sorting prudential reasons concerning the most feasible, sustainable and efficient ways of implementing already justified legal policies in the light of relevant facts; implementation discourses have no control over the normative content used to justify the laws being implemented. The process of applying laws – the paradigmatic function of courts – is grasped in terms of the logic of application discourses, where the syndrome of normative reasons used to legislatively justify general legal norms is reconstructively "unpacked" and impartially applied to the facts of a particular situation, with an eye to both the justice of the particular adjudication and the overall consistency of the system of legal norms.[12]

With respect to institutionalization, the key claim is that different branches of government may in fact take over some of the functions traditionally associated with other branches, as long as they establish discursive forms of participation and communication appropriate to legitimation for that function of law. For instance, when administrative agencies take on basically legislative functions in the elaboration of regulatory schemes in the light of quite general statutes, they must ensure that all those potentially affected have substantive opportunities for communication and participation in the processes of regulatory decision. In other words, to the extent that administrative agencies take on lawmaking powers, they must go beyond mere technocratic consideration of pragmatic issues and establish forms of communication and decision appropriate to justification discourses, if their lawmaking is to be legitimate. The same point applies any time a branch of government takes on one of the distinct functions of lawmaking, law implementing and law applying: it must adopt the discursive processes of legitimation – the forms of communication, openness to reasoning, and participation – appropriate to that function of processing law.

Habermas's discourse theory of legal adjudication, then, spells out the logic of the function of applying laws, a function carried out paradigmatically (but not exclusively) by the judiciary.[13] He develops the theory out of a complex and multifaceted attempt to come to terms with a number of different types of jurisprudential theories – natural law theory, legal realism, hermeneutics, legal positivism and critical legal studies, among others – as well as with the distinctive legal practices of different nations – for the most part, those of Germany and the United States. Simplifying, we can think of Habermas's theory of adjudication as combining three main elements. First, Habermas endorses Günther's (1993) understanding of legal application discourses. Here the goal is to decide among a variety of already justified legal norms, for instance, statutes passed through legislative procedures, by finding the single most appropriate norm for the facts of the case at hand, in the light of an exhaustive description of all of the normatively significant situation features. If a court proceeding conscientiously reconstructs a full description of the facts of the case from an impartial perspective, and selects the most appropriate legal norm relevant to the case from among those available, then justice will be done to individual litigants: their already established and justified legal rights will have been vindicated.

However, in hard cases – the kinds of cases that tend to be appealed up through appellate courts – it is not always clear that there is one uniquely appropriate legal rule for the case: two or more laws might impartially be seen to fit equally well. Here the second main element of Habermas's theory comes into play: namely, his endorsement and modification of Dworkin's (1986) theory of "law as integrity". For in situations where simple considerations of "fit" between the case facts and relevant legal norms – norms variously enshrined in constitutions, statutes, regulations and past judicial precedents – is insufficient to dispose of the case, a judge must consider which of the fitting legal norms actually justify the overall legal system as the best that it can be. Here, Habermas claims, judges must begin to unpack the syndrome of normative reasons employed to justify the various applicable legal norms, in order to attempt to reconstruct interpretively the overall system of law to make it as coherent as possible. With a coherent ranking of the various applicable legal norms in the light of the facts of the case, judges aim for the one right answer to the question of which disposition of the case will make the overall legal system most closely match its inherent principles. Thus, while the element of application discourses ensures justice to individuals, the element of reconstructive legal interpretation ensures the overall coherence and stability of the legal system, especially for legal systems that include both statutory enactments and common law precedents as valid legal sources.

The third element in Habermas's theory is the large role he sees public, legal communication and dialogue playing in producing both rational and legitimate adjudication. In contrast to Dworkin's theory which, in essence, idealizes single judges in the regulative ideal of judge Hercules, a judge with super-human cognitive capacities and unlimited decision time who strives alone to render the right decision, Habermas's theory is attuned more to the actual practice of law, where a number of different players engage in a structured process of claims-making and reasoned argumentation: not only lone judges, but judges on multi-member panels, organized in courts subject to the review of other courts, with lawyers and litigants, and legal academics, all embedded in a broader legal public sphere. For not only do judges render decisions, they often render decisions backed by written opinions laying out the legal reasons for the decisions. And those opinions are subjected to critical scrutiny not only by other judges, but also by the broader legal public sphere involved in more and less formal processes of critical review. It is this institutionalized rational reflexivity of law that Dworkin misses with his monological judge Hercules.

The three elements together largely answer sceptical worries about adjudication as the mere arbitrary disposition of cases according to the subjective whims of individual judges. Habermas agrees with numerous critics of legal formalism who insist that the correct outcomes of many hard cases are not easily or "mechanically" determined by the pure semantic content of legal norms – a range of critics extending from legal realists, to legal positivists, to legal hermeneuticists such as Dworkin, and on to those in the critical legal studies movement. Yet his discourse theory of legal adjudication is intended to answer the charge that such legal underdetermination implies an irrational indeterminacy in law. The ambitious claim of Habermas's account is that specific features of adjudicative processes, including the structure of judicial discourses of application, the coherence of constitutionalized legal systems and the institutional organization of legal experts and courts, together warrant the expectation of a rational processing of individual legal claims. Adjudication in modern legal systems, in other words, can reach rationally justifiable results when carried out under the institutionally mediated conditions analysed by discourse theory.[14]

A different set of worries, however, arises from the fact that judges and court proceedings are not directly accountable to voting citizens in the same way that legislators and members of the executive branch are. These worries about a purported democratic deficit of adjudication can be arranged from least to most troubling. To begin, if courts are only engaged in the particular application of legal norms that have already been justified through open democratic practices, then there is little worry. But, as mentioned above in discussing the separation of powers, judges are also often involved in the positive elaboration and development of legal norms. Furthermore, Habermas argues that judicial elaboration is an ineliminable by-product of the dialectical relationship between the justification of general norms tailored to standardized situations and the application of those norms to the much messier world of concrete situations. Habermas's response to democratic concerns about ordinary judge-made law is basically twofold. First, courts themselves are open to some democratic influence through their place within an institutionalized legal public sphere. Additionally, newly developed judicial doctrine can be relatively easily overridden or modified through normal, electorally accountable legislative processes.

The problem of the democratic deficit of adjudication grows more serious, however, once we consider the work of high courts such as the Supreme Court of the United States or the German Constitutional Court, particularly when they review laws and state actions for constitutionality.[15] Sometimes stylized as the "countermajoritarian difficulty" or as the "paternalist problem" with judicial review, the worry here is that, because such courts do in fact positively develop constitutional law as they apply abstract constitutional provisions to particular laws and cases, they assume the role of constitutional legislators. But in constitutional democracies, the function of constitutional development is legitimately reserved only to the people themselves and their accountable representatives, usually through special democratic procedures for ratification or amendment.

One response to the democratic objection to judicial review, quite prevalent in the literature, is to claim that supreme court judges will be more apt to rule in the light of, say, objectively correct values, or natural law, or the true demands of justice, than democratic actors would be (e.g. Bickel 1986; Dworkin 1996; Perry 1982). But for procedural democrats such as Habermas, this kind of a response ignores both the "postmetaphysical" situation of normative reasoning in the modern world and the fact that modern societies are pluralistic: they contain an ineliminable plurality of reasonable conceptions of what norms and values are substantively correct or true. The whole thrust of Habermas's democratic philosophy is that, under modern conditions of the loss of "metasocial" guarantees for normative claims and of social and ideological pluralism, the only legitimate way to decide questions involving the imposition of state power is through legally constituted, open and deliberative democratic procedures.

Habermas's strategy is to see constitutional courts not as substantive arbiters of the moral law, but rather as guardians of those very procedures that are required for democratically legitimate lawmaking.

There must be, in other words, some way of reviewing the procedures of constitutional democracy, including the assurance of individuals' constitutional civil, membership, legal, political and social rights, if the outcomes of those procedures are to ensue is legitimate laws. According to Habermas, it is at least acceptable to have courts carry out this function, for two main reasons. First, as we have already seen, courts have special competencies for maintaining legal coherence among a complex system of legal norms while impartially interpreting and applying abstract norms, including constitutional norms and rights. Second, the judiciary, precisely because it is *not* directly accountable democratically, is able to police impartially the very procedures of democracy which legitimate laws in the first place. An independent judiciary is in a unique institutional position to guarantee that the procedural conditions of democratic processes are correctly fulfilled.

Turning finally to questions of constitutional jurisprudence – questions, that is, of what kinds of methods, standards and approaches constitutional court judges should use in exercising their powers – Habermas argues that constitutional courts ought to adopt anti-paternalist, proceduralist and democracy-promoting forms of constitutional adjudication. They should be wary of taking on the role of a constitutional legislator, that is, wary of attempting to craft and justify by themselves the most basic norms that are to govern all citizens' common life. Further, they should not attempt to craft constitutional law in the light of ostensibly "natural" pre-political rights nor engage in value-balancing approaches referring to putatively "objective" hierarchies of value. Most importantly, constitutional courts should be concerned to foster and promote democratic procedures: namely, the openness, full inclusion, deliberation and wide dialogue and communicative exchange that are all necessary ingredients of a healthy system of deliberative constitutional democracy.[16]

Notes

1. My thanks to Barbara Fultner and Vic Peterson for their very helpful comments on this chapter. All mistakes are mine.
2. See Chapter 2 of this volume for more explanation of Habermas's philosophical approach and methods.
3. Topics omitted here which are nevertheless important to Habermas's philosophy of law include: the role of background paradigms of law and the attractions of a reflexive paradigm of law; international human rights and the relation between capitalist modernization and the spread of human rights; European-wide constitutionalism and the promotion of European federalism; the interrelations between national, transnational and supranational legal systems; and the

constitutionalization of international law and the prospects for a cosmopolitan global order.

4. TCA 1 and 2 contain the full theory of social modernization. It is summarized and applied to law in BFN chapters 1 and 2. See also Chapter 4 of this volume.
5. In the next section, I touch on some of the crucial theses of Habermas's normative theory as they relate to the philosophy of law. Chapter 3 of BFN contains the central normative arguments of Habermas's political philosophy. See especially Chapters 7 and 10 of this volume for more extensive treatments, but also see Chapter 6 of this volume for discussion of discourse ethics which forms an important background for the political philosophy.
6. Throughout the 1980s (e.g. TCA), he did not view law in these bridging terms, seeing modern positive law as itself a functionally integrated subsystem, with its own distinctive pathological form of the colonization of the lifeworld called "juridification". While Habermas still recognizes the dangers of juridification, he no longer analyses law in solely functional terms, nor has as bleak an assessment of its overall valence in modernity. He is, rather, quite concerned to strike a theoretical balance between idealizing the law as solely a force for legitimate normative control of functional subsystems, and sceptically reducing law simply to an anonymous, self-reproducing system of social control disconnected from non-instrumental social concerns. Luhmann's reductively functionalist systems theory of law is a major theoretical adversary in BFN, and Habermas is concerned to rebut the systems theory presupposition that legal systems are enclosed in upon themselves, sealed in the confining semantics of pure legality (see Luhmann 2004). Thus, Habermas's transmission belt thesis is also intended to rebut an overly objectified view of law, which overlooks law's connections to the rich, complex semantics and values of the lifeworld and everyday life.
7. The principles and institutions of the constitutional state are the focus of chapter 4 of BFN.
8. The most important discussion of the relation between law and morality is in BFN chapter 3, although there are other useful discussions in BFN chapters 4 and 5, as well as other sections.
9. See Chapters 6 and 7 of this volume for discussions of Habermas's moral theory and his normative theory of democracy, respectively. The most up-to-date statements of the principles that I am aware of are as follows. The principle of discursive legitimacy (D) states: "just those action norms are valid to which all possibly affected persons could agree as participants in rational discourses" (BFN: 107). The moral principle of universalization (U) states: "valid moral practical norms must satisfy the condition that the foreseeable consequences and side-effects of their general observance for the interests of each individual must be acceptable by all those possibly affected in their role as participants in discourse" (BNR: 80). The principle of legal legitimacy, the principle of democracy states: "only those laws can claim legitimate validity that meet with the agreement of all citizens in a discursively constituted process of legislation that commands the agreement of all citizens and is itself legally operationalized" (BFN: 80).
10. See Chapters 7 and 10 of this volume for further discussions of Habermas's political philosophy.
11. The principles of the separation of powers are discussed in BFN chapter 4 and applied to the thorny problems of judicial constitutional review in BFN chapter 6.
12. For more on the distinction between justification and application discourses, and

on the varying logics of different kinds of practical discourse – moral, ethical and pragmatic – see Chapter 6 of this volume.

13. The discourse theory of legal adjudication is the topic of BFN chapter 5.
14. For reasons of space, this article skips another imporant component in Habermas's legal theory and his reply to legal sceptics: namely, the character and role of widely shared background "paradigms of law". According to Habermas, the twentieth century saw the progression of three different major legal paradigms – specifically, the liberal, the welfare state and the reflexive paradigms of law – where each paradigm comprises a set of standardized assumptions about individual psychology and motivation, society and the nature of social relations, the proper role and aim of government, the function of law in social and in political life and so on. To the extent that a single paradigm is widely shared among members of the legal public, albeit as a set of unacknowledged presuppositions operating in the background, a legal system is able to achieve a great deal of certainty, stability and closure. When, by contrast, an older paradigm is falling apart and being replaced by a new one, a legal system is increasingly subject to sceptical worries on account of its instability and apparent arbitrariness. In the end, Habermas argues that the time is right for the legal public to fully (and consciously) embrace a reflexive paradigm of law in the wake of the insurmountable problems of the earlier liberal and welfare state paradigms. He accomplishes this, in chapter 9 of BFN, with a fascinating case-study of the dialectic between formal and factual equality as evinced in feminist debates in legal and political theory.
15. While chapter 5 of BFN is concerned with legal adjudication in general, chapter 6 of BFN is concerned specifically with the problems of constitutional courts, judicial review and constitutional jurisprudence.
16. Habermas takes his cue on this score from democracy-promoting forms of jurisprudence recommended by American scholars such as John Hart Ely (1980), Frank Michelman (1986) and Cass Sunstein (1988), and seeks to enrich them with his more capacious and sociologically nuanced account of the various citizen competences, diverse public spheres, formal and informal political institutions, and types of discourse and communication that his political philosophy claims need to be involved in deliberative democratic constitutionalism.

PART III

Politics and social change

NINE

Civil society and social movements

Keith Haysom

This chapter examines the role played by social movements in Jürgen Habermas's social and political theory. Social movements appear as a theme at pivotal moments of certain of his key texts and serve as potential carriers of emancipatory social and political change. Yet their place in Habermas's *oeuvre* has rarely been closely examined, at least not by scholars of Habermas. This may be partially due to the fact that the role he accords to social movements has always been tentative and ambivalent, and that his direct discussions of them are relatively minimal. However, social movements play a functionally vital role within Habermas's political theory, which requires actors such as social movements to generate debate within the public sphere and open avenues within civil society for active citizenship in order to make the abstract ideal of deliberative democracy an empirical reality. As such, they and the role they play in Habermas's writings deserve greater attention.

I will begin with a historical overview of how his account of social movements has evolved from the early writings *circa Toward a Rational Society* and the 1970s-era social theory of *Legitimation Crisis* to his mid-period masterpiece, *The Theory of Communicative Action*, to the more recent and mature political theory of *Between Facts and Norms*. The theoretical frameworks within which social movements appear seem to slowly change as his concern for the crisis of the welfare state cedes ground to an appreciation for the emancipatory potentials of civil society. This marks an overall movement within Habermas's intellectual biography away from the early Frankfurt School topos of "the administered society", with its threat of closure and pathology hanging ominously over potentially emancipatory movements, towards a more open, and American, emphasis on constitutional law as an evolving framework of normative commitments that receives and channels the protests of social movements, even setting aside space within the law to account for civil disobedience against it.

This "liberalization" of Habermas's analytical framework has allowed for the retrieval and expansion of his earliest political-philosophical project, that is, the public sphere, in the form of the twin political/moral philosophical projects of deliberative democracy and discourse ethics.[1] While I will explore some of these themes, particularly as they appear in *Between Facts and Norms*, I will focus on what at first appears to be only a minor theme in this symphonic movement: that is, the formation of social movements in the social lifeworld and the reciprocal intervention of these same movements in the spheres of official political and economic life. Not only are Habermas's thoughts on social movements interesting in their own right, but refracting our understanding of the changing role of the welfare state, civil society and democracy in Habermas's thought through the prism of his partial engagement with social movement theory will offer us a unique vantage point on the whole of that thought. By using social movements as our focal point, we can identify not only the sociological dimensions of Habermas's political theory, but the political dimensions of his social theory as well.

Youth revolt (*Toward a Rational Society*)

Habermas's initial engagement in the post-war politics of the Federal Republic reached a climax in the 1960s. The years 1967, 1968 and 1969 proved to serve as important turning points not only in West German political life, but in the intellectual development of the young critical theorist, who had published his first major work, *The Structural Transformation of the Public Sphere,* in 1962. In the wake of its publication, Habermas had become regarded as an intellectual leader of an increasingly radicalized cohort of German university students, a role that he was generally happy to play, for he saw in the students the possibility of making good upon a promised, but postponed, post-war democratization of the Federal German Republic. By Habermas's account, this process had been way-laid by a pervasive bureaucratic authoritarianism, cultural conservatism and social conformism that remained held over from the Nazi era. On the other hand, according to Habermas, the student generation of the 1960s, as the first generation to have grown up in a post-Nazi era, was not only liberated from the cultural provincialism that had given birth to Nazi extremism, but was also sharply aware of the discrepancy between the stated ideals of the newly democratized Federal Republic and its ossified reality.

Habermas believed that students had "become sensitive to the costs for individual development of a society dominated by competition for status and achievement and the bureaucratization of all regions of life" (TRS: 29). And in an argument to resurface in many later writings (particularly in TCA) he argued that "what is in question [for student radicals] is not the system's productivity and efficiency, but rather the way in which the system's achievements have taken on their own life and become independent of the needs of the people" (TRS: 28). Students therefore concluded that any attempt to change this situation through normal political channels (specifically the bureaucratized Social Democratic Party) was likely to conclude merely in integration and neutralization. Therefore, "protest must assume the form of provocation, of going beyond the legitimate rules of the game" (TRS: 26). Habermas concurred with this analysis, to a point.

As the decade progressed and confrontations between students and society intensified, students began to conceive of themselves as a revolutionary vanguard who, by their commitment to an immanently revolutionary praxis, would not only provide a decisive rupture with their parents' conformism, but also throw aside capitalism and imperialism in one fell swoop of radical democratic enthusiasm. It was here, at the point where the students believed themselves to be on the cusp of revolutionary change, and believed themselves its natural leaders, that Habermas registered his dissent. In June 1967, a mere day after having marched with students to protest the police shooting of unarmed student protester Benno Ohnesorg, Habermas warned students that their revolutionary "actionism" risked becoming a form of "Left Fascism" if their ambitions and confrontational tactics were not scaled back. At that point, Habermas was quickly written off by student leaders as a bourgeois sell-out whose support for the radical democratization of society extended only to theory and not to practice. Habermas protested at the time and later that his "two words" were not intended as denunciation but as a sympathetic critique, but the decisive rupture between past and future intended by the students had now emerged between them and their most sympathetic teachers, with figures like Habermas and Adorno made to stand as a convenient symbols of stuffy academic hypocrisy.

In the meantime, Habermas had presented students with five theses on the student movement (which later grew to six in published form), which he now termed a "phantom revolution".[2] Despite the polemical phraseology, however, Habermas registered his broad sympathy for and agreement with the goals of the student protesters, including the democratization of the university system and the re-politicization of the public sphere. He saluted the innovative character of student protest techniques for their ability to disrupt the facade of authoritarian society, creating incitements to democratization in the broader culture. Yet at the same time he chided students for their delusions of grandeur, for failing to realize that they represented not the oppressed masses of the world, but instead a privileged elite. In the tracts and slogans which sought a direct correspondence between student revolt and national liberation in the Third World, Habermas detected not only an unreconstructed Marxist–Leninist dogmatism, but a dangerous romanticism which allowed students to imagine the coming revolution as a total liberation from the machinery of capitalism, a leap from necessity into freedom manifested in the "actionism" of direct action and revolutionary praxis.

That Habermas found the romanticized Marxism of the "Great Refusal" unsound intellectually as well as politically should be of little surprise to any of his contemporary readers. Habermas would spend much of the following decade coming to terms with his own Marxist and Frankfurt School background, in the process dispensing entirely with both the labour theory of value as an analytical framework and with the revolutionary overthrow of social totality as a political strategy. It seems, in fact, that it was his encounter with the German student movement that in part prompted Habermas to clarify his ambivalent relationship to Marx and Marxism. Nevertheless, the student movement provided him with more than a negative foil in opposition to which he might divest himself of any revolutionary pretentions; even despite his criticisms, he retained the conviction that the student movement had a progressive impact and potential that extended beyond its own self-understanding. To some extent, his attitude is redolent of Kant's second-hand enthusiasm for the French Revolution; Kant believed the latter to be an irreversible world-historical event which could inspire a love for freedom in the minds of those who observed it from afar, even while its terroristic *dénouement* was to be abhorred and revolution in general to be guarded against as sin against legitimate constitutionalism. Similarly, in *Protestbewegung und Hochschulreform*, Habermas cited the potential long-term impact of the rise of "the New Sensibility" of post-materialist youth as possibly "the motive force of a long-term process of transformation that prevents foreseeable catastrophes on an international scale and makes possible a measure of emancipation domestically. This cannot be known, but *we can encourage it with caution*" (TRS: 48, emphasis added).

Cautious and qualified encouragement of the German student movement sets the standard for Habermas's response to anti-systemic revolts against state and economy, and thus to those groups of the 1970s and 1980s soon to be christened the "new social movements". In future writings, anti-nuclear, environmentalist, feminist, autonomist and various radical movements all pass, briefly if suggestively, before Habermas's critical eye, to be treated as one part pathological reaction to various rationality deficits and systemic crises, one part emancipatory alternative to said system and its crises, and one part dangerous throwback to anti-modern atavism – that is, "Left Fascism". Habermas's ambivalence is surely partly explained by his own preference for what he called in 1968 "radical reformism" (TRS: 49). What this meant at the time and subsequently, Habermas's own changing technical formulas aside, is a democratization of decision-making processes throughout society that nevertheless would not fundamentally disturb or endanger those key elements of modernity to which Habermas pledges an unqualified loyalty: political if not parliamentary democracy, human rights and moral universalism, the functional differentiation of society into autonomous spheres (including the definitive dislodging of state and economy from the lifeworld), the maintenance of communicative freedoms (including the autonomy of theory from practice) and ultimately the preservation of the public sphere as a realm of open argumentation where only the force of the better argument triumphs. As we will see, this last commitment is to be mobilized against not only the usual targets of economic and state power, but also against the unconstrained constituent power of *any* popular mobilization set on the radical transformation of social totality; which is to say, any social movement *not* content with accepting a self-limiting role in civil rather than political society.

Crisis of the welfare state (*Legitimation Crisis*)

However, the term *civil society* is conspicuously missing from Habermas's theoretical vocabulary of this period. Even the public sphere is largely absent from Habermas's writings *after* the publication of *The Structural Transformation of the Public Sphere* in 1962, and before 1992's *Between Facts and Norms*. This thirty-year gap in Habermas's theorizing concerning, if not necessarily democracy, then the critical role played within it by the public sphere is more understandable when considering the earlier work's main thesis that the classic bourgeois public sphere of the late eighteenth century had long since been paved over and occupied by forces of both corporate capitalism and the welfare state. In Habermas's mid-period writings, the public sphere remains dominated by corporate mass media and hierarchically organized political parties, for whom it serves as merely a raiding ground for the tribute of votes and market share and not as an independent sphere of critique and discussion.

The structural transformation of the public sphere at the hands of state and economy largely coincides, for Habermas, with the functionalist organization and self-understanding of society. In *Legitimation Crisis*, for example, Habermas writes of the historical supercession of liberal capitalism by "organized or state-regulated" capitalism. What distinguishes the latter from the former, apart from the rise of the corporation, is the intervention of the state in the economic process, on both demand and supply sides. Moreover, the modern welfare state intervenes not only on the side of capital, but as an autonomous broker of a peace accord between capital and labour. Political wage and price settlements, as directly negotiated by the three partners of postwar corporatism, thus "externalize" class conflict by refracting it into issues of fiscal and financial stability, as well as government spending on public programmes.

Politically speaking, the re-coupling of economic and political systems engenders a re-politicization of the economy, but ironically a depoliticization of the public sphere, as the administrative system itself withdraws many of its powers from all but the most perfunctory public scrutiny. Citizens are rendered passive in the process, and their energies redirected toward civil privatism – into career, leisure and consumption. Between civil privatism and public corporatism, there remains no space for either the public sphere or civil society as we currently understand it; that is, as a legally regulated but autonomous space of voluntary citizens' organizations, whose discourse and actions may target political institutions and issues, but remain independent of both the official political sphere and the corporate mass media. Instead, for Habermas of the 1970s and early 1980s, social movements remain the only organized heirs to the radical democratic aspirations of the political Enlightenment. On the other hand, Habermas's conceptual framework locates social movements within a functionalist environment where they are both the direct product of and direct contributors to steering crises in the administration of fully administered societies. This is why their very existence is a matter for both enthusiasm *and* caution for those who, like Habermas, hope for radical reformism but fear the return of fascism. Social movements, *circa* LC, operate at the fault line between psyche, culture and society, and thus their anarchic energies are capable of generating earthquakes of a magnitude great enough to unbalance social order as a whole. Thus the sentence that concludes 1968's "Technology and Science as 'Ideology'" that "in the long run ... student protest could permanently destroy this crumbling achievement ideology [i.e. status competition and possessive individualism], and thus bring down the already fragile legitimation basis of advanced capitalism" must be read as both a promise and as a threat (TRS: 128). That is, the promise of progressive social transformation heralded by the youth revolt of the 1960s also brought with it the attendant threat, still very real to someone of Habermas's generation, of social crisis and cultural counter-revolution.

Social pathology and social movements (*The Theory of Communicative Action*)

The Theory of Communicative Action's landmark contribution to social theory is specifically the notion that in the course of social evolution from primitive to traditional to modern societies, structures of political and economic power have become progressively uncoupled not only from each other, but from the common social lifeworld upon which they nevertheless depend. On Habermas's reading, the functional imperatives of the subsystems, which otherwise admit of no natural principle of limitation, inevitably burrow into the lifeworld itself, in a process that Habermas calls "the internal colonization of the lifeworld" (TCA 2: 332). Roughly, while the capitalist economy is hell-bent on commodifying every last corner of the social world, the welfare state is equally hell-bent on regulating and bureaucratizing not only the formal economy as such, but also those populations who are most disadvantaged by the structural inequalities of the capitalist labour market and the disruptive vicissitudes of the business cycle. In the process of taming the economic process, however, the welfare state finds itself intervening directly in the material reproduction of the lifeworld, bureaucratizing the lives of those it renders as clients and restricting their autonomy, even if in the name of social justice and equal opportunity. As a result of this two-pronged colonization process, subjects who may have once stood as citizens in relation to one another are instead locked into reified social roles as consumer or client.[3]

Moreover, since the internal colonization process reflects not only the unintended consequence of a skirmish between state and economy, but also a one-sided extension of strategic rationality and action at the expense of communicative rationality and action, it inevitably generates what Habermas now calls "social pathologies": a loss of meaning in the everyday lives and life histories of citizens transformed into clients and consumers, the resulting alienation of said clients and consumers from a social totality which they no longer understand, and a social dislocation (or "anomie") of individuals from each other. TCA, moreover, largely trades in LC's language of crisis for this revised language of social pathology; pathologies proliferate on the margins, but do not threaten the structural core, which, it now seems, is impregnable.

Nevertheless, even in TCA there are rumblings of dissent on precisely those margins where social pathologies tend to appear. Indeed, it is in respect of these pathologies, and their perceived causes in the internal colonization of the lifeworld, that the new social movements form and act. As in TRS, here the conflicts ignited by and formative of social movements are no longer related to the questions of material reproduction that motivated the labour movement (the "old" social movement par excellence), but rather "questions having to do with the grammar of forms of life", such as "quality of life, equal rights, individual self-realization, participation and human rights" (TCA 2: 392). Habermas's particular account of the new social movements thus dovetails nicely with his overall movement towards a "post-materialist" theory of society altogether, in which political and social conflicts are generated not by the relationship between labour and capital, but the relationship between the "institutionally unbound" communicative action of the lifeworld and the functional imperatives of the two subsystems taken together.

Not only are the issues aligned along a post-material axis, but the actors engaged in protest neither come from nor migrate to traditional social and political groupings (such as parties and unions). Instead, they arise from among the new post-war middle classes, and from youth and students in particular. These groups provide the membership pool for the feminist, environmentalist, anti-nuclear and various counter-cultural movements. These groups fight not for social justice and the rights of workers, but for autonomous social spaces free from the incursions of either economic or administrative systems.

However, Habermas makes an important, if polemical, distinction between those movements with emancipatory potentials and those that remain limited by their orientation towards resistance and withdrawal as such. The difference between emancipation and resistance itself turns on whether a movement is assertive in its desire to acquire and instantiate new legalized rights and freedoms, or "defensive" in its desire merely to protect currently held rights and freedoms from further subversion by functional imperatives. Feminism as a "struggle against patriarchal oppression and for the redemption of a promise that has long been anchored in the acknowledged universalistic foundations of morality and law" (i.e. the equality of the sexes) is specifially singled out as the only contemporary movement possessing emancipatory potential (TCA 2: 393). Habermas is much more ambivalent with regard to resistance movements, in a manner which bears further explanation.

For example, the positive aims of the sort of radicals whom Habermas associates with "defensive movements" range from the restoration of the natural environment to "the revitalization of possibilities for expression and communication that have been buried alive" by the process of internal colonization (TCA 2: 395). Strategically, such protests seek to create "counter-institutions" which "are intended to de-differentiate some parts of the formally organized domains of action, remove these from the clutches of the steering media, and return these 'liberated areas' to the action-coordinating mechanism of reaching understanding" (TCA 2: 396).

Given the way in which Habermas here interpolates the intentions of "resistance" movements with the terms of his own theory of communicative action, one might have expected an endorsement of their goals, however cautiously. However, Habermas remains cautious to the point of coolness here, and as earlier in his career, sees the spectre of fascism lurking at the edge of the frame. He says of the radical agenda of counter-institution and de-differentiation not only that it is unrealistic, but that the significance of said agenda:

> is obscured, both in the self-understanding of those involved and in the ideological imputations of their opponents, if the communicative rationality of cultural modernity is rashly equated with the functionalist rationality of self-maintaining economic and administrative action systems – that is, whenever the rationalization of the lifeworld is not carefully distinguished from the increasing complexity of the social system. (TCA 2: 396)

In other words, if activists wish to remain true to the radical *normative* heritage of the European Enlightenment, they must also respect the facts of social complexity and structural differentiation with which it has been associated historically. The judgement upon social movements thus remains similar to that formulated during the late 1960s, even if the theoretical framework in which this judgement is housed has expanded. TCA's treatment of social movements is set against the backdrop, not merely of the particular dynamics and struggles of the post-war welfare state, but capitalist modernity as such. Thus the above passage expresses not only Habermas's bottom line with regard to social movement radicalism, but also his ambivalence towards any social and political conflict, not only emergent at the border between lifeworld and system, but threatening to disturb this border, in *either* direction. If modernity is defined by the uncoupling of system and lifeworld, then whatever acts against this uncoupling thus appears to be necessarily anti-modern.

Indeed, the broader implication of the above passage is that Habermas becomes critical of resistance movements where they attempt to directly transform "concrete forms of life", rather than advance universalistic *claims* (made of the political system) concerning the formal status of citizens. That is, he equates the desire or intent to produce a direct structural transformation in everyday life with a particularist anti-modernism that is willing to "rashly" equate cultural modernity with functionalist rationality, and whose political programme culminates in the "de-differentiation" of "formally organized domains of activity". He maintains this rough equation between the desire to transform concrete living arrangements and cultural anti-modernism *even* when the former is sought after in order to "foster the revitalization of possibilities for expression and communication that have been buried alive" by internal colonization, or in order to "return these 'liberated areas' to the action-coordinating mechanism of reaching understanding".[4]

Civil society and the rediscovery of the public sphere (*Between Facts and Norms*)

Much changes in the eleven years between *The Theory of Communicative Action* and *Between Facts and Norms*. For example, if TCA placed social movements within the scope of a broad social-historical theory, and thus attributed to them potentials and perils of a similar scope, BFN locates them within a comparatively modest (for Habermas!) legal-political framework. The overall argument of BFN is that liberal constitutional regimes, composed both of law and civil society, function to mediate between the administrative imperatives of the system and the communicative needs of the lifeworld. This argument remains the most comprehensive articulation of several lines of thinking that Habermas developed through and beyond TCA, particularly discourse ethics and the discourse theory of democracy. Moreover, it has served as a platform on which to re-establish to prominence the public sphere, as both a social theoretical and normative concept. It thereby also serves to re-contextualize the place of social movements within a critical theory of society.

In BFN, Habermas has largely displaced Niklas Luhmann's systems theory with legal and moral theorizing of a neo-Kantian variety.[5] However, he does introduce, as a sort of compromise with empirical models of democratic government, Bernhard Peters's conception of the modern democratic state as a complex defined by a dualism between core and periphery, which are connected by "sluices" that allow information and decisions to travel back and forth between administration and environment. The core of society is, on this reading, composed of the administrative, judicial and parliamentary facets of government, which are then surrounded by a peripheral network of organizations that function either as customers, performing quasi-governmental coordination functions, or suppliers (of votes, of information) to the core. Obviously, this model does not correspond to any classical image of democracy as the tribune of popular will, since not only is the administrative core for the most part dominant with respect to its periphery, but the core is itself internally differentiated and organized only on a polyarchal basis as a constantly re-negotiated set of relations among formally autonomous powers and domains.

This might seem like an inauspicious sociological foundation on which to establish the normative project of deliberative democracy, even if it does correspond with the image of social complexity that has been a hallmark of Habermas's social theory since TCA.[6] Not the least of the problems Habermas sets for himself in reading Peters's model into his own is the question of how what he calls "a constitutionally regulated circulation of power" (i.e. the process of democratic will formation by which public opinion is converted into binding law via the generation of "communicative power" in the public sphere) can be reconciled with an image of politics that sanguinely assigns to the public a marginal role on the periphery (BFN: 327).

Yet it is precisely its *empirically* peripheral position relative to administrative power that allows Habermas to place the public sphere at the centre of a *normative* account of democracy with practical intent. Which is to say that the political potential of the public sphere rests not in its capacity to directly organize the people as an undivided whole, but rather in its capacity to act as a relay for anarchic communications flows among plural citizens: a relay that generates communicative power without submitting discussion and opinion to the functional machinations of actual administrative power. As a result of this indirect relation to power, the public sphere *qua* "supplier" can "give voice to social problems, make broad demands, articulate public interests or needs, and thus attempt to influence the political process more from normative points of view than from the standpoint of particular interests"

(BFN: 355). As generative of normative influence rather than of social power, the public sphere thus serves as a perfect institutionalization of the Kantian propensity, not only to separate out public orientations from private, but also to praise the revolution while simultaneously holding it at a distance. The people can have their cake, in this model, only because they themselves are never directly empowered to divvy and distribute it, or eat it whole, for that matter.

Habermas can only pull off this trick of placing the public sphere at the heart of a normative account of democracy while cordoning it off from any empirical analysis of how administrative power actually operates because, simultaneously with his rediscovery of the public sphere, he has discovered, in the wake of the self-limiting revolutions of 1989, the salience of civil society as a mediator between system and lifeworld. Of course, civil society had played an important supporting role in STPS, but there the concept was *largely* conceived in its classical *bourgeois* form, as an economic market of private individuals.[7] BFN is written in a context, however, in which the term "civil society" had since been reconceived to designate a space of associations and grassroots organizations which arise and develop independently of *both* the state and economy. Habermas is here specifically indebted to Jean Cohen and Andrew Arato's consideration of the intellectual history and future of civil society as a concept, a study itself greatly influenced by Habermas. As extrapolated by Cohen and Arato from a survey of both the material and intellectual history of the term, civil society "has become the indispensable terrain on which social actors assemble, organize, and mobilize" (Cohen & Arato 1994: 502). This is so not because civil society exists in abstraction from the state, in some sort of prelapsarian state of grace absent the corruptions of power and money, but rather because it subsists in the network of legal rights that are institutionalized in modern democratic constitutions. These basic civil and political rights (rights to free assembly and association, freedom of speech and expression, etc.) create a simultaneously legal and thus legally instituted social space in which nongovernmental and non-economic associations can operate free of repression. These legal and associational infrastructures "anchor the communication structures of the public sphere" and allow for the formation of genuine social movements outside the official political sphere (BFN: 366).

As such, civil society provides not only an institutionalized (but never institutional) space for the stabilization of the public sphere of communication flows from periphery to core, but also a public sphere in which social movements proper can form and act to influence the political sphere proper, yet without being drawn into it. On this reading, which

Habermas now reappropriates from Arato and Cohen, social movements "more or less spontaneously emergent" within civil society act with a dual orientation of influencing the political system and revitalizing the public sphere in which and towards which they act. Thus the dualistic distinction drawn in TCA between emancipatory and resistant movements gives way to a more nuanced appreciation of how movements realize (or attempt to realize) both emancipatory and resistant goals.

Moreover, Habermas now argues not only that extra-political actors in civil society are able to influence the political system in everyday policy matters, but that:

> at critical moments of accelerated history [i.e. brought on by some sort of crisis], these actors get the chance to *reverse* the normal circuits of communication in the political system and the public sphere [i.e. the normal circumstances whereby initiative comes from within and communication is dominated by the administrative system itself]. In this way they can shift the entire system's mode of problem solving. (BFN: 381)[8]

For example, acts of civil disobedience, which Habermas had recognized during the 1960s as necessary means by which to force issues onto the political agenda, can themselves now be seen precisely as *civil*: as acts that, although formally in violation of the law, display, by their symbolic, non-violent nature, a high fidelity to the normative ideals upheld by liberal democratic constitutions. Civil disobedience can therefore become not only a means of forcing confrontation, but also, as Habermas quotes Cohen and Arato, "a means for reasserting the link between civil and political society" when the latter has closed itself to the former.[9]

Habermas's treatment of social movements (and like phenomena) in BFN is thus a great deal more optimistic than in TCA or his writings of the late 1960s. In moving beyond the intractable conflict between system and lifeworld, Habermas is able to credit social movements with a constructive rather than merely oppositional role. By introducing into his social theory an explicitly normative theory of democracy with social-theoretical underpinnings, and thus moving away from a crisis model that had been shaped by a (yet) Marxian imaginary towards a pluralist understanding of the political process, Habermas is able to construe social movement activity as a part of this process, necessarily peripheral, but yet vital, to it and preserved in its autonomy from direct political administrative power. Finally, by housing the public sphere within the legal-associational framework of civil society, and construing social movements as agents of its revitalization whose disruptive activity itself catalyzes the constitutional norms that define civil society, Habermas is able to dispel much of the anxiety regarding social movement radicalism present in his earlier writings. If conflict no longer takes place at the border between lifeworld and system, but is contained within the legal framework of civil society as itself a buffer between the functional and communicative, then social conflict and social movements no longer need be haunted by the spectre of "Left Fascism".

A generally deflationary strategy is also at work in BFN to make social movements safe for (liberal, constitutional, representative) democracy by co-opting their radicalism for its own purposes. Rather than being burdened with the task of effecting the emancipatory transformation of society as a whole, social movements are conceived in BFN as participants in a dynamic process of democratization which itself extends far beyond the frequently sectarian concerns of the movements themselves. Moreover, the discourse theory of democracy posits a crucial role for the institutional apparatus of constitutional law and lawmaking, which feeds off the energy of uncontrolled debate in the public sphere and converts it, via the transformation of public opinion into influence and then into law, into a *generalized* communicative power.

The conceit of Habermas's discourse theory of democracy is thus that the opposition of systemic and anti-systemic forces may be exploited for the benefit of the democratic *ideal* that both presumably serve; that is, that the extremes can be played off against each other *in support of* the middle. For although any democratic state must function as a *system*, those discursive practices that constitute it as a *democratic* system must necessarily act as a simultaneous counter-force against its own systemic tendency to close down on discourse. Habermas contends in BFN that:

> the justification of civil disobedience relies on a *dynamic understanding* of the [liberal democratic] constitution as an unfinished project. From this long-term perspective, the constitutional state does not represent a finished structure but a delicate and sensitive – above all, fallible and revisable – enterprise, whose purpose is to realize the system of rights *anew* in changing circumstances, that is, to interpret the system of rights better, to institutionalize it more appropriately, and to draw out its contents *more radically*.
> (BFN: 384, emphasis added)

Conclusion

Just how radical is Habermas's account of democratic constitutionalism? Many critics, sympathetic and otherwise, have suggested that Habermas's gesture towards radical democracy is greatly compromised by his refusal fully to call into question the established parameters of "real-existing" liberal democracy, including the elitism of its representational structure, the capture of the state by social capital and the erosion of formal egalitarianism and civic engagement under pressure by the structural inequalities of a capitalist economy.[10]

However, concerning the matter at hand, let us first take note of the theoretical work that civil society, and social movements and civic associations operating within civil society, do in BFN's analysis. Habermas is often considered, and has proclaimed himself to be, a proponent of a proceduralist account of democratic politics, and is frequently linked in this to the so-called *ideal theory* school of political theory. However, Habermas's recognition of the necessarily contentious dynamic of public contestation as the real basis of deliberative democratic politics is what distinguishes his position from that of purely ideal theorists such as Rawls and Dworkin. For Habermas, the normative potential of democratic politics is released, *not* by a purely procedural mechanism fully incorporated into politics as a *system* of government, but as much by anti- or extra-systemic actors who lay siege to the system and force it to recognize their claims, and the public as a whole. Habermas puts a fine point on this when he claims at the end of the passage excerpted above, that it expresses "the perspective of citizens who are *actively engaged* in realizing the system of rights" (BFN: 384, emphasis added).

So, for Habermas, constitutional democracy depends not only on a routine system of checks and balances or procedural norms governing the making and implementation of law and so on, but on the active intervention of citizens into the political process, whose capability to *restore* the proper normative relationship among citizens, and between the citizen and the state, rests on their ability either to foster or at least exploit a *crisis* situation that impairs the political system's normal operating parameters. As the case of civil disobedience demonstrates, it may be necessary to *break the law* in order to *realize* its normative potential.

Yet, as we have also seen, Habermas's account allows for the fact that in the normal course of events, initiative lies not with civil society, nor even with parliaments and legislatures, but with senior members of government and the administrative bureaucracy, such that "issues will tend to start in, and be managed from the center, rather than following a spontaneous course originating in the periphery" (BFN: 380). It is only in crisis situations that social movements and civil society organizations obtain opportunities to influence the system's agenda. Yet Habermas does not, either in BFN or subsequent writings, provide much indication as to what the source or nature of such crises might be. The most he says in BFN is that they "can at most be explained historically", and are "symptomatic of the peculiar position of political systems as asymmetrically embedded in highly complex circulation processes" (BFN: 386). Whether this is to be understood as a late restatement of the crisis model of earlier writings (first elaborated in LC and carried over into TCA), or merely a loose end, it leaves the empirical significance of social movement activity for democratic governance unresolved.

Moreover, Habermas's continued insistence on the would-be self-imposed limitations on social movement activity corresponds too closely to his own normative-political preference set (for "radical reformism") to be taken as *simply* an analytical rendering of an empirical political dynamic. For despite the privileged place he grants to non-institutional actors outside of the formal political system, Habemas remains a proceduralist in the final (normative) instance, arguing that communicative power only becomes political power to the extent that "it affects the beliefs and decisions of *authorized* members of the political system" (BFN: 363). Politicians and administrators remain, for Habermas, the ultimate arbiters of the public good, because only their actions are governed by explicit and binding democratic *procedures*, which are understood to manifest themselves only in the relationship between the *strong* public sphere of representative legislatures, the political parties that occupy it, the administrative apparatus and the legal judiciary. Debate and dispute in the *weak* publics of the press and the street are "better suited for the 'struggle over needs' and their interpretation" than it is for the resolution of these conflicts (BFN: 314). Moreover, social movements, however important they may be to the instigation of public debate in civil society, are given strict limits that stem from the very legal structures that guarantee their rights. Using language reminiscent of his treatment of social movements from the late 1960s onwards, Habermas cautions ambitious social movements against harbouring "holistic aspirations to [create] a self-organizing society" via the seizure or even partial dismantling of the political system, which he claims possesses "a limited effectiveness in functionally differentiated societies" and in any event is "not a suitable medium for fostering emancipated forms of life" (BFN: 372).

So although the reintroduction of the public sphere and the discovery of a legal-associational civil society in BFN undoubtedly nuance and enrich Habermas's earlier stark dichotomization between lifeworld and system, providing the necessary conceptual space in which "anarchic" democratic politics can develop, it does not seem to alter fundamentally the judgement that Habermas had come to in the late 1960s: that radical reformism is only as radical as the predetermined alienation of administration from society will allow. Within the confines of this "self"-limitation that Habermas sets for his political theory, the public sphere optimally, maximally, serves as both a buffer and a relay between lifeworld and system, but has no latent potential to become a site of either direct democratic self-administration or even the devolution of power from the core to the periphery. And since the public sphere itself is *contained* within the legal-associational matrix of civil society, it only follows that the actors who move within it must themselves forswear also any "holistic demand for the political self-organization of a society". The promise of civil society for extra-institutional actors is a sort of contract: in exchange for constitutionally guaranteed freedoms of speech and assembly, and the prospect of exerting some fluctuating and unquantifiable influence on the political system, grassroots organizations and the movements that emerge from them accept as the legitimate limit of their actions the continued sovereignty of the very legal-administrative system that guarantees those rights, limits which can be breached in a merely symbolic fashion by means of peaceful civil disobedience. And while his support for civil disobedience means that Habermas does not go as far as Kant does to say "*Argue as much as you want and about what you want, but obey!*" Habermas retains from Kant not only the abstract radicalism of his moral universalism, but also the essentially conservative desire to separate public and private, theory and practice, for fear of their mutual corruption and contamination. Ultimately, for Habermas, power must remain in the core (even if under siege there) so that critique can flow freely in the periphery. For this reason, *Between Facts and Norms* might have been tentatively retitled (in translation) *Between Administration and Contention*.

Notes

1. See Chapters 7 and 6, respectively, in this volume.
2. For a discussion of Habermas's five (or six) theses on the student movement, see either Matuštík (2001: 35–64, 89–124) or Holub (1991: 78–105).
3. See also Chapter 4 in this volume.
4. What explains this curious impulse to strangle the resurgence of the very phenomenon to which Habermas's entire philosophy is dedicated? Why must communication be limited to universalistic claims-making in the public sphere? Why

is the impulse to challenge the one-sided rationalization of the lifeworld in daily praxis reproached as anti-modern? The answer, I believe, can be found in Habermas's fetishistic division between lifeworld and system, and the hypostatization of their uncoupling as a social-evolutionary necessity. If, for Habermas, the increasing reliance upon communicative action that is the hallmark of cultural modernity, and upon which the rationalization of the lifeworld depends, comes about *only when the lifeworld is released from the tasks of system-steering* by the emergence and splitting-off of the two subsystems then their autonomy is the price to be paid for the emergence of communicative rationality as such. Therefore, on this interpretation of social history, any attempt to de-differentiate the now differentiated sub-systems can only threaten to bring the whole arrangement down upon the head of communicative reason itself. If political or social movements were to attempt to re-integrate either administrative or economic steering functions directly into the lifeworld, its communicative infrastructure would buckle under the strain, and the rationalization of the lifeworld would stop or regress.

5. See also Chapters 8 and 10 in this volume.
6. In *The Philosophical Discourse of Modernity*, Habermas stresses the analytical insufficiency and political hazard of relying upon holistic models of society when attempting to envisage its democratization. Rather than looking for means by which direct or participatory modes of democracy could replace representative modes of the liberal-democratic state, or means by which the capture of the state itself could be used to effect a radical redistribution of wealth and/or power, Habermas seeks out processes by which and spaces within which the communicative rationality of public debate and deliberation could be converted into what he called "communicative power".
7. Obviously, the public sphere itself appears in STPS as transcending the private spheres of both the bourgeois family and bourgeois marketplace. That is, despite the fact that the emergence of the public sphere "was bound up with a complicated constellation of social preconditions", the nature of which were largely economic or at least determined by the broad *class* interests of the bourgeoisie, Habermas characteristically claims that the public sphere itself was both "ideology and simultaneously more than mere ideology" (STPS: 88). Thus, while the presumption that the classic bourgeois public sphere was open to all and egalitarian in its composition was a fiction, it was a fiction that simultaneously gave birth to critical public opinion as a utopian register of general interest which might transcend its narrow class origins. STPS charts the rise and fall of this delicate and ambivalent balancing act between "mere ideology" and something "more" that was the bourgeois public sphere. This analysis does not, however, present public sphere and civil society as synonymous terms, regardless of their joint bourgeois origins; in fact they differ precisely because of this joint origin. That is, civil society itself (i.e. "narrowly defined") remains, in STPS, essentially defined as the "realm of commodity exchange and social labour", *out of which the public sphere emerges* as an extra-economic realm of public opinion which allows the critical use of public reason (STPS: 30). Indeed, Habermas frequently makes use, in STPS, of the formulation, "the public sphere *of* civil society", to emphasize *both* the material-economic roots of the former in the latter, *and* its relative distinction therefrom.
8. As examples, he cites shifts in public opinion on matters such as nuclear energy, environmental protection, women's rights and multiculturalism, pointing out how: "Hardly any of these topics were *initially* brought up by exponents of

the state apparatus, large organizations, or functional systems. Instead they were broached by intellectuals, concerned citizens, radical professionals, self-proclaimed 'advocates', and the like. Moving in from this outermost periphery, such issues force their way into the newspapers and interested associations, clubs, professional organizations, academies and universities. They find forums, citizen initiatives, and other platforms before they catalyze the growth of social movements and new subcultures. The latter can in turn dramatize contributions, presenting them so effectively that mass media take up the matter ... Sometimes the support of sensational actions, mass protests, and incessant campaigning is required before an issue can make its way ... into the core of the political system and there receive formal consideration" (BFN: 381).

9. Quoted in BFN: 383. The original can be found in Cohen & Arato (1994: 587).
10. For example, William Scheuerman has argued persuasively that Habermas not only concedes too much ground to what Schueuerman calls the "defence model" of deliberative democracy, "in which democratic institutions exercise at best an attenuated check on market and administrative processes, and where deliberative publics most of the time tend to remain, as Habermas himself describes it, 'in dormancy'", but that he simply superimposes "the outlines of an *ambitious* radical democratic polity based on far-reaching social equality, and equipped with wide-ranging capacities for over-seeing bureaucratic and market mechanisms" overtop the defence model, covering over the discrepancy between the two with an abstract normative discourse (Scheuerman 2002: 63). See also Sitton (2003), and also Johnson (2006: 93–6).

TEN

Cosmopolitan democracy

Ciaran Cronin

Over the past two decades Jürgen Habermas has produced a body of writings on international law and politics which represent a major contribution to cosmopolitan political thought at the beginning of the twenty-first century.[1] These writings are highly diverse both in terms of the issues they address – ranging from the impacts of globalization on the welfare state, through developments in international law in the post-war period and European political integration, to reforms of the United Nations and a system of global governance for an emerging world society – and in terms of their style and intended audiences. Theoretically speaking, they involve the extension of the theories of modernization and of deliberative democracy that Habermas developed with reference to the nation-state to international and global relations.[2] Drawing on a universalistic conception of human rights and a corresponding interpretation of the development of international law, Habermas argues that a regime of "global governance without a world government" is both normatively required in response to the political challenges confronting the international community and that it could be realized through a constitutionalization of international law based on reforms of existing international institutions and regimes. The model of global governance he envisages would combine a *supranational* regime with responsibility for global peace and human rights policy with a *transnational* regime in which a global domestic policy would be negotiated and implemented. Nevertheless, Habermas insists that this multilayered system is not a blueprint for a world state: rather than *superseding* existing sovereign nation-states, it would instead *integrate* them into a new global constitutional framework.

Habermas's model of cosmopolitan democracy (IO: 186) combines normative and empirical considerations into a coherent political programme which can serve as a basis for critical reflection on international and global political questions. However, in its current form it does not constitute a fully worked-out theory. Thus any serious critical engagement with it must first attempt to bring its various elements into a sharper focus. The present chapter is intended as a contribution to this endeavour.

Rather than revisiting the theoretical underpinnings of Habermas's approach to cosmopolitan democracy addressed elsewhere in this volume, the first part of this chapter will focus on his analysis of globalization as leading to a "postnational constellation". This analysis lays down the empirical parameters for his extension of the deliberative theory of law and democracy to the international level based on a critical reading of Kant. The second part will examine the architecture of a possible future global political order as advocated by Habermas. It will address, first, his arguments for a system of supranational governance based on the constitutionalization of international law; second, his proposals concerning a global domestic policy to be negotiated and implemented at the transnational level; third, the implications of the resulting system of global governance for the nation-state and national sovereignty; and, fourth, his account of how the resulting tripartite model of global governance could acquire democratic legitimacy.

In conclusion, I will briefly examine some of the most pertinent critical challenges to Habermas's version of cosmopolitan democracy under three headings. First, does Habermas succeed in presenting a coherent alternative to competing realist and pluralist approaches to international relations, on the one hand, and to more ambitious models of cosmopolitanism, on the other? Second, Habermas assumes that national governments and their peoples would have to undergo "learning processes" through which their identities would acquire an additional cosmopolitan dimension. Can the relevant conceptions of political identity and social solidarity be convincingly extended to the global level? And, finally, Habermas insists that future global political institutions must enjoy democratic legitimacy in fundamentally the same sense as national constitutional systems. But does his deliberative conception of democratic legitimation have any application beyond the nation-state?

Kantian cosmopolitanism as a response to the postnational constellation

Habermas began to deal systematically with international political questions during the 1980s as the impacts of globalization on the nation-state and the international system were becoming a major focus of debates. He was particularly concerned that the growing influence of neo-liberal economic policy and ideology were sapping the utopian energies that had sustained constitutional democracy and the welfare state during the post-war period.[3] For Habermas this raised the question of whether a critical social theory commensurate with the emerging global constellation was still possible and whether the project of modernity was still viable as a politically directed process. At the latest, the events of 1989 made clear that the socially divisive effects of capitalism could no longer be contained effectively at the national level, even within the wealthy OECD (Organization for Economic Cooperation and Development) countries. What was required was the coordination of social and economic policy within larger political units, such as a future, politically integrated European Union and, ultimately, a new global political regime.

Not surprisingly, Habermas turned to Kant when reflecting on the normative implications of this shifting global constellation. With Kant he shares a commitment to enlightenment as a historical and political process and a conception of human rights as intrinsically *legal* or *juridical* rights that need to be institutionalized through a system of positive and coercive law.[4] Kant's cosmopolitan extension of classical social contract theory remains an important point of reference for thinkers such as Habermas who reject the "realist" assumption that international relations are not subject to the same normative requirements as domestic politics.

The postnational constellation

The "postnational constellation" is Habermas's term for the transformations that the international system of sovereign states is undergoing as a result of globalization. Whether they like it or not, he argues, nation-states are becoming integrated at a variety of levels – economic, political, cultural and environmental – into an increasingly interdependent world society. Globalization can be understood in Habermasian terms as a global phase of the "colonization" of the communicatively mediated reproduction of the "lifeworld" by "systemic" mechanisms of social coordination based on "steering media", in particular money and administrative power.[5] If these impersonal systemic forces are not brought back under effective political control, contemporary societies are in danger of losing their ability to govern themselves in accordance with requirements of justice and equality and, as a result, of succumbing to fatalism in the face of global operations of power that increasingly escape their control.

Of particular relevance in the present context is Habermas's analysis of the threat to democratic forms of political organization posed by economic globalization. The latter, he argues, is leading to a structural transformation of each of the four major historical functions fulfilled by the nation-state, namely its functions as an *administrative state* that funds its programmes through taxation revenue, as a *sovereign territorial state* that claims a monopoly over the legitimate means of violence, as a *national state* that depends on a shared national identity as a basis of social solidarity, and as a *constitutional state* and a *welfare state* whose legitimacy depends on guaranteeing the material preconditions of private and public autonomy (PNC: 62–5). In particular, by eroding the ability of the nation-state to guarantee its citizens the "fair value" of their civil rights, economic globalization raises the question of whether a genuinely *political* response is possible at all.

On the "deliberative" conception of democracy favoured by Habermas, the individual liberties and rights of political participation enshrined in democratic constitutions can confer legitimacy on the political system only if citizens enjoy the "fair value" of these rights. Formal guarantees of rights in law ("paper rights") are not sufficient; in addition no social groups may be deprived of the necessary resources to make active use of their liberties and to participate in the political process. But there is a fundamental tension between these requirements of deliberative democracy and capitalism as a system of economic organization. A capitalist economy obeys a logic of prices and competition that is not sensitive to the material requirements of democratic legitimation; thus unless the political system intervenes to "tame" its dynamics through market regulations and redistributive social programmes (to ensure, among other things, sufficient levels of welfare and of access to education and health care for all), the result will be the emergence of disadvantaged social groups and, at the extreme, of an "underclass" whose members lack adequate social resources to mobilize effectively in support of their viewpoints and interests. On Habermas's analysis, the welfare state, as it developed in the OECD countries during the post-war period, was designed to defuse this inherent conflict between capitalism and popular sovereignty. But this "social welfare compromise" is now being undermined by economic globalization, and the resulting threat to democratic legitimacy can be averted only through corresponding reforms of the international political system.

The globalization of production, labour and financial markets is undermining the bases of social solidarity in ways that overtax existing political institutions both at the national and the international levels. Faced with the increased international mobility of investment capital, for example, nation-states have been drawn into competition to secure jobs and investment, among other things, through competitive reductions in corporate tax rates and by shifting social costs onto employees. As the ability of national governments to extract revenue from their national economies diminishes, their scope for intervening in society through legal and political channels is being eroded. But, as we have seen, the democratic legitimacy of national governments depends on their ability to secure the material preconditions of citizens' enjoyment of their rights: unless citizenship also "pays off" in terms of social, ecological and cultural rights, democratic governments are in danger of losing legitimacy in the eyes of their subjects (PNC: 76–7). This smouldering crisis of democracy poses a similar issue for Habermas to the one raised by Karl Polanyi in his important study, *The Great Transformation* (2001), at the end of the Second World War: will the political response to the erosion of social solidarity assume a repressive form (as in pre-war fascism) or a progressive, democratic form (as in post-war social democracy)?[6] This time around, however, a progressive democratic option is no longer available within the limits of individual nation-states. The impacts of globalization cannot be cushioned through protectionist economic policies or Keynesianism within a single state, Habermas argues, because the emerging world society cannot be divided back up into its national segments. Instead democratic governments must try to regain their ability to intervene politically in society above the level of the nation-state through a *transnational* policy attuned to the dynamics of opening and closure of socially integrated lifeworlds analysed by Polanyi (PNC: 81–2).[7]

This analysis of economic globalization is emblematic of Habermas's view that globalization is leading to profound structural transformations of the international system of "sovereign" nation-states (DW: 176–9). The institutions and policies through which modern states have upheld their internal and external autonomy, such as standing armies, citizenship regulations and externalizing the environmental costs of industrialization and urbanization, are losing their effectiveness under the conditions of the postnational constellation. The kinds of military conflicts that have become prevalent in recent decades, for example, cannot be brought under control, let alone "won", by traditional armies, however technologically sophisticated these may be (as the United States has recently learnt to its cost in Iraq and Afghanistan).[8] The traditional mechanisms of passport controls, residence permits and forcible expulsion are looking increasingly ineffective, or, in their more aggressive and exclusionary forms, repressive, in the face of the waves of economic migrants in search of a decent standard of living for themselves and their families. And the threat of catastrophic climatic change due to deforestation and the burning of fossil fuels cannot be met effectively by national, or even regional, policies, since climate change knows no political boundaries. These developments have led to an explosion in the number of international regimes, nongovernmental organizations and multinational alliances in recent decades; yet international governance remains weakly institutionalized because it lacks a unifying legal framework through which collective political responses could be mobilized and legitimized. The question raised by the postnational constellation, therefore, is whether world society will continue to develop in an anarchic fashion or whether its most powerful members (which, for the foreseeable future, will remain nation-states and alliances of states) will be forced by circumstances, and possibly by political pressure from their own citizens and global public opinion, to cooperate in constructing global political institutions commensurate with these global challenges.

Kantian cosmopolitanism

The foregoing argument for cosmopolitan reforms of the international system must face essentially the same problems concerning national sovereignty as Kant wrestled with at the end of the eighteenth century. Kant's importance as a political thinker rests largely on his development of social contract theory into an international and cosmopolitan political theory. Kant interpreted the basic rights to freedom and equality of modern social contract theory as juridical rights that also call for binding forms of legal and political regulation above the level of the state. Thus "Kantian cosmopolitanism" is the view that the implementation of basic rights calls for a republican or democratic constitution not only within individual states but also at the international level (i.e. in relations between states) and at the cosmopolitan level (i.e. in relations between individuals, states and peoples everywhere in the world) (Kant 1996: 322 [Ak 8: 349]). In his most important political writings, however, Kant was concerned less with the theoretical justification of this cosmopolitan ideal than with the form in which it could be realized under the specific historical conditions of his time.[9] Thus, whereas Kant argued that the application of the social contract argument to international and cosmopolitan relations calls for a cosmopolitan republican constitution or a state of nations (*Völkerstaat*), he did not think that a global republic was possible at his time. The most that could be realized was a "surrogate" for this ideal which would take the form of a peaceful but *voluntary* alliance or league of nations (*Völkerbund*) which, he argues, could form around a single powerful republic and gradually attract new members. Although Kant's arguments for the voluntary alliance raise a number of difficult interpretive problems,[10] his main concern seems to have been that, whereas a world state would destroy the sovereignty of the member states, the proposed surrogate alliance would preserve their autonomy as separate states.

However, Habermas criticizes the proposed voluntary alliance as self-contradictory. For if we ask why its members would uphold the alliance in the absence of the threat of coercion, the only answer open to Kant would seem to be that they would do so out of a sense of moral obligation; but this contradicts his stipulation that a legal order can only regulate *external* relations between legal subjects and must not rely on their acting out of a sense of moral duty (IO: 168–70; see also Wood 1998: 67–8). Kant failed to resolve a latent tension between his cosmopolitan ideal and the reigning conception of state sovereignty of his time, Habermas contends, because he was unable to conceive of how states could accept the binding authority of cosmopolitan law without fatally compromising their sovereignty. His failure to challenge the dominant conception of state sovereignty as necessarily absolute and undivided may be understandable in the light of the international relations of his time. But by accepting the primacy of foreign over domestic policy, Kant allowed the autonomy of citizens (i.e. internal sovereignty) to be pre-empted by state sovereignty, so that the rights of individuals as world citizens shrank to the single right to be treated hospitably when visiting foreign countries.[11] If Kantian cosmopolitanism is to remain relevant for the contemporary world, therefore, we must abandon the classical conception of state sovereignty in favour of one which allows that certain functions of the state can be delegated to transnational or supranational institutions without undermining the autonomous political identity of states as such.

In recent writings Habermas has refined this criticism of Kant in ways that reveal an important underlying commonality in their views of the role of states in any future cosmopolitan order. Kant, Habermas argues, was misled by the examples of the American and French revolutions into conceptualizing the legal regulation of relations between states in terms of a *second* social contract. Just as individuals in the state of nature must submit to a common political authority, Kant assumed that states are also under an obligation to leave their "lawless condition" by creating a world state. However, this reiteration of the social contract argument obscures an important difference between the actual historical problems that democratic constitutions are supposed to address at the two levels. In the case of national constitutions, the problem was to subject *existing* absolutist or despotic regimes to constitutions in accordance with the principle of popular sovereignty; at the international level, by contrast, *prima facie* legitimate states *already exist* and the problem is how they could *first create* a higher-level political authority (DW: 123, 129ff.; BNR: 315–7).[12] The point is that, contrary to Kant's tacit assumption, there is no need for a revolution in political relations above the level of the state because legitimate political actors already exist who can cooperate in constructing a global constitutional system.

Habermas devotes particular attention to Kant's philosophy of history, because, in spite of its shortcomings, it proves to be surprisingly relevant to the contemporary global situation. Surveying the course of world history at the end of the eighteenth century, Kant identified three historical developments which he argued could promote a cosmopolitan condition in the long run, in spite of the unwillingness of the states and peoples of his time to embrace the idea. In the first place, he conjectured that republican constitutions would tend to foster international peace. As states acquired republican constitutions, wars between them would become less frequent because those who have to bear their costs, namely, the ordinary citizens, would gain increasing influence over foreign policy and would not permit wars to be conducted for questionable motives (1996: 323–4 [Ak 8: 350–1]). Against this Habermas objects that Kant failed to anticipate the rise of nationalism during the nineteenth century and its role in winning mass support for wars of national self-assertion, so that, far from being peaceful, the intervening two centuries have been blighted by wars of unprecedented scope and destructiveness. However, in the revised form of the "liberal" or "democratic" peace hypothesis, there is a considerable body of empirical evidence that tends to support Kant's conjecture. For, although democratic states have proven to be no less inclined to engage in wars with nondemocratic states, they are much less likely to go to war against other democratic states.[13] This tendency of democracy to promote peace could be explained in terms of the influence that Habermas's deliberative conception of democracy attributes to public opinion over the foreign policy of democratic states, which can lead over time to a transformation of their understanding of their role in the international arena. Through such communicatively mediated "learning processes" cosmopolitan norms can become part of the identities of democratic states, so that the latter come to see themselves as agents of international law and no longer as exclusively pursing their national self-interest in their foreign policy.

Kant's second major historical conjecture was that the growth in international trade would foster a "spirit of commerce" which would give all states an interest in preventing war and promoting peace, and thereby help to bring about a cosmopolitan condition over time (1996: 336–7 [Ak 8: 368]). Here, too, Kant remained a prisoner of his historical horizon, Habermas argues, because he failed to foresee that the rise of capitalism would promote class antagonism and conflicts of interest between different global regions. Nevertheless, the assumption that increasing economic interdependence can promote peaceful relations acquires renewed relevance within the postnational constellation. Thus, although economic globalization is accentuating the inequalities and divisions within global society and is undermining the material basis of state sovereignty, it also has the potential to foster an awareness of global interdependence and the recognition that the risks of the globalized economy call for fair and inclusive transnational regulatory regimes. Thus globalization could also stimulate collective learning processes that lead states and their populations to regard themselves as members of a global political order (DW: 176ff.).

The third conjecture of Kant's philosophy of history addressed by Habermas is the claim that the freedom of moral and political thinkers to make public use of their reason would have an enlightening influence on public policy over time, and thereby promote international peace. It would be easy to dismiss this conjecture with hindsight as naive, given that the influence of intellectuals in public spheres dominated by the mass media is tenuous at best and that intellectuals have proved to be enthusiastic advocates of belligerent ideologies during the nineteenth and twentieth centuries (IO: 171ff.; DW: 145–6). Nevertheless Habermas maintains that it is also open to an interpretation that lends it a surprising relevance for contemporary cosmopolitan thought. Globalization in the dimensions of culture, the media and electronic communication in general has gradually given rise to a global public sphere, in particular by making what used to be self-enclosed national public spheres "permeable" to inputs from other national spheres and from the international media. Although this emerging global public sphere remains vulnerable to subversion by images and "virtual realities", Habermas thinks that it could play a comparable role in shaping global public opinion to the one Kant attributed to the public use of reason.

These criticisms of Kant's philosophy of history nevertheless reveal a shared underlying commitment to a progressive view of history, which Habermas reinterprets in terms of his theory of communication. With regard to each of Kant's historical conjectures, he emphasizes the potential of public communication at both the national and international level to transform the self-understanding of nation-states. Thus whereas Kant had to appeal to "providence" to ground his progressive interpretation of human history, Habermas appeals to the power of communicative processes to transform social relations under conditions of expanding democracy.

Global governance without a world government

Although Habermas thinks that a system of cosmopolitan democracy is both a normative requirement and a practical possibility, he agrees with Kant that it should not take the form of a world government. Apart from the obvious practical objections to a world government – that it would be too remote, too unwieldy and too unresponsive to govern effectively, and that it would tend to become oppressive (or, in Kant's memorable phrase, to degenerate into a "soulless despotism") – it would also violate the claim of existing democratic states to be recognized as legitimate subjects of cosmopolitan law. As an alternative to world government, therefore, Habermas proposes a tripartite model of global governance in which the *national* level would retain a considerable degree of autonomy from the *transnational* and *supranational* levels, and all three levels would form integral parts of a unified constitutional system.

Supranational governance: a constitution for world society

Rather than a world government, the supranational level of Habermas's proposed model would assume the form of a world organization with responsibility for global human rights and peace policy, which could be brought about by a constitutionalization of international law involving reforms of the existing UN institutions. In arguing that modern law can play an analogous role in regulating and legitimizing political power beyond the state as it does within the state, Habermas relies on a conceptual distinction between *state* and *constitution*.[14] The legitimizing or rationalizing force of law, he argues, is not confined to the state but can also apply in principle to political institutions or networks that are not organized as states, such as the treaty-based organizations and regimes of the international system.[15] In fact, international law already fulfils the function of a constitution for world society in part, according to Habermas. During the post-war period, international law assumed characteristic features of national law and in the process shed its status as *soft law*. The UN Charter, the Nuremberg and Tokyo war crimes tribunals, and the role of the UN Security Council in authorizing humanitarian interventions and establishing war crimes tribunals after 1989 are part of a long-term trend towards a constitutionalization of international law at the level of human rights and peace policy.[16]

This analysis of international law as developing towards a constitution for world society assumes that the same republican conceptions of political justice and legitimacy that inform state constitutions also apply above the level of the state. Thus Habermas takes issue with accounts of international law and politics based on traditional liberal conception of the constitution as regulating the relations among social actors by setting mutual restrictions on their power. A corresponding liberal conception of the international rule of law would have to appeal to an extra-legal or pre-political conception of human rights as religious or metaphysical endowments, which would be at odds with the cultural and religious pluralism of world society. Habermas's republican constitutional model, by contrast, offers a "postmetaphysical" account of political legitimation based on the principle of the co-originality of the rule of law and popular sovereignty (DW: 139–40). According to this view, the legitimacy of a possible supranational constitutional system depends on its remaining connected to the *same* sources of democratic legitimation as state constitutions.

If this differentiation between state and constitution and the presumption in favour of a monistic, republican constitutional model are not to remain merely abstract requirements, however, Habermas needs to provide a credible programme of political reform through which they could find concrete institutional embodiment. This, he argues, could be achieved through suitable reforms of the UN. In a detailed discussion of a report presented by a UN high-level panel in 2004, he argues in "A Political Constitution for the Pluralist World Society?" that the reforms proposed by the panel represent a logical continuation of a commitment to the constitutionalization of international law implicit in the UN Charter (BNR: 336–7).[17] Among the reforms he endorses are proposals to regularize the role of the Security Council in authorizing armed interventions to protect human rights. In this way humanitarian interventions would acquire the character of police operations instead of a series of irregular – and shamefully inconsistent – military interventions (BNR: 339–40). In addition, Habermas believes that full recognition of the International Criminal Court would contribute to the development of international human rights law, exercise a judicial controlling (and hence legitimating) function with respect to the Security Council, strengthen the autonomy of the UN *vis-à-vis* the nation-states, and provide a point around which global public opinion concerning political crimes and unjust regimes could crystallize (BNR: 341–2).

These remarks yield a clear picture of the shape that the supranational tier of global governance would assume on Habermas's model. The world organization, in effect a reformed UN, would have chief responsibility for securing peace and guaranteeing human rights throughout the world, although in a constitutionally regulated division of labour with the nation-states and regional alliances. Its "legislative branch" would consist of a reformed General Assembly comprising delegates elected directly by world citizens in addition to representatives of national governments. It would administer peace and human rights policy in accordance with a constitution based on the UN Universal Declaration of Human Rights and the UN Charter. The "executive branch" of the world organization would consist primarily of a Security Council with responsibility for authorizing and organizing police operations to protect human rights. And the "judicial branch" would be based on a combination or amalgamation of the International Court of Justice and the International Criminal Court, and would function as the court of final appeal in cases involving human rights violations.

In none of these core areas of competence, however, would the world organization need to exercise the kind of authority typical of modern states. It would not have a standing army, since it would depend on the member states to supply it with the necessary means of coercion, nor would it need a cumbersome administrative apparatus to implement global policies. The task of the General Assembly would not be to implement global economic, environmental, security or social policies, but to establish the legal framework within which such policies could be negotiated at the transnational level. Moreover, the judicial branch of the world organization would be authorized to prosecute crimes against humanity only when national courts or other international tribunals were unable or unwilling to prosecute such crimes themselves. Here the legal system of the European Union provides a model for how a multi-level supranational constitutional system, in which each tier retains a large degree of legislative and adjudicative autonomy, could work at the global level.[18]

Transnational governance: a global domestic policy for world society

A major reason why the UN institutions do not exercise direct control over international economic policy, and why Habermas's reformed world organization would not do so either, is that economic policy involves controversial questions of distribution on which a broad international consensus is difficult to achieve, to say the least. The same holds true for other fields such as environmental policy, social policy and health and migration policy. Thus on Habermas's scheme the political challenges facing the international community in these areas would instead become the focus of a "global domestic policy" to be worked out through negotiation at a *transnational* level of global governance.

Here we must distinguish between *domain-specific networks* specializing in technical questions and a central *negotiation system* responsible for genuinely political tasks.[19] There already exists a multiplicity of formal and informal networks of government officials and experts from different fields who cooperate in establishing standards and regulations in such areas as communications and information exchange and combating epidemics and international terrorism. As long as such networks specialize in technical questions they can operate successfully within a relatively thin and informal regulatory framework. However, policy areas with major implications for distribution, such as international economic regulation, poverty reduction, development, or environmental, health and migration policy, involve genuinely *political* matters that cannot be dealt with effectively by networks of experts. At the same time, such issues do not admit of democratic regulation based on inclusive forms of political consultation geared to consensus because states and peoples with different histories and cultures, which in addition may be at different stages of social and economic development, are not likely to agree on a single set of policies. The political will to redistribute resources from "haves" to "have-nots" on a global scale, which is in effect what would be required, would call for much higher levels of social solidarity between donor and recipient countries, regions or peoples, than currently exist or, Habermas seems to assume, are likely to develop in the foreseeable future.

As an alternative to full-scale democratic deliberation and decision-making, therefore, he proposes that the required "global domestic policy" should be based on negotiated compromises among a limited number of major powers which take account of their interests and relative positions of power. Such a negotiation system would produce stable compromises only if there were a sufficient level of equilibrium among the parties; for example, none of the parties could be so powerful that they would not have a strong motivation to accept "fair" compromises, and none of them could be so weak that they could be permanently marginalized by the others. These kinds of considerations are reflected in Habermas's proposed design for the transnational negotiation system. It would involve a limited number of regional or continental regimes, or "global players", with mandates to negotiate for whole continents and with sufficient power to implement policies throughout large territories. They would have to be "strong enough to form shifting coalitions, to negotiate and implement binding compromises – above all on issues concerning the structure and boundary conditions of the global ecological and economic systems" (BNR: 325).

At present no major powers or regional alliances exist that would be capable of serving as a counterweight to the United States in such a system. Nevertheless Habermas thinks that the EU could play such a role, provided that it acquired an effective common foreign and security policy which would enable its members to speak with a single voice on global economic and security issues.[20] Habermas's proposals are more than a European intellectual's fantasies of future European global influence to rival that of the US. The recent evidence of the limits of American military and economic power, coupled with the inexorable march of China and India towards superpower status, mean that it is also in the interest of the US to act now to bind future rivals into a global regulatory regime such as the one Habermas proposes.

Although Habermas's model of a transnational negotiation system bears more than a passing resemblance to traditional notions of a "balance of powers", his global domestic policy is not simply great power politics in a new guise.[21] A crucial difference is that, under the supranational peace and human rights regime, the global players would lose the traditional right of sovereign states to go to war in pursuit of national interests. Moreover, global domestic policy would be based on *multilateral* negotiated agreements from which the parties could not simply withdraw when they considered them to be no longer in their national interest. Furthermore, the acceptance of the human rights regime by all of the negotiating parties would set limits on their ability to exploit their negotiation power, because it would prohibit patently immoral or unjust negotiation strategies. For example, the parties would have to accept responsibility for the externalities of their own policies, such as the risks to the global financial system of a lax national financial oversight regime, and not exploit them as a bargaining chip to exact concessions from other parties who would otherwise have to bear the brunt of these externalities.

The nation-state and the future of sovereignty

This model of global governance without a world government would have far-reaching implications for nation-states. Although the world would remain a world of sovereign nation-states, "sovereignty" would take on a new meaning in both its external aspect (recognition by the community of states) and its internal aspects (control over the legitimate means of violence and popular sovereignty).[22] As regards the former, the transition to the proposed global political regime would reinforce the development in international law away from the *principle of effectivity*, according to which a state is recognized as sovereign if it maintains law and order within its borders, towards the *principle of legitimacy*, whereby "outlaw" regimes would no longer be recognized by the community of states (BNR: 341).

As regards internal sovereignty, although states would retain control over the means of legitimate violence, they would be obliged to make these means available to the world organization when called upon to lend support to armed interventions and peacekeeping missions. Although Habermas does not discuss the implications of the latter change in detail, the majority of militarily weaker states would clearly lose a large degree of effective control over their armies, for they would not be in a position to resist the will of the world community if called upon to make their armed forces available to the Security Council. Moreover, as the envisaged regime of global governance became established, the resort to military violence in self-defence, the only legitimate case in which a country could claim a right to go to war on Habermas's model, would gradually lose its practical relevance. For in the face of the concerted force of the world community, outlaw states would cease to exist and international terrorist organizations or organized crime could be combated more effectively through regional or global security alliances than through unilateral military operations. Thus the envisaged system of global governance is, in effect, a plan for "perpetual peace", because the global police and security order would eventually render standing armies, and the associated bloated military budgets, pointless. At any rate, it seems likely that the locus of military power would shift from nation-states to the global players of the transnational level.

As regards the other dimension of internal sovereignty, namely popular sovereignty, by contrast, Habermas assumes that the envisaged global regime would expose non-democratic countries to pressure to reform their constitutions along democratic lines. In addition, existing democratic states would regain the political ability to shape their destinies at the transnational level (in most cases as members of regional multinational organizations, such as the EU), thereby counteracting the threat to democratic legitimacy posed by economic globalization. In the process, popular sovereignty and citizenship would acquire new cosmopolitan meanings (BNR: 314). Thus Habermas's model of global governance, like Kant's, should not be understood as the imposition of additional layers of transnational and supranational governance on a world of states that would remain largely unaltered. It would also involve processes of democratization at the national level through which citizenship and membership would acquire new cosmopolitan meanings.

Democratic legitimation

The role of democratization in Habermas's reflections brings us to a final important issue concerning the proposed system of global governance, namely, how its institutions could acquire democratic legitimacy. Although the account of legitimation is different for each level of governance, as we have seen Habermas insists that his model is a unitary or monistic one: that is, the same underlying conception of legitimacy is operative at all levels. Moreover, since nation-states would remain the primary units of political organization and democratic participation, governance above the national level would depend on legitimation from the national level (DW: 140–41).

As regards the *transnational* level, Habermas maintains that the negotiated regulations and regimes could "dispense with the familiar forms of legitimation through the will of an organized citizenry" (BNR: 316). Since the issues of global domestic policy cannot be the focus of a democratic consensus, the operative criterion of validity at this level would be the *fairness* of negotiated compromises rather than the democratic validity of norms of justice. Nevertheless even the negotiated agreements would acquire indirect democratic legitimacy from the democratic mandates of the global players who would negotiate on behalf of their citizens. This would assume in turn that debates concerning transnational political issues within national public arenas should become responsive to each other in ways that promote transparency concerning transnational policies.[23] Furthermore, the world organization would be responsible for establishing and implementing the legal framework within which the negotiation system operated. Thus in so far as its legislative institutions enjoyed democratic legitimacy this would also confer a degree of indirect democratic legitimacy on the transnational regulations and regimes.

The requirements of democratic legitimation at the *supranational* level would be relatively modest because the relevant issues are legal rather than political in nature.[24] Although world citizens would enjoy a form of democratic political participation through the election of representatives to the General Assembly, the deliberations of the world organization would acquire legitimacy in large part from being embedded in a global public sphere. In this respect, the decisions of the General Assembly could rely on a worldwide background consensus based on "the exemplary histories of proven democracies", on the one hand, and on a universalistic morality of justice with roots in all cultures, on the other (BNR: 343–4).

Taken together, this amounts to a "two-track" model of legitimation, with one path leading from cosmopolitan citizens via the international community of democratic states to the peace and human rights policy of the world organization, and a second, from national citizens via their nation-states (and regional alliances) to the transnational negotiation system, where both paths converge in the General Assembly of the world organization.[25] As the embodiment of the community of states and world citizens, the world organization would represent the *unity* of the global constitutional system and thus ensure the monistic character of the global constitutional system as a whole.[26]

This account of democratic legitimation assumes that all of the agents concerned – national citizens, national governments, the regional regimes and major powers, and the United Nations – would have to undergo changes in their identities, and hence in their understandings of their political roles and obligations. National citizens would have to overcome their nationalistic mindsets and come to view themselves as cosmopolitan citizens who have obligations to their fellow human beings throughout the world. Here Habermas's conception of constitutional patriotism provides an "abstract", procedural model of civic identity based on loyalty to constitutional principles, and hence one that can in principle be extended to constitutional orders beyond the nation-states.[27] Nation-states would have to learn to see themselves not only as defending their national interests but also as agents of the international community in the worldwide implementation of human rights. The emergence of a small group of global players would also call for learning processes on the part of the respective "players". Whereas the United States would have to overcome the temptation to impose its own conception of democracy unilaterally on a recalcitrant world and to abandon its policy of regional hegemony as formulated in the Monroe Doctrine, the EU would first need to equip itself with the necessary political competences to function effectively as a global player by adopting a constitution. Finally, the proposed reforms of the United Nations would also amount to a learning process through which the world body would finally make good on the commitment to the constitutionalization of international law implicit in its Charter (BNR: 312–13).

Towards a critical assessment

Given the scope and complexity of the issues involved, I cannot offer a detailed critical assessment of Habermas's writings on cosmopolitan democracy here. Instead I will conclude with a review of three interrelated sets of controversies prompted by Habermas's proposed architecture for the global political system.

Given that Habermas's position attempts to occupy an intermediate terrain between realism and more ambitious models of global governance, it is not surprising that it is open to criticisms concerning its internal coherence, as well as to challenges from the more extreme positions. The classical challengers to all forms of cosmopolitanism are so-called realist positions which view international relations as an anarchic system whose actors, that is, nation-states and, in particular, "great powers", are divided by unbridgeable cultural and historical differences which make durable agreements on collective political goals impossible. For realists, international relations are irreducibly competitive and international law cannot be based on anything more normatively robust than voluntary agreements; thus for realists, the idea of a "constitutionalization" of international law, which would involve major powers delegating part of their sovereignty to a supranational body, is simply at odds with the nature of the international system.

Habermas's chief engagement with the realist tradition takes the form of a protracted polemic against Carl Schmitt, the controversial German constitutional lawyer and political philosopher who defended a radical version of the realist position on international relations. Although the details of this polemic would take us far beyond the scope of the present discussion, one of Habermas's central criticisms of Schmitt is of broader relevance for his critical stance on realism in general. Although Schmitt claims to oppose a human rights-based international peace policy on the grounds that it would lead to a moralization of war and thereby justify total war against a demonized and dehumanized enemy, Habermas argues that he cannot justify even minimal moral constraints on the self-assertion of governments, since, according to his conception of "the political", such self-assertion constitutes the essence of politics.[28] This has wider relevance because realists generally assume that human rights set at least minimal constraints on all actors in the international system and thus can provide a basis for cooperation in combating outlaw states or criminal or terrorist groups that commit serious human rights violations or crimes against humanity. The problem, as Habermas sees it, is that they are not able to provide a coherent justification of the human rights principles on which they nevertheless rely. At best they can represent them as values with roots in different cultural or religious traditions, so that an "overlapping consensus" on human rights among peoples with different histories and cultures is conceivable. However, even granting the possibility of a global convergence on human rights principles, this would not provide a sufficient basis for global political cooperation unless the interpretation and implementation of human rights were tied to democratic procedures of deliberation and decision-making.[29] It is precisely this requirement that Habermas's approach is intended to satisfy by extending the principle of popular sovereignty to the global level.

Habermas's position is also open to challenge from more ambitious positions which argue that only a world government in a more substantive sense than he is willing to allow is either normatively required or empirically inevitable[30] in response to globalization. Suffice it to say that Habermas's intermediate position represents an attempt to combine two strategies for meeting the potentially fatal criticism that all schemes for world government are hopelessly unrealistic and that a world government would inevitably be remote, unrepresentative and ultimately oppressive. He seeks to defuse this kind of scepticism by building on already existing institutions at both the transnational and the supranational levels; thus the European Union serves him as a model for the formation of regional multinational federations that could function as global players in the negotiation system and, as we have seen, he provides a roadmap for reform of the UN into a supranational regime. This might be dubbed a "push from behind" aspect of his model. On the other hand, his proposals concerning the constitutionalization of international law "pull from in front" in that constitutionalization would serve as a catalyst for developments towards global political integration at other levels (such as the reform of the UN and fostering an effective global public opinion). A key strength of Habermas's approach, therefore, is the way it combines elements of gradualist and constitutional approaches into a unified model.

Whether this constitutes a viable alternative to other approaches to global governance, however, depends on its ability to meet potentially damaging criticisms of its internal coherence. Thus William Scheuerman, in particular, has argued in effect that the separate components of Habermas's model pull in opposing directions. Somewhat ironically in view of Habermas's hostility to realism, Scheuerman points out that the idea of a transnational negotiation system is indebted to the realist tradition because it is predicated on a kind of "balance of negotiation power" among the global players in question. At any rate, the role that Habermas assigns to a politically integrated European Union as a counterweight to the United States creates the impression that the proposed negotiation system would involve a kind of legally constrained power politics at the transnational level.[31] But is such a large dose of realism at the transnational level compatible with cosmopolitanism at the supranational level?

The underlying tension comes to the fore in the case of military policy. As we have seen, Habermas maintains that human rights and peace policy can be entrusted to a reformed General Assembly and Security Council because it concerns relatively uncontroversial human rights principles on which a global consensus could be reached; moreover, the world organization would not need a standing army of its own but could "borrow" the necessary military assets from its member states. However, the history of UN interventions and peacekeeping operations suggests that decisions concerning "humanitarian" interventions are highly controversial and that appeals to human rights are far from unproblematic. Moreover, from the perspective of the member states which would be expected to "lend" out their armies, decisions over when and where troops should be deployed and over who should bear the human and financial costs, are among the most controversial and divisive in contemporary democracies; thus it is not realistic to expect that governments, and especially those of the major powers such as the US or China, would voluntarily transfer command over their forces to a supranational organization. And, even assuming that the major powers were to buy into a system of pooling military resources, Habermas's model would probably lead to a concentration of control over military power at the level of regional alliances or global players. Thus, with regard to control over the means of legitimate violence – although not just this – there is a legitimate question concerning how much sovereignty the average nation-state would in fact enjoy in the reformed global political order.[32]

Habermas might respond that his model assumes that the self-understandings of states and their populations would undergo a transformation in the transition to the new global regime as a result of learning processes.[33] But this raises a second set of objections which focus on the coherence of his conceptions of political identity and social solidarity in general, and their cosmopolitan credentials in particular. Democratic forms of political organization, according to Habermas, depend on high levels of social solidarity because democratic citizens must be willing to adopt the standpoint of others in judging controversial political questions and, when necessary, they must be ready to make corresponding sacrifices. Although, historically speaking, these requirements were met in fledgling democracies by shared national identities, Habermas insists that the interdependence between nationalism and democracy was a contingent historical matter (IO: 105–27, 129–53). Against the claim that a shared national identity is a necessary precondition of democracy, he argues that, as democratic principles put down roots in a society, the role of patriotism founded on nationalism can be taken over by "constitutional patriotism". The assumption is that through participation in democratic discursive and deliberative procedures political attachment can shift over time from the nation conceived in ethnocultural terms to the values, norms and procedures enshrined in the constitution (IO: 117ff.).[34]

The fact that constitutional patriotism nevertheless remains rooted in the *national* political cultures and traditions of particular countries, however, has raised doubts concerning its suitability as a basis for *cosmopolitan* identification and solidarity, because countries with different democratic traditions would inevitably clash over their respective, culturally differentiated interpretations of democratic values and principles.[35] However, Habermas could respond that this objection does not take the *procedural* character of democracy on his deliberative conception seriously enough. The assumption is not that the world's diverse populations and their governments must already come to the process of constructing global institutions with a shared understanding of cosmopolitanism, but that a shared identity, and the associated mutual identification that could strengthen global solidarity, could develop in the process of constructing and implementing a constitution for world society.[36]

In fact, focusing too much on Habermas's institutional proposals could lead us to overlook the extent to which his model of global governance also revolves around a broadening and deepening of democracy at the local and national levels, because the learning processes to which he appeals would involve citizens putting pressure on their governments to cooperate in establishing trans- and supranational regimes. However, this raises in turn a question concerning the model of historical development that informs his proposals: his "philosophy of history", as it were. In particular, in reflecting on how a constitutionalization of international law could be achieved, Habermas proceeds from an idealized image of world society as composed of democratic nation-states. Only states with democratic political systems can be expected to demonstrate the necessary political will to cooperate in constructing a global political regime, since only democratic governments will feel pressure to adopt an understanding of themselves as agents of the world organization in enforcing human rights. But the fact that some of the most powerful and populous states in the world currently do not have democratic constitutions (e.g. China), or have only very fragile democratic institutions (e.g. Russia), or are riven by deep social divisions (e.g. India and Brazil), might suggest that Habermas's theory is utopian in a problematic sense. At any rate it must explain how developments towards the envisaged global regime could go hand-in-hand with a broadening and deepening of democracy in countries and regions where it does not yet exist, or has at best a tenuous foothold.

This brings us, finally, to the question of whether the deliberative model of democratic legitimation ultimately has any purchase above the national level. Habermas is committed to "monistic" conceptions of justice and legitimacy which hold that political authority, and the associated duties of citizens, must be founded on the same principles of human rights and popular sovereignty regardless of the level of governance in question. Thus, even though the competences of the supranational regime, and the corresponding duties of cosmopolitan citizens, would be strictly limited, they require essentially the same kind of democratic legitimation as national political systems. The two-track model of legitimation outlined above in the section "Democratic legitimation" is intended to explain how this is possible. Its success would depend, among other things, on the emergence of an influential global public opinion that would exert effective pressure on the world organization and the players in the transnational negotiation system. Habermas cites cases in which such a global public opinion has already found expression in worldwide protest movements, a recent example being the worldwide protests against the US invasion of Iraq in 2003. However, as Habermas acknowledges, until now a global public opinion has emerged only concerning specific issues and for limited periods of time, so that its long-term influence, and its resistance to ideological manipulation, is open to question. An enduring and influential global public opinion would have to be founded on a transnational public sphere, for only this would ensure that relevant issues would be addressed simultaneously, and in more or less the same terms, within the existing national public arenas. But even if the formidable obstacles to the realization of internationally networked, yet independent and critical, media and fora of public debate could be overcome,[37] the reliance on *impersonal* procedures and "circuits" of communication sustained by professional media and expert publics seems to reinforce a trend away from popular, participatory forms of democratic politics in Habermas's democratic theory which some critics find problematic. The fact that democratic legitimation above the national level would be chiefly *indirect* because it would be mediated by journalists and experts raises the question of what is left of *popular* sovereignty in Habermas's conception of cosmopolitan democracy.

This might lead us to wonder, in conclusion, whether the tension between human rights and popular sovereignty which Habermas claims neither classical liberalism (Hobbes, Locke) nor classical republicanism (Rousseau, Kant) manage to resolve, and which his deliberative theory of democracy is intended to overcome, does not break out again at the cosmopolitan level. It is striking that when discussing democratic institutions at the level of the state Habermas stresses the republican credentials of his procedural model, whereas when he discusses deliberation and decision-making in the future world organization he focuses almost exclusively on human rights and their interpretation.

Given that Habermas's theory of cosmopolitan democracy is still a work in progress, it is perhaps too early to draw any definitive conclusions on these and related criticisms. Only when the various elements of his approach have been developed in greater detail will we be in a position to offer a conclusive critical assessment of Habermas's cosmopolitanism as a response to the postnational constellation. There can be no doubt, however, that his work on international law and politics is an indispensable resource for critical reflection on current global political developments.

Notes

1. I am indebted to Barbara Fultner for detailed comments on and criticisms of earlier drafts of this chapter.
2. For relevant discussions in the present volume, see Chapter 4 (modernization, lifeworld vs. system), Chapter 7 (deliberative democracy), Chapter 8 (law) and Chapter 11 (modernization and postsecularism).
3. Habermas (1985b: 59–76); "The New Obscurity: The Crisis of the Welfare State and the Exhaustion of Utopian Energies" (1989a: 48–70). For an illuminating analysis of this phase in the development of Habermas's political thought (although one that ignores its cosmopolitan dimension) see Specter (2009).
4. For a discussion of Habermas's discourse theory of law see this volume, Chapter 8.
5. On Habermas's theory of modernization as a process of the colonization of the "lifeworld" by the "system" see this volume, Chapter 4.
6. Habermas's analysis of globalization as involving the colonization of the lifeworld by economic rationality is deeply indebted to Polanyi's historical account of successive waves of capitalist modernization which led to "social openings"

(i.e. the radical disruption of established forms of social reproduction through market mechanisms) that necessitated compensatory "political closures" in order to protect the integrity of social forms of life.

7. See also, among numerous other discussions, Habermas, "Does Europe Need a Constitution?" (2006: 94ff.).
8. On transformations in warfare in recent decades see, for example, Kaldor (2006); Shaw (2005).
9. This is the central concern of his most celebrated political work, "Toward Perpetual Peace" (1996).
10. In a world state, he argues, the individual member states would be fused into a single nation and as a result lose their identities as individual nations (1996: 326, Ak 8: 354); furthermore states that already have lawful internal constitutions are not subject to external coercion and hence cannot be forced to submit to a higher political authority (*ibid.*: 327, Ak 8: 356); and in any case states are unwilling to accept the idea of a cosmopolitan republic because it conflicts with their understanding of their rights (*ibid.*: 328, Ak 8: 357). For a perceptive account of interpretive problems posed by this essay see Wood (1998).
11. Kant (1996: 328–31 [Ak 8: 357–60]). See DW: 127–9. This also prevented Kant from conceiving of war *itself* as a crime; thus Kant's politics of peace deals exclusively with restrictions on the *conduct* of war.
12. See also the rebuttal of Thomas Nagel's conceptual objections to the idea of a democratic world constitution without a state in Habermas, "The Constitutionalization of International Law and the Legitimation Problems of a Constitution for World Society" (2009a: 118–9).
13. The democratic peace hypothesis is difficult to prove conclusively because, among other things, democracy is an exacting normative ideal and it is impossible to specify in uncontroversial ways what empirical criteria a country must fulfil in order to count as "democratic" in the relevant sense; for a sceptical view see, for example, Archibugi (2000: 142–3). Nevertheless, it is widely accepted that there are no clear historical examples of two democratic states going to war against one another. For a contemporary assessment of the "liberal" version of Kant's conjecture, see Doyle (1983).
14. Habermas follows Rousseau and Kant in viewing modern law as not simply the *medium* through which political power is exercised but as the institution through which political power is "tamed" and "rationalized" in constitutional democracies. Indeed, he argues further that political power as a system of binding authority is *constituted* by law, since it is only in the medium of law that political power can be organized as a rule-governed system of behavioural expectations, and law provides a resource of justice through which political power can be legitimized; conversely, political power, in the guise of the sanctioning power of the state, endows law with the necessary means of coercion for its implementation. On the relation between political power and law see BFN: 133–51.
15. DW: 131–2; and Habermas, "The Constitutionalization of International Law and the Legitimation Problems of a Constitution for World Society" (2009a: 112–6). See also Scheuerman (2008a: 137–9); Brunkhorst (2008: 494ff.).
16. DW: 147ff.; BNR: 335ff.; Habermas, "The Constitutionalization of International Law and the Legitimation Problems of a Constitution for World Society" (2009a: 109ff.).
17. For Habermas's most extensive treatment of the UN reform agenda see BNR: 334ff. For the UN reform proposals see United Nations (2004).

18. On EU law as a constitutional system see MacCormick (1993); Grimm (1995); Brunkhorst (2006).
19. BNR: 323–4; Habermas, "The Constitutionalization of International Law and the Legitimation Problems of a Constitution for World Society" (2009a: 113–14).
20. Thus Habermas has been a vocal advocate of the initiatives to lend the EU a constitution, and thereby establish a formal legal framework for further European political integration. For two representative discussions among others see Habermas, "Does Europe Need a Constitution?" (2006) and "European Politics at an Impasse: A Plea for a Politics of Graduated Integration" (2009a: 78–105).
21. Habermas, "The Constitutionalization of International Law and the Legitimation Problems of a Constitution for World Society" (2009a: 125–6).
22. On the external and internal aspects of sovereignty see Maus (2006: 465).
23. Habermas, "The Constitutionalization of International Law and the Legitimation Problems of a Constitution for World Society" (2009a: 126).
24. They turn on the legal elaboration of the meaning of human rights; see BNR: 342–3.
25. Habermas, "The Constitutionalization of International Law and the Legitimation Problems of a Constitution for World Society" (2009a: 118).
26. *Ibid.*, 119–20.
27. *Ibid.*, 128–9. For an interpretation of constitutional patriotism as based on a procedural conception of political identity see Cronin (2003).
28. See Schmitt (1996). According to Habermas, a consistent application of Schmitt's notorious "friend/foe" distinction would lead to the suppression of political opponents as enemies in the domestic sphere and to wars of annihilation against those foreign countries deemed "enemies" by the official state ideology (a fact that explains Schmitt's enthusiastic support for National Socialism); DW: 187ff.
29. This is what underlies Habermas's objections, on the one hand, to philosophical positions, such as those of John Rawls and Thomas Nagel, which argue that the requirements of justice beyond the state are much weaker than duties towards fellow-citizens, and, on the other, to contemporary versions of realism, such as Amitai Etzioni's model of "semi-empire" or Anne-Marie Slaughter's model of "disaggregated sovereignty", which agree that globalization necessitates reforms of the international system but argue that these must be based on extensions of existing intergovernmental networks. See Rawls (1999); Nagel (2005); Etzioni (2002); Slaughter (2004).
30. See, respectively, Lafont (2008) and Wendt (2003).
31. See Scheuerman (2008a: 140ff.). Elsewhere Scheuerman argues that Habermas does insufficient justice to the realist tradition which, at least as represented by Hans Morgenthau, is less wedded to an anti-reformist, conservative position on international relations than Habermas assumes; see Scheuerman (2008c).
32. For an argument that Habermas's supranational regime would have to have more pronounced state-like characteristics in order to fulfil the tasks Habermas assigns it see Scheuerman (2008b).
33. For a critique of the assumption that individual learning through participation in discursive democratic procedures can serve as a conduit for societal learning see Eder (1999: 197ff.),
34. On constitutional patriotism see Cronin (2003) and Müller (2007).
35. See, in particular, Fine & Smith (2003: 470–73).
36. On the associated conception of a constitutional order as a project that unfolds over time, see Cronin (2006).

37. In a recent essay Habermas has argued that empirical research on the media tends to support the possibility of a transnational public sphere: see "Political Communication in Media Society: Does Democracy still Have an Epistemic Dimension? The Impact of Normative Theory on Empirical Research" (2009a: 138–83).

ELEVEN

Rationalization, modernity and secularization

Eduardo Mendieta

The question of religion is at the centre of not just sociology and philosophy, but also political theory. With respect to sociology, it can be said that modern sociology emerged precisely through an attempt to make sense of how social order was forged from a religiously sanctioned social and political matrix, and how in turn religion itself had been sublimated and transcended through the development of profane structures of subjective, interpersonal and worldly interaction. At the heart of sociology is the notion that the modern social order emerged through the dual processes of privatization of religion and the disenchantment of a world that had been rendered profane and thus both knowable and manipulable by humans. For Émile Durkheim and Max Weber, social solidarity takes the place of religion, and an ethos of frugality and industry becomes a secular version of religious orientations and practices. For most social theorists after Marx, Durkheim and Weber, the modern social order is predicated on the secularization of both the social and natural worlds that entailed and anticipated the eventual withering of religion. With respect to philosophy, it can be said that there has been no philosopher who has not grappled with the question of the dependence of philosophy on religious notions. From Plato through Derrida, and of course up to Habermas, the question has been posed in terms of the possibility of a dialogue, or subterranean co-dependence, between Athens and Jerusalem, where each is a metonym for reason and faith respectively. One of the distinctive aspects of the Western philosophical tradition is precisely this millennial dialogue between faith and reason. Even as sociology anticipated the eventual abolition of religion, philosophy continues to have an ever intense dialogue with religion and theology. With respect to political theory, religion has been and continues to be a major point of reference. There is no theory of the state that does not address the ways in which political power emerged through the secularization of religious institutions. As with Plato's *Republic*, which formulated the need of what we now call a "civil religion" for the stabilization of the social order, so with Thomas Hobbes, Jean-Jacques Rousseau, John Locke, as well as G. W. F. Hegel and Immanuel Kant, who all linked the possibility of an autonomous political order to the separation between church and state, the privatization of religion, and the development of institutions that made space for the fact of religious pluralism.

The modern state rose out of the ashes of the religious wars and yet it remains uncomfortably dependent on the motivational resources that are renewed within churches and faiths (BNR). Yet, it is the negotiation of the dependence on and autonomy of the state from religion that makes of religion a ceaseless source of preoccupation for political theory, as John Rawls's (2009) work illustrates most recently. In short, how secularization is conceived in relation to the social order, the sources of normative concepts and the very foundations and limits of political power, discloses strikingly and pointedly how social evolution is conceptualized. Alternatively, secularization theory becomes a seismograph that registers the links between rationalization and the evolution of society, and with them, personality structures and ever more transparent social institutions of political self-legislation. At play, then, are descriptions, theoretical models and, expectedly, ideologies.

For this reason secularization has to be understood in at least three ways: first, as the description of a historical process that names precisely the separation of the state from the church that took place in Europe and the Americas between the sixteenth and eighteenth centuries; second, as a theoretical model that normatively links the secularization of the social order to a process of rationalization, which in turn is conceived as a process of modernization; and third, as a particular ideological formation that derides those societies that are thought not to have undergone rationalization and modernization as results of secularization, and which simultaneously assumes certain social formations to have achieved the highest stage of the secularization. In this third sense, we can talk about secularization as secularism, that is, as an invidious and differential naming that places societies in a temporal sequence of more or less rationalization and modernization. As we examine these three different senses of secularization, we can note the connections between rationalization and modernization and recognize that one of the central tenets of Western sociological theory has been to tie intimately the rationalization of the social order to its secularization in such a way that a society only merits being called modern if its social structure has been secularized. Modernity, as a particular epochal noun that names a type of social order based on rationality and self-reflexivity, is to be conceived as the telos of secularization. Modernity, indeed, becomes the temporal and rational telos of all social order. At the same time, we note how rationalization is conceived as the profanation of both the social and natural worlds. There is no cognitive and social progress without the disenchantment and de-sacralization of the worlds through which we move as secular and lay social agents.

The centrality of religion to social theory in general and philosophy in particular explains why Jürgen Habermas has dealt with it in all of his work in both substantive and creative ways from the beginning; it has been a constant theme in Habermas's philosophical, sociological and, more recently, political-philosophical work.[1] Indeed, religion can be used as a lens through which to glimpse both the coherence and transformation of his distinctive theories of social development and his rethinking of a philosophy of reason as a theory of social rationalization. In this chapter, I will rely on the periodization of Habermas's intellectual itinerary in terms of four periods, as was elaborated in the introduction to this book. Each period, furthermore, will be referred to Habermas's evolving views and conceptualization of religion. Before, however, I discuss how religion was treated differently during each stage, I want to provide a brief overview of two treatments of religion that were determining for the early Frankfurt School. Such a discussion is necessary not just because many of the key figures of the Frankfurt School dealt with religion substantively, but because these views provided the background against which Habermas's own views were developed. In fact, there are serious continuities and discontinuities from the first generation to Habermas's own take on religion. The chapter will conclude with an analysis of Habermas's development of what he calls a "postsecular" self-understanding of modern societies, which is tied to a rethinking of the traditional tethering of rationalization to modernization, and these in turn to secularization. I will defend the thesis that Habermas's work has undergone serious modifications and that these changes are tied to how he has conceptualized religion. In tandem, I will defend the claim that Habermas's work must be placed along with that of Bloch, Adorno, Benjamin and Horkheimer as it concerns the tradition's treatment of religion, in this tradition's distinctive way, and that, more specifically, Habermas's work, like that of Durkheim, Weber, Parsons and Luhmann, offers an alternative way to rethink secularization that rejects Western social theory's Eurocentrism and that opens itself ecumenically and with a cosmopolitan intent to the different religious faiths of the world in a parsimonious and respectful way.

Religion as critique

"The Frankfurt School" is an eponym for the Institute for Social Research that had been established in the German city of Frankfurt am Main by a wealthy grain merchant. The aims of the institute were to engage in empirical and interdisciplinary research on the conditions of the working class and to aid with the edition of Karl Marx and Friedrich Engels's complete works.[2] The director of the institute was also appointed as a professor at Frankfurt's Goethe University. The institute thus had a quasi-academic, quasi-independent status. From the outset, however, the members of the institute thought of themselves as socialists in the broadest sense of the term, but also as "Marxists" in a non-doctrinaire sense. In the 1920s, partly in response to the failures of the socialist revolution to materialize in the industrially advanced countries of Europe, namely Germany, France and England, and partly in response to the triumph of the Russian revolution, many sympathizers undertook the task of rethinking, actualizing and critiquing from within Marxism. This general movement of the self-critique of Marxism was called "Western Marxism". The members of the Frankfurt School were Western Marxists. What makes this movement cohesive is the application of Marxist methods to Marxism itself, that is, if ideas reflect both particular configurations of modes of production and social relations, then Marxism itself has to be historicized and "updated". This "update" took the form of a philosophical reflection on the philosophical assumptions of Marxism itself. Western Marxism, in short, sought to engage in a critical self-reflection of the fundamental philosophical tenets and assumptions of Marxism as a philosophical method.

Nothing expresses the Frankfurt School's relationship to both Marxism in general and Western Marxism in particular as clearly as Adorno's first line from *Negative Dialectics*: "Philosophy, which once seemed obsolete, lives on because the moment to realize it was missed" (1983: 3). Here, Adorno is inverting Karl Marx's famous eleventh thesis on Feuerbach: "The philosophers have only *interpreted* the world, in various ways; the point is to *change* it" (1992: 423). The world was to be transformed by having philosophy realize itself. But since we failed to change the world, philosophy remained unrealized. Whereas philosophy was seen by Karl Marx as a practical tool of the proletariat for the transformation of the world, for Adorno philosophy takes on a non-instrumental character; so long as philosophy remains autonomous from immediate political and practical aims, it can do its work: to prefigure a transformed world.

In addition to Western Marxism, another factor determined the critical identity of the first generation of Frankfurt School thinkers, namely the fact that they were almost all assimilated German European Jews (Löwy 1992). The most immediate consequence of their being Jews was that as soon as the National Socialist Party took power in Germany, most of them had to go into exile. Thus most of their work was to be produced in exile in England and eventually in the US. Their Jewish, albeit secular, background, however, made them particularly sensitive to questions of the relationship between religious motifs and philosophical concepts. The contributions to the study of religion by various members of the Frankfurt School are extensive and an overview of their collective achievement is beyond the scope of this chapter.[3] For our purposes, however, it is important to indicate two key figures in Habermas's own philosophical development: Ernst Bloch and Walter Benjamin. These two figures are singled out because in many ways they exemplify the conceptual extremes between which Habermas seeks to negotiate a middle path.

While Ernst Bloch was not strictly a member of the Institute for Social Research, he is one of the philosophers who had the most intense and enduring impact on the intellectual formation of the first generation of the Frankfurt School. Bloch is arguably one of the most distinct and representative figures of that large and amorphous group of Western Marxists who set out to re-philosophize Marxism. Bloch also developed an extremely original style of writing and articulating his ideas, one that can be called "philosophical expressionism". This style was already articulated in his *Spirit of Utopia*, a book written shortly after the First World War, and republished in an expanded edition in 1923. Here Bloch offers the basic elements of his philosophy of hope, his re-articulation of Marxism with Jewish messianism, and the lineaments of an ontological phenomenology of the human being's fundamental openness. *The Spirit of Utopia* was in fact a manifesto that proclaimed the need to rethink Marxism not simply as a philosophy of revolution, but also as a philosophy that is nourished and informed by utopian dreams that lay latent and preserved in different cultural configurations: art, music, painting, literature. Historical materialism is at the service of the process of the translation, elucidation, extraction and realization of the many yearnings, hopes, dreams that have sedimented, crystallized and congealed in the different cultural productions of humans.

All culture is not mere ideology, proclaims Bloch, and even as ideology, culture points, either negatively or positively, towards a future in which humans can stand fully upright.

What Marx said about religion in his introduction to the "Critique of Hegel's Philosophy of Right" (1843–4) was generalized by Bloch. Marx wrote:

> *Religious* suffering is at one and the same time the *expression* of real suffering and a protest against real suffering. Religion is the sigh of the oppressed creature, the heart of a heartless world and the soul of soulless conditions. It is the *opium* of the people. The abolition of religion as the *illusory* happiness of the people is the demand for their *real* happiness. To call on them to give up their illusion about their condition is to *call on them to give up a condition that requires illusions*. The critique of religion is therefore in *embryo* the *criticism of that vale of tears* of which religion is the *halo*. Criticism has plucked the imaginary flower on the chain not in order that man shall continue to bear the chain without fantasy or consolation but so that he shall throw off the chain and pluck the living flower. (1992: 244)

Every cultural production and formation is a reservoir, a compendium, an encyclopedia of humanity's illusions, as well as the expression of their sigh of distress and suffering. For Bloch, in contrast to Feuerbach and even Marx, the transcendent, that which is posited in the future, that to which all critique aims, is already immanent in history. The radical otherness of the Christian God is not a transcendent and transmundane otherness. This otherness is latent and operative in the very materiality of culture. As against a salvation or saviour that irrupts from without history, from a transcendent beyond, emancipation is operative in the profane world. God, as the name for what Bloch called *Mannesalter*, the coming of age or accomplished maturity of the human, is at work in history (2000: 266). If for Feuerbach and Marx God is the figure of alienated humanity, for Bloch God is the name for a potency and force already latent and at work in history. In a phrase, one that will be echoed by Habermas, there is transcendence, but only from within: "Hope alone is what we want, and thought serves hope, hope is its only space, its semantic content and its object scattered into every part of the world, hidden in the darkness of the lived moment, promised in the shape of the absolute question" (*ibid.*: 276). Theodicy is the name we give to this absolute question: why do we suffer? Why do we crouch in the darkness of uncertainty crying after a redeeming God? Philosophy's goal is to rescue and decipher the "semantic" contents scattered through the ruins and objects of human culture.

It was precisely this kind of positive orientation towards religion in particular and culture in general that allowed Bloch to engage in a critical manner with the manipulation of cultural imagery and illusions by national socialists. In what turned out to be a prophetic work, *Heritage of Our Times*, published in 1935, Bloch offered a trenchant critique of the uses of religion and mythologies by the Nazis (1991). The blunt communist rejection of popular culture turned out to be both short-sighted and above all self-defeating, for it prevented socialists and communists from addressing the dreams, hopes and language of the German working classes. Social reality is always shot through with what Bloch called non-contemporaneous "impulses and reserves" that are preserved and that remain latent in culture that may condition in subterranean ways our times. Critical thinking has to be attuned to their unresolved potential. Critical thought takes a stance against present oppression while being attentive to what remains non-contemporaneous in society:

> The foundation of the non-contemporaneous contradiction is the unfulfilled fairytale of the good old times, the unsolved myth of dark ancient being or of nature; there is here, in places, not merely a past which is not past in class terms, but also a past which is not yet wholly discharged in material terms. (*ibid.*: 112)

A critical transformation of Marxism betrays itself when it does not appropriate both the promised dreamed in past times and the material dimension of those contradictions that remain operative in our time.

Almost on the opposite of the theological spectrum, from transcendence from within to transcendence from without, Walter Benjamin has remained a fascinating though tragic figure, and the one who provided Habermas with the occasion to formulate what he called "rescuing critique" (1983: 129). Like Bloch, Benjamin also wanted to wrest from social reality the elements that would point the way out from alienation and exploitation. Like no one else, Benjamin sought to develop a materialist aesthetic that would decipher in the commodity those contradictions that could unleash revolutionary potentials. It was for this reason that Benjamin paid such close attention to the figure of the *flâneur*, the French term for what today we would call a shopper who goes window shopping, strolling through the malls of hyper-consumerism. In Benjamin's view, however, the *flâneur* became a figure of pilgrimage to the world of commodities, whose gaze aims to rescue the promise of happiness and redemption reified and crystallized in the wares and products of aestheticized consumption. In a more decidedly materialist fashion than Bloch, Benjamin seeks to release the utopian and critical potential frozen in the very commodities that stand for the alienation of the proletariat.

Walter Benjamin provided the twentieth century with one of the most original materialist analyses of works of art with his notion of the loss of the "aura" of works of art by means of their "mechanical reproducibility" (Benjamin 1968). Works of art can be said to have occupied a *sui generis* place and time, a location that was imbricated with religious and ritualistic connotations and functions. They could be copied, but the original remained that, the origin, that according to which everything else followed. This originality, the source of their authenticity, was what Benjamin called the aura. Works of arts were grounded in an ontology of authenticity. With the advent of the industrial means of production, that is, with the invention of mass production by means of the reproducibility of parts, works of art lose their aura, that is, works of art are no longer grounded in an ontology of origin and authenticity. Post-auratic work has no original because now everything is a copy of a copy. It is a simulacrum, in Baudrillard's sense, a copy of a copy that has no referent to an original. "The technique of reproduction detaches the reproduced object from the domain of tradition" (*ibid.*: 223). For Benjamin, the loss of aura of the work of art allows it to be integrated in everyday life. In fact, the profanation of works of art allows commodities to become works of art and in turn works of art to become commodities. The release of the aesthetic from tradition allows it to be manipulated into aestheticizing politics, of which the aestheticization of war is the epitome. As against this Nazi aestheticization of politics, Benjamin called for a politicization of art: which meant at the very least, to see art as an expression of the material contradictions of society. Works of art become both registers of those contradictions and partly their critique.

There is an almost directly inverse relationship between the fragmentary character of Benjamin's work and the generative provocation of his work. The more fragmentary, the more provocative; the more tragically incomplete, the more ceaselessly generative. This is indeed how we should read Benjamin's so-called theses on history. Thesis one is particularly important for understanding Habermas's own work on religion. In this thesis Benjamin uses the allegory of a hunchback guiding the hands of an automaton chess player who always wins against any human contender. The automaton or puppet is to "historical materialism", which is to win all the time, as the hunchback is to theology, "small and ugly and has to be kept out of sight" (2003: 389). If "historical materialism", that is the critique of an unjust and dehumanizing social order, is to win and bring about the establishment of a just and human order, then it must enlist the services of theology. Theology is here a synecdoche for all religious critique of a reality that is taken to be final, ineluctable and irreversible. As against a notion of progress that entails that the past is irrevocably past, and the victims of history are buried and forgotten, theology raises the question of a well-being and happiness without resignation to or reconciliation with the slaughter bench of history. A historical materialism that accepts Hegelian theodicy promises a future empty of happiness. The concept of history presupposed by such a notion of progress is one of history as a continuous homogeneous time. In contrast, a historical materialism guided by the ugly hunchback of theology approaches history as though approaching a monad, that is, it approaches historical objects and events as "constellation saturated with tensions", as "signs" of a messianic halting of time which can disrupt the continuance of the empty homogenous time of bourgeois progress (*ibid.*: 396). Less important is how theology is to be enlisted at the service of historical materialism than how Benjamin challenges the way progress has been conceptualized.

> There is no document of culture which is not at the same time a document of barbarism. And just as such a document is never free of barbarism, so barbarism taints the manner in which it was transmitted from one hand to another. The historical materialist therefore dissociates himself from this process of transmission as far as possible. (*ibid.*: 392)

History has to be thought of as a storm that piles up the debris of human tragedy. When the historical materialist sees through the eyes of religion, she can see that what we call progress must be unmasked as an ideology that reconciles us to human sacrifice. Theodicy must be renounced and history must be held open for the promise of redemption. The rejection of theodicy means that we must be relentlessly critical of any promise of the resolution of social conflict in our time. It is significant that one of the key ideas Habermas takes from Benjamin is precisely this utter negativity towards any kind of self-certain and insouciant historical materialism.

Religion as a catalyst of rationalization

Notwithstanding the shifts that have taken place in Habermas's long intellectual itinerary, his work has remained steadfastly focused on two central issues: the public sphere and the rationality of this public sphere. In perhaps his most autobiographical text, a speech he gave when he received the Kyoto Prize in 2004, he wrote:

> On my seventieth birthday, my students honored me with a *Festschrift* that bore the title *Die Öffenlichkeit der Vernunft und die Vernunft der Öffenlichkeit* –"The public sphere of reason and the reason of the public sphere." The title is not a bad choice, because the public sphere as a space of reasoned communicative exchanges is the issue that has concerned me all my life. (BNR: 12)

Indeed, there are two words that come up when one mentions Habermas's name: communicative reason and above all the public sphere. *Öffenlichkeit* does refer in English to public sphere, as a space in which citizens give each other reasons and in which the only admissible force is that of the better argument. *Öffenlichkeit* can also be translated as "publicness", or that which possesses a public character. The term also refers to "publicity" and in general the "public". The term is a noun derived from *offen*, that is, that which is open to everyone, and *öffnen*, the verb. Thus, the "publicness" or openness of reason means reason is for everyone and is everyone's. Reason occurs in the midst of a public dialogue; this dialogue is indeed its most exalted embodiment. Conversely, reason does not exist apart from an institutional, material, social context: a space of reasons. This is the meaning of the inverse formulation: the reason of the public, of publicness, of the public sphere. As the embodiment of reason, the public sphere itself becomes the locus for the release of rationality. For this reason, we can say that Habermas's focus on both the public sphere and communicative rationality is driven by the intersubjective, and thus always already public release of reason, a reason that in turn commands and requires its preservation in both institutions and the competencies of social agents (see Chapter 7).

For Habermas religion has been a continuous concern precisely because it is related to both the emergence of reason and the development of a public space of reason. The overview of the four stages of Habermas's intellectual itinerary sketched in the introduction shows slight shifts in emphasis and perspective, without a corresponding diminishing of the treatment of religion. We could say that in his earliest, anthropological-philosophical stage Habermas approached religion from a predominantly philosophical perspective. The text that best illustrates this philosophical approach is an essay from 1961, published in the German edition of *Theory and Praxis*, but not included in the

English translation. "Dialectical Idealism in Transition to Materialism: The Historical-Philosophical Consequences of Schelling's Idea of God's Contraction" (1963) takes up and summarizes many ideas from Habermas's own doctoral dissertation *The Absolute and History* (1954). In this essay Habermas traces how Schelling's idea of God's contraction gave rise, on the one hand, to the Hegelian idea of the sociality of reason and, on the other, to the emergence of Marx's own historical materialism. At the centre of the text is an analysis of Schelling's appropriation and translation of an idea present in Protestant and Jewish mysticism, namely, that God creates the world by retracting, contracting, withdrawing within himself. God makes space for creation by contracting himself. For Habermas, however, this idea of God's contraction became a metaphor, or a philosopheme, that expresses the principle of all dialectics: only with reason, in the midst of a material history. That God retracts and withdraws becomes the clearing for the history of the world and thus for the creativity of humans. At the centre of this theologume is the claim "Nemo contra Deum nisi Deus ipse" (Nothing can oppose God except God himself). But if God withdraws, then it is humans that carry on his generative task. God's creative labour is turned over to humans and this opens the way, in Habermas's view, to Marx's own ideas about the humanization of nature and the naturalization of humanity. For Habermas these mystical ideas are never mere irrational speculation. They possess a form, a grammar or syntax, that unleashes rational insights, even arguments. Religious ideas possess not just specific semantic contents about God, but also a particular structure that catalyzes rational argumentation. This view is also eloquently expressed in another major text from the same year, "The German Idealism of Jewish Philosophers", now in *Philosophical-Political Profiles* (1983). In this extremely important essay, Habermas argues that German idealism, and its philosophical aftermath, would have been unthinkable without the fruitful dialogue with themes in Jewish thinking. German idealism and Jewish thinking are so interwoven that it is difficult to think the one without the other.

In the second stage, as Habermas undertakes the task of "transforming historical materialism" that will culminate in his magnum opus, *The Theory of Communicative Action*, there is a shift from philosophy to sociology and more generally social theory. In this shift, religion is treated now not in terms of being a germinal for philosophical concepts, but instead in terms of being the source of the social order. This approach is of course shaped by the work of the classics of sociology: Weber, Durkheim and even Freud. Thus, for instance, in his 1968 essay "Technology and Science as 'Ideology'", Habermas writes with respect to Weber's understanding of secularization:

> First, traditional world-views and objectivations lose their power and validity *as* myth, *as* public religion, *as* customary ritual, *as* justifying metaphysics, *as* unquestionable tradition. Instead, they are reshaped into subjective belief systems and ethics which ensure the private cogency of modern value-orientations (the "Protestant ethic"). Second, they are transformed into constructions that do both at once: criticize traditions and reorganize the released material of tradition according to the principles of formal law and the exchange of equivalents (rationalist natural law).
> (1970: 98–9)

What is noteworthy about this passage is that here secularization is being explained as "pressure for rationalization" from "above" that meets the force of rationalization from below, from the realm of technical and practical action oriented towards instrumentalization. Additionally, here secularization is not simply the process of the profanation of the world, that is, the withdrawal of religious perspectives as worldviews, and the privatization of belief, but perhaps most importantly, that religion itself becomes the mean for the translation and appropriation of the rational impetus released by its secularization. Here religion becomes its own secular catalyst, or rather secularization itself is the result of religion. This approach will mature in the most elaborate formulation of what Habermas called the "linguistification of the sacred" in volume two of *The Theory of Communicative Action*. There, basing himself on Durkheim and Mead, Habermas shows how ritual practices and religious worldviews release rational imperatives through the establishment of a communicative grammar that conditions how believers can and should interact with each other, and how they relate to the idea of a supreme being. Habermas writes there:

> worldviews function as a kind of drive belt that transforms the basic religious consensus into the energy of social solidarity and passes it on to social institutions, thus giving them a moral authority. What is of primary interest in analyzing the interrelation between normative consensus, worldview, and institutional system, however, is that the connection is established through channels of linguistic communication. Whereas ritual actions take place at a pregrammatical level, religious worldviews are connected with full-fledged communicative actions. (TCA 2: 56)

The thrust of Habermas's argumentation in this section of *The Theory of Communicative Action* is to show that religion is the source of the normative binding power of ethical and moral commandments. Yet there is an ambiguity here. While the contents of worldviews may be sublimated into the normative binding of social systems, it is not entirely clear that the structure, the grammar of religious worldviews is itself exhausted. Indeed, in an essay now included in *The Inclusion of the Other: Studies in Political Theory*, titled "A Genealogical Analysis of the Cognitive Content of Morality" (IO: 3–46), Habermas resolved this ambiguity by claiming that the horizontal relationship among believers and the vertical relationship between each believer and God shapes the structure of our moral relationship to our neighbour, but now under two corresponding aspects: that of *solidarity* and that of *justice* (IO: 10). Here the grammar of one's religious relationship to God and the corresponding community of believers are like the exoskeleton of a magnificent species, which once the religious worldviews contained in them have desiccated under the impact of the forces of secularization leave behind a casing to be used as a structuring shape for other contents.

In the third, "postmetaphysical" stage in the periodization of Habermas's intellectual itinerary, Habermas turned his attention away from sociology and towards philosophy once again, in particular political and moral philosophy. These are the years when Habermas is working assiduously on the elaboration of his discourse ethics and a discourse theory of law and democracy (see Chapters 6, 7, and 9 of this volume). At the heart of this work is the development of what Habermas called postmetaphysical thinking (see Chapter 2). Metaphysical thinking, which in Habermas has become untenable by the very logic of philosophical development, is characterized by three aspects: identity thinking or the philosophy of origins that postulated the correspondence between being and thought; the doctrine of ideas, which becomes the foundation for idealism that postulates the tension between what is perceived and what can be conceptualized; and a concomitant strong concept of theory, where the *bios theoretikos* takes on a quasi-sacred character, and where philosophy becomes the path to salvation through dedication to a life of contemplation. After the scientific revolution, the rise of the hermeneutical-humanistic sciences and the emergence of pragmatism, existentialism and Marxism out of the ashes of idealism, three main norms are established for thought: first, reason can only be understood in a procedural and non-substantive way, which forces philosophy to enter into dialogue and cooperation with the different sciences, being attentive to the different procedures of verification and justification; second, all reason is situated, which is partly a consequence of the hermeneutical or so-called linguistic turn. Third, and as a cumulative effect of the prior two norms, we have the deflation of the extra-ordinary and a corresponding demotion of theory. Thus, by postmetaphysical Habermas means that new self-understanding of reason that we are able to obtain after the collapse of the Hegelian idealist system, the historicization of reason, the desubstantivation of reason turning it into a procedural rationality, and above all, its humbling. Postmetaphysical thinking is parsimonious *vis-à-vis* the social and human sciences, retaining only its power to arbitrate among competing claims.

One of the main aspects of the new postmetaphysical constellation is that in the wake of the collapse of metaphysics, philosophy is forced to recognize how it must coexist with religious practices and language:

> Philosophy, even in its postmetaphysical form, will be able neither to replace nor to repress religion as long as religious language is the bearer of semantic content that is inspiring and even indispensable, for this content eludes (for the time being?) the explanatory force of philosophical language and continues to resist translation into reasoning discourses. (PMT: 51)

In contrast to metaphysical thinking, with its overvaluation of philosophy's power, and thus believing itself to be the voice of the truth of being, postmetaphysical thinking would neither dismiss religion as mere myth, and thus as the other of reason, nor assimilate itself to religion, usurping religious language and contents (as with mystical philosophies, such as that of the late Heidegger with his call for a God who would save us). In other words, metaphysical thinking either surrendered philosophy to religion or sought to eliminate religion altogether. In contrast, postmetaphysical thinking recognizes that philosophy can neither illegitimately replace nor dismissively reject religion, for religion continues to articulate a language whose syntax and content elude philosophy, and from which philosophy continues to derive insights into the universal dimensions of human existence.

Since 2001, however, when he was awarded the Peace Prize by the German Booksellers Association, Habermas has been engaging religion even more directly, deliberately and consistently. In the speech he gave on the occasion of this prize, for instance, Habermas claims that even moral discourse cannot translate religious language without something being lost. Thus, the parenthetical question "for the time being?" that meant to qualify philosophy's ability to capture and translate the semantic contents of religious languages has now received an unambiguous answer: never! "Secular languages which only eliminate the substance once intended leave irritations. When sin was converted to culpability, and the breaking of divine commands to an offence against human laws, something was lost" (Habermas 2003b: 110). Still, Habermas's concern with religion is no longer solely philosophical, nor merely socio-theoretical. I argued above that as a philosopher Habermas has always been attentive to the dependence of philosophy on religion. More recently, the philosophical and sociological concerns with religion have taken on a political immediacy and urgency. Indeed, he now asks whether modern rule of law and constitutional democracies can generate the motivational resources that nourish them and make them endurable. In a series of essays, now gathered in *Between Naturalism and Religion* (2008), as well as his *Europe: The Faltering Project* (2009), Habermas argues that as we have become members of a world society (*Weltgesellschaft*), we have also been forced to adopt a societal "post-secular self-consciousness" (Mendieta 2010). By this term Habermas does not mean that secularization has come to an end, or even less that it has to be reversed. Instead, he now clarifies that secularization refers very specifically to the secularization of state power, and to the general dissolution of metaphysical overarching worldviews (among which religious views are to be counted). Additionally, as members of a world society that has if not a fully operational at least an incipient global public sphere, we have been forced to witness the endurance and vitality of religion. As members of this emergent global public sphere, we are also forced to recognize the plurality of forms of secularization. Secularization did not occur in one form, but in a variety of forms and according to different chronologies.

With respect to his preoccupation that "the liberal state depends in the long run on mentalities that it cannot produce from its own resources" (BNR: 3), through a critical reading of Rawls, Habermas has begun to translate the postmetaphysical orientation of modern philosophy into a postsecular self-understanding of modern rule of law societies in such a way that religious citizens as well as secular citizens can coexist not just by force of a *modus vivendi*, but out of a sincere mutual respect. "Mutual recognition implies, among other things, that religious and secular citizens are willing to listen and to learn from each other in public debates. The political virtue of treating each other civilly is an expression of distinctive cognitive attitudes" (BNR: 3). The cognitive attitudes Habermas is referring to here are the very cognitive competencies that are distinctive of modern, postconventional, social agents. Habermas's recent work on religion, then, is primarily concerned with rescuing for the modern liberal state those motivational and moral resources that it cannot generate or provide itself. At the same time, his recent work is concerned with foregrounding the kind of ethical and moral concerns, preoccupations and values that can guide us through the Scylla of a society administered from above by the system imperatives of a global economy and political power and the Charybdis of a technological frenzy that places us on the slippery slope of a liberally sanctioned eugenics.

In autumn 2008, Habermas gave a series of lectures at Yale, which were followed the next autumn by another set of lectures, and a seminar at Stony Brook University on "Political Theology". That same autumn a workshop was organized on Habermas's recent work on religion for which he made available several large manuscripts of what appears to be the working draft for a book on religion.[4] The workshop yielded a large manuscript of essays engaging Habermas's comprehensive rethinking of some of his earlier ideas and formulations on religion. One of the centrepieces of this working draft is a critique of modernization theory that links social progress to secularization. Here Habermas aims to show why secularization theory has been mistaken on several accounts and why we must attenuate and revise some of its major claims. At the very least if we are to hold on to the basic claims of modernization theory, we must uncouple them from strong "secularist" assumptions. This critique of modernization theory is matched by a turn towards the latest work on anthropology, ethnography and archeology that is theorizing the relationship between ritual, the emergence of mythological narratives and the evolution of the human mind. There is also a long chapter on the Axial Age and the simultaneous emergence of universal, monotheistic religions and world-transcending philosophical perspectives. Even in this preliminary form, it can be surmised that Habermas is working on a massive book that aims to bring together the philosophical position that he argues he has held consistently at least since 1988 when he presented the essay "Transcendence from within, Transcendence in this World" written for a conference organized at the Divinity School at the University of Chicago, with an appropriation of the most recent work on developmental neurobiology, and a rethinking of Karl Jaspers's provocative thesis about the Axial Age cognitive breakthrough of humanity (Habermas 2009b: vol. 5, 32).

The project in its present form is unmistakably guided by the hermeneutical key of not merely talking about religion in the third person perspective, but of talking with religious co-citizens and co-participants in a global public sphere. This talking with, which has obvious political consequences as Habermas has sought to make explicit, presupposes two irreducible but complementary attitudes on both sides of the divide between faith and knowledge:

> ...the religious side must accept the authority of "natural" reason as the fallible result of the institutionalized sciences and the basic principles of universalistic egalitarianism in law and morality. Conversely, secular reason may not set itself up as the judge concerning truths of faith, even though in the end it can accept as reasonable only what it can translate into its own, in principle universally accessible, discourses. (Habermas *et al.* 2010: 16)

If this dialogue is to be successful and non-instrumentalizing, then the dialogue partners must know that the dialogue is not a zero sum game in which what one gains is a loss for the other (Habermas 2009b: vol. 5, 30).

It is surely premature to anticipate what the final book will look like, but this much can be anticipated, as with most of Habermas's work: it will be another major contribution to social theory and philosophy. Habermas has already earned his place in the pantheon of great philosophers. This soon-to-be-published work will complement *The Theory of Communicative Action*, without question securing his place along that of Max Weber and Émile Durkheim as one of the classics of the sociology of religion, which has always been the heart of Western sociology. At the same time, however, with the published work on religion, Habermas has already also earned a prominent place next to the great philosophers in the Western tradition who have contributed to the ceaselessly generative dialogue among Athens, Jerusalem and Rome: Kant, Hegel, Bloch, Benjamin and, more recently, Levinas and Derrida.

Notes

1. See my introduction to Habermas (2002a); see also Mendieta (2007).
2. The best and most extensive treatment of the Frankfurt School is Wiggershaus (1994).
3. Interested readers can turn to Mendieta (2005).
4. Habermas presented a long essay on "The Political", which is a critique of the way in which "political theology" is being received today. The essay is published with essays by Judith Butler, Charles Taylor and Cornel West, who also spoke at a one-day "Public Dialogue" on the issue of the power of religion in contemporary society. For the text and an introduction to the discussion, see Mendieta & Van Antwerpen (2010). The essays that were written on the basis of Habermas's still unpublished manuscripts for the book on religion will be published in a volume edited by Craig Calhoun, Eduardo Mendieta and Jonathan Van Antwerpen.

Chronology of life and work

1929	Born 18 June in Düsseldorf, Germany
1933	Hitler becomes Chancellor of Germany Roosevelt becomes President of the United States
1938	9 November: Kristallnacht
1939	Second World War begins
1944	Joins Hitler Youth
1945	Second World War ends
1946	Nuremberg Trials
1949	Studies in Göttingen Establishment of NATO First government of Federal Republic of Germany under Konrad Adenauer
1950	Studies in Zurich
1951	Studies in Bonn (until 1954)
1952	Freelance journalist for *Frankfurter Allgemeine Zeitung* until 1956
1954	Doctoral dissertation on Friedrich Schelling
1956	Research Assistant to Theodor Adorno at Institute of Social Research, Frankfurt
1958	Moves to Marburg to study with Wolfgang Abendroth
1961	Habilitation, *Structural Transformation of the Public Sphere* (English 1989) Professor of Philosophy (Privatdozent) in Heidelberg Berlin Wall is erected
1963	*Theory and Practice* (English 1971)
1964	Professor of Philosophy and Sociology at the University of Frankfurt
1968	*Knowledge and Human Interests* (English 1971)

1971	Becomes Director of Max Planck Institute, Starnberg Gauss Lectures, Princeton University
1973	*Legitimation Crisis* (English 1975)
1974	Hegel Prize
1976	Sigmund Freud Prize
1981	*The Theory of Communicative Action* (English 1984/1987)
1982	Returns to Frankfurt
1983	*Moral Consciousness and Communicative Action* (English 1990)
1986	Historikerstreit (Historians' Dispute) (lasts into 1989) Tanner Lectures ("Law and Morality"), Harvard University
1987	Sonning Prize
1989	Fall of the Berlin Wall
1990	German reunification Gulf War begins (ends 1991)
1991	Beginning of Yugoslav Wars
1992	*Between Facts and Norms* (English 1996)
1994	First annual guest professorship at Northwestern University Retires from Goethe-Universität, Frankfurt
1996	Karl Jaspers Prize *The Inclusion of the Other* (English 1998)
1999	NATO bombing in Kosovo *Truth and Justification* (English 2003)
2000	Joint seminar with Jacques Derrida in Frankfurt
2001	Peace Prize of the German Booktrade Association
2003	US-led invasion of Iraq and beginning of Iraq War
2004	Kyoto Prize
2005	Holberg International Memorial Prize *Between Naturalism and Religion* (English 2008)
2007	*The Dialectics of Secularization* (dialogue with then Joseph Ratzinger, now Pope Benedict XVI)
2008	*Europe: the Faltering Project* (English 2009)
2010	Ulysses Medal, Dublin

Bibliography

Works by Jürgen Habermas

Most of Habermas's writings are available in English and references in this volume are to English translations where available. German publication information has been included here in square brackets. Occasionally, the contents of a collection of essays in English varies slightly from the German original; a few collections are drawn from multiple sources and therefore do not correspond to any German editions.

Habermas, J. 1954. *Das Absolute und die Geschichte von der Zwiespältigkeit in Schellings Denken*. Bonn: H. Bouvier.

Habermas, J. 1963. "Dialektischer Idealismus im Übergang zum Materialismus: Geschichtsphilosophische Folgerungen aus Schellings Idee einer Contraction Gottes". In *Theorie und Praxis; Sozialphilosophische Studien*. Neuwied am Rhein: Luchterhand.

Habermas, J. 1970. *Toward a Rational Society; Student Protest, Science, and Politics*, J. Shapiro (trans.). Boston, MA: Beacon Press. [From *Technik und Wissenschaft als "Ideologie"* (Frankfurt: Suhrkamp, 1968) and *Protestbewegung und Hochschulreform* (Frankfurt: Suhrkamp, 1958)]

Habermas, J. 1971. *Knowledge and Human Interests*, J. Shapiro (trans.). Boston, MA: Beacon Press. [*Erkenntnis und Interesse* (Frankfurt: Suhrkamp, 1968)]

Habermas, J. 1974. *Theory and Practice*, J. Viertel (trans.). Boston, MA: Beacon Press. [*Theorie und Praxis* (Frankfurt: Suhrkamp, 1971)]

Habermas, J. 1975. *Legitimation Crisis*, T. McCarthy (trans.). Boston, MA: Beacon Press. [*Legitimationsprobleme im Spätkapitalismus* (Frankfurt: Suhrkamp, 1973)]

Habermas, J. 1979. *Communication and the Evolution of Society*, T. McCarthy (trans.). Boston, MA: Beacon Press. [From *Zur Rekonstruktion des historischen Materialismus* (Frankfurt: Suhrkamp, 1976) and *Sprachpragmatik und Philosophy*, K.-O. Apel (ed.) (Frankfurt: Suhrkamp, 1976)]

Habermas, J. 1980. "The Hermeneutic Claim to Universality". In *Contemporary Hermeneutics: Hermeneutics as Method, Philosophy, and Critique*, J. Bleicher (ed.), 181–211. London: Routledge & Kegan Paul. [Originally published in 1970, reprinted in the expanded edition of *Zur Logik der Sozialwissenschaften* (Frankfurt: Suhrkamp, 1985)]

Habermas, J. 1981. *Kleine Politische Schriften (I–IV)*. Frankfurt: Suhrkamp.

Habermas, J. 1983. *Philosophical-Political Profiles*, F. G. Lawrence (trans.). Cambridge, MA: MIT Press. [*Philosophisch-politische Profile* (Frankfurt, Suhrkamp, 1981); essays from the period 1958–79]

Habermas, J. 1984a. *Vorstudien und Ergänzungen zur Theorie des Kommunikativen Handelns*. Frankfurt: Suhrkamp.

Habermas, J. (ed.) 1984b. *Observations on "the Spiritual Situation of the Age": Contemporary German Perspectives*, A. Buchwalter (trans.). Cambridge, MA: MIT Press. [*Stichworte zur geistigen Situation der Zeit* (Frankfurt: Suhrkamp, 1979)]

Habermas, J. 1984/1987. *The Theory of Communicative Action*, 2 vols, T. McCarthy (trans.). Boston, MA: Beacon Press. [*Theorie des kommunikativen Handelns*, 2 vols (Frankfurt: Suhrkamp, 1981)]

Habermas, J. 1985a. "Reply to Skjei". *Inquiry* 28 (March): 105–12.

Habermas, J. 1985b. "Konservative Politik, Arbeit, Sozialismus und Utopie heute (1983)". In *Die Neue Unübersichtlichkeit: Kleine Politische Schriften V*, 59–76. Frankfurt: Suhrkamp.

Habermas, J. 1986. *Autonomy and Solidarity: Interviews with Jürgen Habermas*, P. Dews (ed.). London: Verso.

Habermas, J. 1987. "Geschichtsbewußtsein und posttraditionale Identität: Die Westorientierung der Bundesrepublik". In *Eine Art Schadensabwicklung*, 161–79. Frankfurt: Suhrkamp.

Habermas, J. 1988a. *On the Logic of the Social Sciences*, S. Weber Nicholsen & J. A. Stark (trans.). Cambridge, MA: MIT Press. [Originally published in 1967, reprinted as *Zur Logik der Sozialwissenschaften*, exp. ed. (Frankfurt: Suhrkamp, 1985)]

Habermas, J. 1988b. "Law and Morality". In *The Tanner Lectures on Human Values*, vol. 8, S. McMurrin (ed.), K. Baynes (trans.), 217–79. Salt Lake City: Utah University Press.

Habermas, J. 1989a. *The New Conservatism: Cultural Criticism and the Historians' Debate*, S. Weber Nicholson (trans.). Cambridge, MA: MIT Press. [Mostly from *Kleine Politische Schriften V* and *VI* (Frankfurt: Suhrkamp, 1985, 1987)]

Habermas, J. 1989b. *The Structural Transformation of the Public Sphere: An Inquiry into a Category of Bourgeois Society*, T. Burger (trans.). Cambridge, MA: MIT Press. [*Strukturwandel der Öffentlichkeit* (Neuwied: Luchterhand, 1962)]

Habermas, J. 1990a. *The Philosophical Discourse of Modernity: Twelve Lectures*, F. Lawrence (trans.). Cambridge, MA: MIT Press. [*Der philosophische Diskurs der Moderne: Zwölf Vorlesungen* (Frankfurt: Suhrkamp, 1985)]

Habermas, J. 1990b. "Justice and Solidarity". In *The Moral Domain: Essays in the Ongoing Discussion Between Philosophy and the Social Sciences*, T. E. Wren (ed.), 224–52. Cambridge, MA: MIT Press.

Habermas, J. 1990c. *Moral Consciousness and Communicative Action*, C. Lenhardt & S. Weber Nicholsen (trans.). Cambridge, MA: MIT Press. [*Moralbewusstsein und kommunikatives Handeln* (Frankfurt: Suhrkamp, 1983)]

Habermas, J. 1991. *Texte und Kontexte*. Frankfurt: Suhrkamp.

Habermas, J. 1992. *Postmetaphysical Thinking: Philosophical Essays*, W. Hohengarten (trans.). Cambridge, MA: MIT Press. [*Nachmetaphysisches Denken* (Frankfurt: Suhrkamp, 1988)]

Habermas, J. 1993. *Justification and Application: Remarks on Discourse Ethics*, C.

Cronin (trans.). Cambridge, MA: MIT Press. [From *Erläuterungen zur Diskursethik* (Frankfurt: Suhrkamp, 1991) and *Die Nachholende Revolution: Kleine Politische Schriften VII* (Frankfurt: Suhrkamp, 1990)]

Habermas, J. 1994. *The Past as Future*, M. Pensky (trans.). Lincoln, NE: University of Nebraska Press. [*Vergangenheit Als Zukunft: Das Alte Deutschland im neuen Europa?*, M. Haller (ed.) (Munich: Piper, 1993)]

Habermas, J. 1997. *A Berlin Republic: Writings on Germany*, S. Rendall (trans.). Lincoln, NE: University of Nebraska Press.

Habermas, J. 1998a. *The Inclusion of the Other: Studies in Political Theory*, C. Cronin (trans.). Cambridge, MA: MIT Press. [*Die Einbeziehung des Anderen: Studien zur politischen Theorie* (Frankfurt: Suhrkamp, 1996)]

Habermas, J. 1998b. *Between Facts and Norms: Contributions to a Discourse Theory of Law and Democracy*, W. Rehg (trans.). Cambridge, MA: MIT Press. [*Faktizität und Geltung: Beiträge zur Diskurstheorie des Rechts und des demokratischen Rechtsstaats* (Frankfurt: Suhrkamp, 1992)]

Habermas, J. 1998c. *On the Pragmatics of Communication*, M. Cooke (ed.). Cambridge, MA: MIT Press.

Habermas, J. 2001a. *The Postnational Constellation: Political Essays*, M. Pensky (trans.). Cambridge, MA: MIT Press. [*Die postnationale Konstellation: Politische Essays* (Frankfurt: Suhrkamp, 1998)]

Habermas, J. 2001b. *The Liberating Power of Symbols: Philosophical Essays*, P. Dews (trans.). Cambridge, MA: MIT Press. [*Vom sinnlichen Eindruck zum symbolischen Ausdruck* (Frankfurt: Suhrkamp, 1997)]

Habermas, J. 2001c. *On the Pragmatics of Social Interaction: Preliminary Studies in the Theory of Communicative Action*, B. Fultner (trans.). Cambridge, MA: MIT Press. [Selections from *Vorstudien und Ergänzungen zur Theorie des kommunikativen Handelns* (Frankfurt: Suhrkamp)]

Habermas, J. 2001d. "Intentions, Conventions, and Linguistic Interactions" [1976]. In *On the Pragmatics of Social Interaction: Preliminary Studies in the Theory of Communicative Action*, B. Fultner (trans.), 105–28. Cambridge, MA: MIT Press.

Habermas, J. 2001e. "Constitutional Democracy: A Paradoxical Union of Contradictory Principles?" *Political Theory* 29(6): 766–81.

Habermas, J. 2002a. *Religion and Rationality: Essays on Reason, God and Modernity*. Cambridge, MA: MIT Press.

Habermas, J. 2002b. "Resentment of US Policies is Growing". *The Nation* 275(21): 15.

Habermas, J. 2003a. *Truth and Justification*, B. Fultner (trans.). Cambridge, MA: MIT Press. [*Wahrheit und Rechtfertigung* (Frankfurt: Suhrkamp, 1999)]

Habermas, J. 2003b. *The Future of Human Nature*, H. Beister, W. Rehg & M. Pensky (trans.). Cambridge: Polity. [*Die Zukunft der menschlichen Natur: Auf dem Weg zu einer liberalen Eugenik?* (Frankfurt: Suhrkamp, 2001)]

Habermas, J. 2003c. "On Law and Disagreement: Some Comments on 'Interpretive Pluralism'". *Ratio Juris* 16(2): 193–4.

Habermas, J. 2004. "The Moral and the Ethical: A Reconsideration of the Issue of the Priority of the Right over the Good". In *Pragmatism, Critique, Judgment: Essays for Richard J. Bernstein*, S. Benhabib & N. Fraser (eds), 29–43. Cambridge, MA: MIT Press.

Habermas, J. 2006. *Time of Transitions*, C. Cronin & M. Pensky (trans.). Cambridge: Polity. [*Zeit der Übergänge* (Frankfurt: Suhrkamp, 2001)]

Habermas, J. 2007a. *The Divided West*, C. Cronin (trans.). Cambridge: Polity. [*Der gespaltene Westen* (Frankfurt: Suhrkamp, 2004)]

Habermas, J. 2007b. "The Language Game of Responsible Agency and the Problem of Free Will: How Can Epistemic Dualism Be Reconciled with Ontological Monism?", J. Anderson (trans.), *Philosophical Explorations* **10**(1): 13–50.

Habermas, J. 2008. *Between Naturalism and Religion: Philosophical Essays*, C. Cronin (trans.). Cambridge: Polity Press. [*Zwischen Naturalismus und Religion: Philosophische Aufsätze* (Frankfurt: Suhrkamp, 2005)]

Habermas, J. 2009a. *Europe: The Faltering Project*, C. Cronin (trans.). Cambridge: Polity.

Habermas, J. 2009b. *Philosophische Texte: Studienausgabe in fünf Bänden*. Frankfurt: Suhrkamp.

Habermas, J. & N. Luhmann 1971. *Theorie der Gesellschaft oder Sozialtechnologie: Was Leistet die Systemforschung?* Frankfurt: Suhrkamp.

Habermas, J. & J. Derrida 2005. "February 15, or, What Binds Europeans Together". In *Old Europe, New Europe, Core Europe: Transatlantic Relations After the Iraq War*, D. Levy, M. Pensky & J. C. Torpey (eds), 3–13. London: Verso.

Habermas, J., M. Reder, J. Schmidt, N. Brieskorn & F. Ricken 2010. *An Awareness of What Is Missing: Faith and Reason in a Post-Secular Age*, C. Cronin (trans.). Cambridge: Polity. [*Ein Bewusstsein von dem, was fehlt* (Frankfurt: Suhrkamp, 2008)]

Habermas, J. & J. Ratzinger 2006. *Dialectics of Secularization: On Reason and Religion*, B. McNeil (trans.). San Francisco: Ignatius Press. [*Dialektik der Säkularisierung: Über Vernunft und Religion* (Freiburg im Breisgau: Herder, 2005)]

Works by others

Aboulafia, M., M. O. Bookman & C. Kemp (eds) 2002. *Habermas and Pragmatism*. London: Routledge.

Adorno, T. W. 1983. *Negative Dialectics*, E. B. Ashton (trans.). New York: Continuum.

Alexy, R. 1989. *A Theory of Legal Argumentation: The Theory of Rational Discourse as Theory of Legal Justification*. Oxford: Clarendon Press.

Allen, A. 2008. *The Politics of Our Selves: Power, Autonomy, and Gender in Contemporary Critical Theory*. New York: Columbia University Press.

Anderson, J. 1996. "A Social Conception of Personal Autonomy: Volitional Identity, Strong Evaluation, and Intersubjective Accountability". PhD thesis, Northwestern University.

Anderson, J. (ed.) 2007. *Free Will as Part of Nature: Habermas and his Critics*. Special issue of *Philosophical Explorations* **10**(1).

Anderson, J. 2008. "Disputing Autonomy: Second-Order Desires and the Dynamics of Ascribing Autonomy". *Sats – Nordic Journal of Philosophy* 9(1): 7–26.

Apel, K.-O. 1980. *Towards a Transformation of Philosophy*, G. Adey & D. Frisby (trans.). London: Routledge & Kegan Paul.

Apel, K.-O. 1994. *Karl-Otto Apel: Selected Essays*, E. Mendieta (ed.). Atlantic Highlands, NJ: Humanities Press.

Archibugi, D. 2000. "Cosmopolitical Democracy". *New Left Review* **4**: 137–51.

Austin, J. L. 1962. *How to do Things with Words*. Cambridge, MA: Harvard University Press.

Baynes, K. 1992. *The Normative Grounds of Social Criticism: Kant, Rawls, and Habermas*. Albany, NY: SUNY Press.

Beck, U. 1992. *Risk Society: Towards a New Modernity*, M. Ritter (trans.). London: Sage.

Benhabib, S. 1986. *Critique, Norm, and Utopia: A Study of the Foundations of Critical Theory*. New York: Columbia University Press.

Benhabib, S. 1992. *Situating the Self: Gender, Community, and Postmodernism in Contemporary Ethics*. New York: Routledge.

Benhabib, S. (ed.) 1996. *Democracy and Difference: Contesting the Boundaries of the Political*. Princeton, NJ: Princeton University Press.

Benhabib, S. 2002. *The Claims of Culture: Equality and Diversity in the Global Era*. Princeton, NJ: Princeton University Press.

Benhabib, S. & N. Fraser (eds) 2004. *Pragmatism, Critique, Judgment: Essays for Richard J. Bernstein*. Cambridge, MA: MIT Press.

Benjamin, W. 1968. *Illuminations*, H. Zohn (trans.). New York: Harcourt, Brace & World.

Benjamin, W. 2003. *Selected Writings*, vol. 4, H. Bullock & M. W. Jennings (eds). Cambridge, MA: Harvard University Press.

Berger, P. L. & T. Luckmann 1966. *The Social Construction of Reality: A Treatise in the Sociology of Knowledge*. Garden City, NY: Doubleday.

Bernard, Thomas J. 1983. *The Consensus–Conflict Debate: Form and Content in Social Theories*. New York: Columbia University Press.

Bernstein, R. J. (ed.) 1985. *Habermas and Modernity*. Cambridge, MA: MIT Press.

Bickel, A. M. 1986. *The Least Dangerous Branch: The Supreme Court at the Bar of Politics*, 2nd edn. New Haven, CT: Yale University Press.

Bloch, E. 1991. *Heritage of Our Times*, N. Plaice & S. Plaice (trans.). Berkeley, CA: University of California Press.

Bloch, E. 2000. *The Spirit of Utopia*, A. A. Nassar (trans.). Stanford, CA: Stanford University Press.

Bohman, J. & W. Rehg (eds) 1997. *Deliberative Democracy: Essays on Reason and Politics*. Cambridge, MA: MIT Press.

Bourdieu, P. 1990. "Objectification Objectified" and "The Imaginary Anthropology of Subjectivism". In his *The Logic of Practice*, R. Nice (trans.), 23–51. Stanford, CA: Stanford University Press.

Borradori, G. (ed.) 2003. *Philosophy in a Time of Terror: Dialogues with Jürgen Habermas and Jacques Derrida*. Chicago, IL: University of Chicago Press.

Brandom, R. 1994. *Making It Explicit: Reasoning, Representing, and Discursive Commitment*. Cambridge, MA: Harvard University Press.

Brunkhorst, H. 2006. "The Legitimation Crisis of the European Union". *Constellations* 13(2): 165–80.

Brunkhorst, H. 2008. "State and Constitution – A Reply to Scheuerman". *Constellations* 15(4): 493–501.

Bühler, K. 1990. *Theory of Language: The Representational Function of Language*, D. Fraser Goodwin (trans.). Amsterdam: J. Benjamins.

Calhoun, C. J. (ed.) 1997. *Habermas and the Public Sphere*. Cambridge, MA: MIT Press.

Christmann, F. 2004. "Motivation Factors in Discourse Ethics: Conscience Formation". PhD thesis, Saint Louis University.

Cohen, G. A. 1982. "Functional Explanation: Reply to Elster". *Political Studies* 28(1): 129–35.

Cohen, J. L. & A. Arato 1994. *Civil Society and Political Theory*. Cambridge, MA: MIT Press.

Cooke, M. 1992. "Habermas, Autonomy, and the Identity of the Self". *Philosophy and Social Criticism* 18(3–4): 269–91.
Cooke, M. 1994a. "Realizing the Post-Conventional Self". *Philosophy and Social Criticism* 20(1–2): 87–101.
Cooke, M. 1994b. *Language and Reason: A Study of Habermas's Pragmatics*. Cambridge, MA: MIT Press.
Cronin, C. 2003. "Democracy and Collective Identity: In Defence of Constitutional Patriotism". *European Journal of Philosophy* 11(1): 1–28.
Cronin, C. 2006. "On the Possibility of a Democratic Constitutional Founding: Habermas and Michelman in Dialogue". *Ratio Juris* 19(3): 343–69.
Crossley, N. & J. M. Roberts (eds) 2004. *After Habermas: New Perspectives on the Public Sphere*. Oxford: Blackwell.
Davidson, D. 2001. *Subjective, Intersubjective, Objective*. Oxford: Clarendon Press.
Davidson, D. 2005. "A Nice Derangement of Epitaphs". In his *Truth, Language, and History*, 89–107. Oxford: Clarendon Press.
Dews, P. (ed.) 1999. *Habermas: A Critical Reader*. Oxford: Blackwell.
Doyle, M. 1983. "Kant, Liberal Legacies, and Foreign Affairs". *Philosophy and Public Affairs* 12(3): 205–35.
Dummett, M. A. E. 1993. "What is a Theory of Meaning? (II)". In his *The Seas of Language*, 34–93. Oxford: Clarendon Press.
Durkheim, É. 1984. *The Division of Labor in Society*, W. D. Halls (trans.). New York: Free Press.
Duvenage, P. 2003. *Habermas and Aesthetics: The Limits of Communicative Reason*. Cambridge: Polity.
Dworkin, R. M. 1986. *Law's Empire*. Cambridge, MA: Belknap Press.
Dworkin, R. M. 1996. *Freedom's Law: The Moral Reading of the American Constitution*. Cambridge, MA: Harvard University Press.
Eder, K. 1999. "Societies Learn and Yet the World is Hard to Change". *European Journal of Social Theory* 2(2): 195–215.
Elster, J. 1985. *Making Sense of Marx*. Cambridge: Cambridge University Press.
Ely, J. H. 1980. *Democracy and Distrust: A Theory of Judicial Review*. Cambridge, MA: Harvard University Press.
Etzioni, A. 2002. "Implications of the American Anti-Terrorism Coalition for Global Architectures". *European Journal of Political Theory* 1(1): 9–30.
Euben, J. P., J. Wallach & J. Ober (eds) 1994. *Athenian Political Thought and the Reconstruction of American Democracy*. Ithaca, NY: Cornell University Press.
Fine, R. & W. Smith 2003. "Jürgen Habermas's Theory of Cosmopolitanism". *Constellations* 10(4): 469–87.
Finlayson, J. G. 2005. *Habermas: A Very Short Introduction*. Oxford: Oxford University Press.
Flynn, J. 2009. "Book Review: Between Naturalism and Religion (Polity Press 2008)". *Notre Dame Philosophical Reviews* (May), http://ndpr.nd.edu/review.cfm?id=16205 (accessed October 2010).
Forst, R. 2002. *Contexts of Justice: Political Philosophy Beyond Liberalism and Communitarianism*, J. Farrell (trans.). Berkeley, CA: University of California Press.
Freundlieb, D., W. Hudson & J. F. Rundell (eds) 2004. *Critical Theory After Habermas*. Leiden: Brill.
Fultner, B. 1996. "The Redemption of Truth: Idealization, Acceptability and Fallibilism in Habermas' Theory of Meaning". *International Journal of Philosophical Studies* 4(2): 233–51.

Fultner, B. 2002. "Inferentialism and Communicative Action: Robust Conceptions of Intersubjectivity". *Philosophical Studies* 108(1): 121–31.

Gauthier, D. P. 1986. *Morals by Agreement*. Oxford: Clarendon Press.

Gilligan, C. 1993. *In a Different Voice: Psychological Theory and Women's Development*. Cambridge, MA: Harvard University Press.

Glüer, K. 2001. "Dreams and Nighmares: Conventions, Norms and Meaning in Davidson's Philosophy of Language". In *Interpreting Davidson*, P. Kotátko, P. Pagin & G. Sega (eds), 53–74. Stanford, CA: CSLI Publications.

Gottschalk-Mazouz, N. 2000. *Diskursethik: Theorien, Entwicklungen, Perspektiven*. Berlin: Akademie.

Grice, H. P. 1989. *Studies in the Way of Words*. Cambridge, MA: Harvard University Press.

Grimm, D. 1995. "Does Europe Need a Constitution?" *European Law Journal* 1(3) (November): 282–302.

Gunnarsson, L. 2000. *Making Moral Sense: Beyond Habermas and Gauthier*. Cambridge: Cambridge University Press.

Günther, K. 1993. *The Sense of Appropriateness: Application Discourses in Morality and Law*, J. Farrell (trans.). Albany, NY: SUNY Press.

Hahn, L. E. (ed.) 2000. *Perspectives on Habermas*. Chicago, IL: Open Court.

Hart, H. L. A. 1994. *The Concept of Law*, 2nd edn. Oxford: Clarendon Press.

Hattiangadi, A. 2007. *Oughts and Thoughts: Rule-Following and the Normativity of Content*. Oxford: Clarendon Press.

Heath, J. 1995. "The Problem of Foundationalism in Habermas's Discourse Ethics". *Philosophy & Social Criticism* 21(1): 77–100.

Heath, J. 1996. "Rational Choice as Critical Theory". *Philosophy and Social Criticism* 22(5): 43–62.

Heath, J. 1998. "What Is a Validity Claim?" *Philosophy and Social Criticism* 24(4): 23–41.

Heath, J. 2001. *Communicative Action and Rational Choice*. Cambridge, MA: MIT Press.

Heath, J. 2008. *Following the Rules: Practical Reasoning and Deontic Constraint*. Oxford: Oxford University Press.

Heath, J. & J. Anderson 2010. "Procrastination and the Extended Will". In *The Thief of Time: Philosophical Essays on Procrastination*, C. Andreou & M. D. White (eds), 233–52. New York: Oxford University Press.

Hohengarten, W. 1996. "Translator's Introduction". In J. Habermas, *Postmetaphysical Thinking*, vii–xx. Cambridge, MA: MIT Press.

Holmes, O. 1897. "The Path of the Law". *Harvard Law Review* 10(8): 478.

Holub, R. C. 1991. *Jürgen Habermas: Critic in the Public Sphere*. London: Routledge.

Honneth, A. & H. Joas (eds) 1991. *Communicative Action: Essays on Jürgen Habermas's The Theory of Communicative Action*, J. Gaines & D. L. Jones (trans.). Cambridge: Polity.

Horkheimer, M. 1972. *Critical Theory: Selected Essays*, M. J. O'Connell *et al.* (trans.). New York: Seabury Press.

Horkheimer, M. & T. W. Adorno 2002. *Dialectic of Enlightenment: Philosophical Fragments*, G. Schmid Noerr (ed.), E. Jephcott (trans.). Stanford, CA: Stanford University Press.

Horster, D. 1992. *Habermas: An Introduction*, H. Thompson (trans.). Philadelphia, PA: Pennbridge Books.

Ikenberry, G. 2002. "Review of The Postnational Constellation: Political Essays". *Foreign Affairs* 81(2): 177.

Ingram, D. 1987. *Habermas and the Dialectic of Reason*. New Haven, CT: Yale University Press.

Johnson, P. 2006. *Habermas: Rescuing the Public Sphere*. Florence: Routledge.

Kaldor, M. 2006. *New and Old Wars*, 2nd edn. Cambridge: Polity.

Kant, I. 1993. *Grounding for the Metaphysics of Morals; with, On a Supposed Right to Lie Because of Philanthropic Concerns*, 3rd edn, J. W. Ellington (trans.). Indianapolis, IN: Hackett.

Kant, I. 1996. *Practical Philosophy*, M. J. Gregor (trans.). Cambridge: Cambridge University Press.

Kant, I. 1999. *Metaphysical Elements of Justice: Part I of The Metaphysics of Morals*, 2nd edn, J. Ladd (trans.). Indianapolis, IN: Hackett.

Kay, J. A. 2003. *The Truth About Markets: Their Genius, Their Limits, Their Follies*. London: Allen Lane.

Kelly, M. (ed.) 1994. *Critique and Power: Recasting the Foucault/Habermas Debate*. Cambridge, MA: MIT Press.

Kettner, M. 1996. "Discourse Ethics and Health Care Ethics Committees". *Jahrbuch für Recht und Ethik* 4 (January): 249–72.

Kittay, E. F. & D. T. Meyers (eds) 1987. *Women and Moral Theory*. Lanham, MD: Rowman & Littlefield.

Kripke, S. A. 1982. *Wittgenstein on Rules and Private Language: An Elementary Exposition*. Oxford: Blackwell.

Kujundzic, N. & W. Buschert 1993. "Staging the Life-World: Habermas and the Recuperation of Austin's Speech Act Theory". *Journal for the Theory of Social Behaviour* 23(1): 105–16.

Lafont, C. 1999. *The Linguistic Turn in Hermeneutic Philosophy*, J. Medina (trans.). Cambridge, MA: MIT Press.

Lafont, C. 2008. "Alternative Visions of a New Global Order: What Should Cosmopolitans Hope For?" *Ethics and Global Politics* 1(1) (January): 41–60.

Lance, M. & H. Heath White 2007. "Stereoscopic Vision: Persons, Freedom, and Two Spaces of Material Inference". *Philosopher's Imprint* 7(4): 1–21.

Levy, D., M. Pensky & J. C. Torpey (eds) 2005. *Old Europe, New Europe, Core Europe: Transatlantic Relations After the Iraq War*. London: Verso.

Lippincott, B. E. 1938. *On the Economic Theory of Socialism*. Minneapolis, MN: University of Minnesota Press.

Löwy, M. 1992. *Redemption and Utopia: Jewish Libertarian Thought in Central Europe: A Study in Elective Affinity*, H. Heaney (trans.). Stanford, CA: Stanford University Press.

Luhmann, N. 2004. *Law as a Social System*. Oxford: Oxford University Press.

MacCormick, N. 1993. "Beyond the Sovereign State". *Modern Law Review* 56(1): 1–18.

MacIntyre, A. C. 1984. *After Virtue: A Study in Moral Theory*. Notre Dame, IN: University of Notre Dame Press.

Mackie, J. L. 1977. *Ethics: Inventing Right and Wrong*. New York: Penguin.

Markell, P. 2000. "Making Affect Safe for Democracy? On 'Constitutional Patriotism'". *Political Theory* 28(1): 38–63.

Marx, K. 1977. *Critique of Hegel's "Philosophy of Right"*, A. Jolin & J. O'Malley (trans.). Cambridge: Cambridge University Press.

Marx, K. 1992. *Early Writings*, R. Livingstone & G. Benton (trans.). New York: Penguin.

Matuštík, M. J. 2001. *Jürgen Habermas: A Philosophical–Political Profile*. Lanham, MD: Rowman & Littlefield.

Maus, I. 2006. "From Nation-State to Global State, or the Decline of Democracy". *Constellations* 13(4): 465–84.

McCarthy, T. A. 1993. *Ideals and Illusions: On Reconstruction and Deconstruction in Contemporary Critical Theory*. Cambridge, MA: MIT Press.

McCarthy, T. A. 1994. "Reason in a Postmetaphysical Age". In D. C. Hoy & T. McCarthy, *Critical Theory*, 31–62. Cambridge, MA: Blackwell.

McCarthy, T. A. 1996. *The Critical Theory of Jürgen Habermas*. Cambridge, MA: MIT Press.

McCarthy, T. A. 1998. "Legitimacy and Diversity: Dialectical Reflections on Analytical Distinctions". In *Habermas on Law and Democracy: Critical Exchanges*, M. Rosenfeld and A. Arato (eds), 115–53. Berkeley, CA: University of California Press.

Medina, J. 2005. *Language*. London: Continuum.

Meehan, J. (ed.) 1995. *Feminists Read Habermas: Gendering the Subject of Discourse*. New York: Routledge.

Mendieta, E. (ed.) 2005. *The Frankfurt School on Religion: Key Writings by the Major Thinkers*. New York: Routledge.

Mendieta, E. 2007. *Global Fragments: Globalizations, Latinamericanisms, and Critical Theory*. Albany, NY: SUNY Press.

Mendieta, E. 2010. "A Postsecular World Society? An Interview with Jürgen Habermas". *The Immanent Frame*. http://blogs.ssrc.org/tif/2010/02/03/a-postsecular-world-society (accessed October 2010).

Mendieta, E. & J. Van Antwerpen (eds) 2010. *The Power of Religion in the Public Sphere*. New York: Columbia University Press.

Michelman, F. 1986. "The Supreme Court, 1985 Term". *Harvard Law Review* 100(1): 1.

Moses, A. D. 2007. *German Intellectuals and the Nazi Past*. Cambridge: Cambridge University Press.

Müller, J.-W. 2007. "Three Objections to Constitutional Patriotism". *Constellations* 14(2): 197–209.

Nagel, T. 2005. "The Problem of Global Justice". *Philosophy & Public Affairs* 33(2): 113–47.

Offe, C. 1992. "Bindings, Shackles, Brakes: On Self-Limitation Strategies". In *Cultural-Political Interventions in the Unfinished Project of Enlightenment*, A. Honneth, T. McCarthy, C. Offe & A. Wellmer (eds), B. Fultner (trans.), 63–94. Cambridge, MA: MIT Press.

Olson, K. 2006. *Reflexive Democracy: Political Equality and the Welfare State*. Cambridge, MA: MIT Press.

Ott, K. 2004. "Noch einmal: Diskursethik". In *Perspektiven der Diskursethik*, N. Gottschalk-Mazouz (ed.), 143–73. Würzburg: Königshausen & Neumann.

Outhwaite, W. 1994. *Habermas: A Critical Introduction*. Cambridge: Polity.

Parfit, D. 1986. *Reasons and Persons*. Oxford: Oxford University Press.

Parsons, T. 1951. *The Social System*. New York: Free Press.

Passerin d'Entrèves, M. & S. Benhabib (eds) 1997. *Habermas and the Unfinished Project of Modernity: Critical Essays on The Philosophical Discourse of Modernity*. Cambridge, MA: MIT Press.

Perry, M. J. 1982. *The Constitution, the Courts, and Human Rights: An Inquiry into the Legitimacy of Constitutional Policymaking by the Judiciary*. New Haven, CT: Yale University Press.

Polanyi, K. 2001. *The Great Transformation: The Political and Economic Origins of Our Time*, 2nd edn. Boston, MA: Beacon Press.

Putnam, H. 1981. *Reason, Truth, and History*. Cambridge: Cambridge University Press.
Rasmussen, D. M. & J. Swindal (eds) 2002. *Jürgen Habermas*. London: Sage.
Rasmussen, D. M. 1984. "Explorations of the Lebenswelt: Reflections on Schutz and Habermas". *Human Studies* 7(2): 127–32.
Rawls, J. 1971. *A Theory of Justice*. Cambridge, MA: Belknap Press.
Rawls, J. 1999. *The Law of Peoples*. Cambridge, MA: Harvard University Press.
Rawls, J. 2001. "The Law of Peoples". In *Collected Papers*, S. Freeman (ed.). Cambridge, MA: Harvard University Press.
Rawls, J. 2001/2009. *A Brief Inquiry into the Meaning of Sin and Faith: With "On My Religion"*. Cambridge, MA: Harvard University Press.
Rehg, W. 1994. *Insight and Solidarity: A Study in the Discourse Ethics of Jürgen Habermas*. Berkeley, CA: University of California Press.
Rehg, W. 2004. "Discourse Ethics and Individual Conscience." In *Perspektiven der Diskursethik*, N. Gottschalk-Mazouz (ed.), 26-40. Würzburg: Königshausen & Neumann.
Renn, O., T. Webler & P. M. Wiedemann (eds) 1995. *Fairness and Competence in Citizen Participation: Evaluating Models for Environmental Discourse*. Dordrecht: Kluwer Academic.
Richardson, H. S. 1990. "Specifying Norms as a Way to Resolve Concrete Ethical Problems". *Philosophy and Public Affairs* 19(4): 279–310.
Rockmore, T. 1989. *Habermas on Historical Materialism*. Bloomington, IN: Indiana University Press.
Rorty, R. 1998. *Truth and Progress*. Cambridge: Cambridge University Press.
Rosenfeld, M. & A. Arato (eds) 1998. *Habermas on Law and Democracy: Critical Exchanges*. Berkeley, CA: University of California Press.
Rummens, S. 2006. "Debate: The Co-originality of Private and Public Autonomy in Deliberative Democracy". *Journal of Political Philosophy* 14(4): 469–81.
Scheuerman, W. 2002. "Between Radicalism and Resignation: Democratic Theory in Habermas's *Between Facts and Norms*". In *Discourse and Democracy: Essays on Habermas's Between Facts and Norms,* R. von Schomberg & K. Baynes (eds), 61–89. Albany, NY: SUNY Press.
Scheuerman, W. 2008a. "Global Governance without Global Government? Habermas on Postnational Democracy". *Political Theory* 36(1): 133–51.
Scheuerman, W. 2008b. "All Power to the (State-less?) General Assembly!" *Constellations* 15(4): 485–92.
Scheuerman, W. E. 2008c. "Realism and the Left: the Case of Hans J. Morgenthau". *Review of International Studies* 34(1): 29–51.
Schmitt, C. 1996. *The Concept of the Political*, G. Schwab (trans.). Chicago, IL: University of Chicago Press.
Schomberg, R. von & K. Baynes (eds) 2002. *Discourse and Democracy: Essays on Habermas's Between Facts and Norms*. Albany, NY: SUNY Press.
Schutz, A. & T. Luckmann 1973. *The Structures of the Life-World*, R. M. Zaner & H. T. Engelhardt (trans.). Evanston, IL: Northwestern University Press.
Sarle, J. 1969. *Speech Acts*. Cambridge: Cambridge University Press.
Searle, J. R. 1995. *The Construction of Social Reality*. New York: Free Press.
Searle, J. R. 2010. *Making the Social World*. Oxford: Oxford University Press.
Sellars, W. 1956. *Empiricism and the Philosophy of Mind*. Cambridge, MA: Harvard University Press.
Shaw, M. 2005. *The New Western Way of War: Risk-Transfer War and Its Crisis in Iraq*. Cambridge: Polity.
Sieyès, E. J. [1789] 2003. "What is the Third Estate?" In *Political Writings: Including*

the Debate Between Sieyès and Tom Paine in 1791, M. Sonenscher (ed.), 92–162. Indianapolis, IN: Hackett.

Sitton, J. 2003. *Habermas and Contemporary Society*. New York: Palgrave Macmillan.

Skjei, E. 1985. "A Comment on Performative, Subject, and Proposition in Habermas's Theory of Communication". *Inquiry: An Interdisciplinary Journal of Philosophy* 28: 87–104.

Slaughter, A.-M. 2004. "Disaggregated Sovereignty: Towards the Public Accountability of Global Government Networks". *Government and Opposition* 39(2): 159–90.

Specter, M. 2009. "Habermas's Political Thought, 1984–1996: A Historical Interpretation". *Modern Intellectual History* 6(1): 91–119.

Steinhoff, U. 2009. *The Philosophy of Jürgen Habermas*, K. Schöllner (trans.). Oxford: Oxford University Press.

Strawson, P. F. 1974. "Freedom and Resentment". In his *Freedom and Resentment and Other Essays*, 1–25. London: Methuen.

Sunstein, C. 1988. "Beyond the Republican Revival". *Yale Law Journal* 97(8): 1539.

Swindal, J. 1999. *Reflection Revisited: Jürgen Habermas's Discursive Theory of Truth*. New York: Fordham University Press.

Taylor, C. 1985. *Human Agency and Language: Philosophical Papers, vol. 1*. Cambridge: Cambridge University Press.

Taylor, C. 1989. *Sources of the Self*. Cambridge: Harvard University Press.

Taylor, C. 1992. *The Ethics of Authenticity*. Cambridge: Harvard University Press.

Thomas, A. 2006. *Value and Context: The Nature of Moral and Political Knowledge*. Oxford: Oxford University Press.

Thomassen, L. (ed.) 2006. *The Derrida–Habermas Reader*. Edinburgh: Edinburgh University Press.

Thompson, J. B. 1981. *Critical Hermeneutics: A Study in the Thought of Paul Ricoeur and Jürgen Habermas*. Cambridge: Cambridge University Press.

Thompson, J. B. & D. Held (eds) 1982. *Habermas: Critical Debates*. Cambridge, MA: MIT Press.

United Nations 2004. *A More Secure World: Our Shared Responsibility: Report of the High-Level Panel on Threats, Challenges, and Change*. New York: United Nations.

Wallace, R. J. 1994. *Responsibility and the Moral Sentiments*. Cambridge, MA: Harvard University Press.

Warren, M. E. 1995. "The Self in Discursive Democracy". In *The Cambridge Companion to Habermas*, S. K. White (ed.), 167–200. Cambridge: Cambridge University Press.

Webler, T. & S. Tuler 2004. "Fairness and Competence in Citizen Participation: Theoretical Reflections from a Case Study". In *Perspektiven der Diskursethik*, N. Gottschalk-Mazouz (ed.), 41–64. Würzburg: Königshausen & Neumann.

Wellmer, A. 1991. "Ethics and Dialogue: Elements of Moral Judgment in Kant and Discourse Ethics". In *The Persistence of Modernity: Essays on Aesthetics, Ethics, and Postmodernism*, D. Midgley (trans.), 113–231. Cambridge, MA: MIT Press.

Wellmer, A. 1992. "What Is a Pragmatic Theory of Meaning?" In *Philosophical Interventions in the Unfinished Project of Enlightenment*, A. Honneth, T. McCarthy, C. Offe & A. Wellmer (eds), W. Rehg (trans.), 171–219. Cambridge, MA: MIT Press.

Wendt, A. 2003. "Why a World State is Inevitable". *European Journal of International Relations* 9(4): 491–542.

Wenzel, J. 1990. "Three Perpectives on Argument: Rhetoric, Dialectic, and Logic".

In *Perspectives on Argumentation: Essays in Honor of Wayne Brockriede*, R. Trapp & J. Schuez (eds), 9–26. Prospect Heights, IL: Waveland Press.

White, S. K. (ed.) 1995. *The Cambridge Companion to Habermas*. Cambridge: Cambridge University Press.

Wiggershaus, R. 1994. *The Frankfurt School: Its History, Theories, and Political Significance*, M. Robertson (trans.). Cambridge, MA: MIT Press.

Wittgenstein, L. 1953. *Philosophical Investigations*, G. E. M. Anscombe (trans.). Oxford: Blackwell.

Wikforss, A. M. 2001. "Semantic Normativity". *Philosophical Studies* **102**(2): 203–26.

Wingert, L. 1993. *Gemeinsinn und Moral: Grundzüge einer intersubjektivistischen Moralkonzeption*. Frankfurt: Suhrkamp.

Wolin, S. S. 1994a. "Fugitive Democracy". *Constellations* 1(1): 11–25.

Wolin, S. S. 1994b. "Norm and Form: The Constitutionalizing of Democracy". In *Athenian Political Thought and the Reconstruction of American Democracy*, J. P. Euben, J. Wallach & J. Ober (eds), 29–58. Ithaca, NY: Cornell University Press.

Wood, A. W. 1998. "Kant's Project for Perpetual Peace". In *Cosmopolitics: Thinking and Feeling Beyond the Nation*, Pheng Cheah & B. Robbins (eds), 59–76. Minneapolis, MN: University of Minnesota Press.

Zurn, C. F. 2007. *Deliberative Democracy and the Institutions of Judicial Review*. New York: Cambridge University Press.

Index